Yankee Red

Yankee Red
NONORTHODOX MARXISM IN LIBERAL AMERICA

Robert A. Gorman

PRAEGER

New York
Westport, Connecticut
London

Library of Congress Cataloging-in-Publication Data

Gorman, Robert A.
    Yankee Red : nonorthodox Marxism in liberal America / Robert A.
  Gorman
      p. cm.
    Bibliography: p.
    Includes index.
    ISBN 0–275–92766–0 (alk. paper)
    1. Communism—United States. I. Title.
HX86.G734 1989
335.43'0973—dc19   88–25882

Library of Congress Catalog Card Number: 88–25882
ISBN: 0–275–92766–0

First published in 1989

Praeger Publishers, One Madison Avenue, New York, NY 10010
A division of Greenwood Press, Inc.

Printed in the United States of America

The paper used in this book complies with the Permanent
Paper Standard issued by the National Information Standards
Organization (Z39.48—1984).

10 9 8 7 6 5 4 3 2 1

To Elaine

Contents

Prologue: The Two Cultures of Marxism

Some things, it is said, only intellectuals are crazy enough to believe. History, of course, will ultimately decide whether Marxism in any of its current forms is one of these things. Indisputably, the Marxist left in America is today, and was in the past, extremely small, with intellectuals over-represented. Most Americans wonder if anything new can or should be said about a social theory that promised to emancipate the powerless and, in practice, delivered a tyrant; one that guaranteed a worker's paradise and delivered instead regimes that persecuted and jailed labor leaders; and one that worshipped egalitarianism but nevertheless institutionalized an elite corps of bureaucrats. Given what is, on balance, its bleak and disillusioning history, is Marxism even worth talking about?

Thoughtful Marxists today are painfully aware that dogma—of the left, center, or right—engenders self-righteous reigns of terror. They also believe, however, that silence perpetuates injustice by default. Theirs is an awkward existence, constantly vacillating between commitment and caution, prophetic vision and a terrible awareness of human finitude.

This dilemma has generated a new culture of the left. Thinkers and activists, bypassing the Bolshevik tradition, have returned to Marx to see what is of value, and what isn't. They have redefined key terms and refocused on the dynamic, inscrutable social qualities that so fascinated and motivated Marx himself. In America, this new Marxism has been quietly gelling since the turn of the century. Unheralded, it struggles to change the ways we think and live, our ideas and activities. By arguing that theory and practice are inseparably linked, it attaches economic change to a new and critical subjectivity, willingly chosen and democratically expressed. Revolution and democratic procedure, consequently, are two aspects of one reality. Marxism, in this revised sense, completes and fulfills America's democratic tradition.

This last assertion is vexing. Can one political movement, which calls itself Marxist, alternately claim to obliterate and fulfill American democracy? "Yes," we answer, because two cultures (that is, two distinct, internally con-

sistent sets of ideas, each of which rationalizes a pertinent set of institutions) coexist within the one movement labeled "Marxist." Modern capitalism, C. P. Snow reminded us, similarly embodies two potentially antagonistic cultures: the razor-sharp realm of science, and the sensuousness of art. Marxism also is a churning entity comprising potboilers and poems, dictators and democrats, nervously cohabiting on socialist turf. Each culture traces its roots into Marx, and both claim to be dialectical, socialist, and revolutionary. Yet beyond these shared ambitions lie fundamental theoretical and practical disagreements. These are exposed only by disconnecting Marxism's two cultures and examining their distinctive features.

Orthodoxy is firmly anchored in philosophical materialism, and emphasizes what it sees as the irreducible core of Marxist social theory: the science of historical materialism. Objective laws govern humanity's social evolution and lead inexorably to proletarian rebellion. These laws are linked to society's level of technological development, which determines its productive capacity and conditions relations of production. This economic base, or material substructure, consists of classes that perform system-maintaining functions, but whose material interests clash. Culture reflects and rationalizes the base. Antagonistic economic classes, therefore, produce social classes with opposing interests, expressed in conflicting ideologies. Society's institutions and ideas reflect the interests of its dominant economic class. As technology improves and material conditions ripen, the class struggle intensifies. The resulting conflict between means and relationships of production is resolved when the exploited class seizes the productive apparatus and replaces existing institutions—including the state—with its own. In this manner history has evolved from pre-feudal to feudal to capitalist stages, and cultural hegemony has passed from tribes to landlords to entrepreneurs. Human behavior is thus directly determined by society's stage of economic development, and indirectly by history's inclusive material laws. In capitalism, workers are the exploited class. They are thus destined to achieve economic and cultural hegemony. Classes, private property, even commodity production will all disappear as workers socialize production and distribution, and realize their potentials in socially useful labor.

Marx described matter's dynamic movement concretely, rejecting theoretical discussion of any kind. Friedrich Engels completed Marx's unfinished picture by connecting materialism to social theory. Dialectics, for Engels, embodied three universal laws that governed matter in motion: the law of the transformation of quantity into quality, and vice versa; the law of the interpenetration of opposites; and the law of the negation of the negation. These three principles functioned impersonally and explained all of reality. They defined class struggle and worker rebellion, as well as the economic contradictions of capitalism, as incontrovertably true and inevitable. The Second International eventually recognized Engels as

Marxism's official philosopher, and his "dialectical materialism" became the philosophy of orthodox Marxism. However, orthodoxy still lacked a praxis by which it could politically realize its theoretical promise. V. I. Lenin transformed dialectical materialism from a frozen formula into a dynamic series of events. His thoughts on epistemology, which reactivated the subjective component of history's material dialectic, nourished a pragmatic politics. Successful revolutionary strategies, he argued, blossomed from creative, goal-oriented actions by knowledgeable and organized human agents triggering history's objective mechanisms. Lenin's activism and secretive, hierarchical Party were quickly adopted by CPs everywhere, and became a permanent feature of orthodoxy. Today, orthodox philosophy and politics direct mainstream Communist Parties throughout the world.

In spite of its successes, orthodoxy has proved a mixed blessing to leftists primarily because it is neither democratic nor individualist enough to attract disillusioned liberal democrats. Turning Marx's weakest link, that is, his unwillingness to argue abstractly and his incomplete philosophy, to their own advantage, radical theorists have discovered the roots of a revised, subjectively relevant, nonmaterialist dialectic. As I have more fully argued in *Neo-Marxism*, Marxism's new, nonorthodox culture was thus born in Marx's ambiguous theoretical legacy and nurtured by practical exigencies, which generated new Marxian theories when circumstances judged old ones lacking. As critical self-consciousness replaced stampeding matter, heretofore bourgeois theories were coopted by the left. Religion, idealism, existentialism, structuralism, empiricism, psychoanalysis, even mysticism, were carefully blended with Marx's class-critique of capitalism, and then peddled among dissatisfied western intellectuals. Orthodoxy's predominantly Russian and German legacy was replaced by the bold new formulations of Lukács, Gramsci, Adorno, Bloch, Sartre, Althusser, Colletti, Mounier, Paci, and many others. Marxism had confronted western culture on its own terms. Where orthodoxy would unthinkingly annihilate the enemy, neo-Marxists proffered a critical hug and a self-conscious, popular insurrection.

Unbeknownst to many supporters and critics alike, American leftism now embodies these two cultures. One, orthodoxy, has failed dismally despite a high profile and a cohesive, disciplined organization. The other, theoretically and institutionally unfocused, learns from friends and enemies alike, grows increasingly popular, and waits anxiously in the wings. Slowly, almost imperceptibly, this decentered, diffused cluster of nonorthodox ideas has become a beacon of hope for America's democratic left.

Yankee Red

Learning From Failure:
Orthodoxy in America

If the Bible's instruction to honor thy parents is well founded, then orthodoxy's bleak history in America is roundly deserved, and nonorthodox Marxism can anticipate a glorious future. Socialism in America originated in an early nineteenth century cultural environment that combined strong doses of Jeffersonian and Jacksonian democracy with ideas from critics of capitalism such as Robert Owen, Charles Fourier, William Thompson, Thomas Spence, William Godwin, and Robert Gray. The emerging intellectual confection was a uniquely American kind of radicalism toward which contemporary neo-Marxists are, perhaps unconsciously, pointing.

This chapter will trace the origins and evolution of mainstream American Marxism, accenting its European flavor. By sacrificing America's indigenous cultural background to an imported materialist formula, orthodoxy sealed its fate. Conversely, the roots of American neo-Marxism lie in a renewed awareness among radicals of uniquely American institutions and values, and the potentially crucial role these must play in a successful political movement. This last insight, we shall see, provided disillusioned Marxists a framework for their unconventional contributions to radical theory and practice.

I

By the early 1820s, American liberal democracy was firmly established, external threats to the Republic dissipated, urbanization and industrialization begun, and the family-owned farm secured as the heart and soul of a thriving economy. With time on their hands, America's expanding middle class detected social and economic blemishes heretofore obscured by the exigencies of frontier life. A small number of educated Americans decided to struggle politically to end slavery, enfranchise women, establish state-supported schools, ban alcohol and tobacco, and secure peace among all the world's nations. American socialism was born in this idealistic environment, especially among starry-eyed utopians who decided to build their own com-

munities. These included Shaker villages, Zoar and Amana settlements, Owenite communities, Fourieristic phalanxes, and several non-attached efforts such as Adin Ballou's Hopedale, Bronson Alcott's Fruitlands, Etienne Cabet's Icaria, and John Humphrey Noyes's Oneida.[1] All believed that earthly utopias—moral communities of equal citizens—were possible, and each propagated abstract, ideal, unchanging religious or secular values. For the most part, they were disengaged from reality, simply ignoring political parties, labor organizations, law, and economics. In such unlikely sources we discover the first American critique of unfettered capitalism. Competitive individualism was condemned by the utopians as brutalizing and inhuman, and replaced by a profound sense of social solidarity. American justice was redefined as a collectivist community of free citizens living, working, and loving in cooperative bliss.

Although utopian communities came and went rapidly, their sentiments endured in the anti-capitalist social theories of several contemporary patriots, including Cornelius Blatchly, Daniel Raymond, Langdon Byllesby, Thomas Skidmore, William Heighton, and William Maclure.[2] Rather than foolishly discarding liberalism, the lifeblood of American culture, Blatchly argued that everyone had a natural right to an equal share of property. Locke was correct, but capitalist America wasn't Lockian enough. Disparities in wealth, argued Raymond, generated political and social inequities which prevented workers from receiving the full value of their labor. Consequently, they lacked the equality their revolution had promised. Byllesby demanded that the poor use their constitutional rights to act politically in their own collective interest. Jefferson and Paine, America's own liberal revolutionaries, were correct, and Skidmore believed they too would support a working class electoral revolution. By voting to redistribute property, workers could initiate a democratic revolution that would fulfill the pledge of 1776. Private property, in Skidmore's view, violated our rights to life and liberty, and hence was immoral, undemocratic, and un-American. Because workers were denied the full value of their labor and suffered from capitalism's mal-distribution of wealth, they constituted a suppressed majority that could employ constitutional freedoms to democratically and peacefully transform the economic system. Here was indigenous radicalism that praised the Declaration of Independence as a noble but unrealized dream. These early radicals tried to mobilize Americans of all classes to complete the Founding Fathers' democratic experiment.

The first trade unions in America appeared in 1827–28, primarily among workers in the Northeast who were protesting unsatisfactory factory and living conditions. Heighton in Philadelphia, and Skidmore in New York, became leaders in their respective unions. They fought hard, but apparently with only limited success, for the workers they represented. By the late 1840s, newly arrived German Marxists, many fleeing the Revolutions of 1848, supported and consolidated the incipient trade union movement. As

the numbers of immigrant workers increased, the complexion of union leadership changed, with native radicals losing much of their power. These early immigrant socialists were flexible Marxists. They apparently sought practical political and organizational reforms leading to short-term worker benefits.[3] Since, for the most part, they weren't intellectuals, they anticipated applying Marxism to local conditions rather than advocating doctrinal purity.

On 7 November 1851, however, a friend, colleague, and follower of Marx named Joseph Weydemeyer landed in America with Marx's and Engels's suggestions on how to spread scientific socialism among workers. Weydemeyer became a leading orthodox propagandist in America until his death in 1866, when his associate Friedrich Adolph Sorge, also a German emigré, took over. Both Weydemeyer and Sorge rejected the utopian mentality of native American radicalism. After the American section of the First International was established in 1869, Sorge, under Marx's direction, purged it of reformists and non-scientific radicals.

Even the post-1869 influx of Lassalean German immigrants, who believed that the capitalist state was capable of redistributing wealth to workers if pressured politically, could not bend orthodox purists. Lassaleans clashed with orthodox Marxists, who insisted unions alone could mobilize American workers and catalyze the revolution. The former fluorished during depressions, when widespread unemployment weakened unions and intensified workers' political demands; the latter, in times of full employment, when unions were powerful. In 1874, Lassaleans established the Social Democratic Party of North America, which, with the Working Men's Party of the U.S., was renamed, in 1877, the Socialist Labor Party of North America. Years of fratricidal struggle ensued, involving orthodox trade unionists, Lassalean socialists, radical anarchists, and reformist labor organizers. Lassaleans saw trade unionism corrupting the socialist movement by isolating workers and capitalists from the rest of society, appealing only to organized trades and workers, and thereby abandoning great masses of non-unionized citizens. Orthodoxy felt ideological purity would, in the long run, unite American workers. Although the tactical struggles survived well into the twentieth century, Daniel DeLeon's emergence, in 1890, as Socialist Labor Party (SLP) leader secured the institutional victory of orthodox Marxism. Henceforth, the organized left unquestioningly accepted materialist orthodoxy and became insulated from native radicals with cultural links to American workers.

The SLP remained the preeminent Marxist party in America only until 1899, primarily because DeLeon's rigid policies and behavior encouraged factionalism. Born in Curaçao, educated at the University of Leyden and Columbia University, where he was a professor of international law, DeLeon was brilliant, charismatic, arrogant and tyrannous—a man said to have expelled his own son from the SLP for doubting his father's interpretation of

Marx's theory of value.[4] Single-handedly, he purged his party of all theoretical and personal opposition. Predictably, DeLeon resolutely opposed making immediate demands on the capitalist state. This Lassalean tactic, he felt, turned revolutionary leaders into "labor lieutenants of capitalism." Shrewdly, however, he acknowledged the necessity of Marxists competing electorally for power in America's non-unionized society. The contradiction was resolved opportunistically: DeLeon would work for electoral victory even as he organized industrial struggles, and would liquidate the capitalist state immediately following the success of either tactic. A Leninist before Lenin, DeLeon believed that revolutionary unions, led by a radical elite, had to educate workers, cultivate class consciousness, and leave no tactic—even electoral politics—unturned.

Some nineteenth century socialists, bothered by orthodoxy's rigid materialism and outraged by DeLeon's heavy-handedness, rallied around a new group of utopians led by Laurence Gronlund and Edward Bellamy. Gronlund was a German emigré Marxist whose *The Cooperative Commonwealth* (1887) openly extolled scientific socialism. On only one crucial point did Gronlund deviate from orthodoxy: as an ethical idealist, he rejected Marx's class struggle thesis, arguing instead that all Americans—capitalists and workers—were equally oppressed by material conditions. Gronlund hoped to convince his readers that decaying capitalism would inevitably be replaced by a socialist commonwealth of cooperating Americans from all economic classes. This "organic union of us all"[5] would be a nonexploitative association of decent, friendly, optimistic, and rational individuals: a uniquely American kind of socialism that would protect cherished individualist traditions by collectivizing the means of production and distribution, not private property.

Edward Bellamy's *Looking Backward* (1887) tells the story of Julian West, a young Bostonian who awakens from an hypnotic trance in 2000 A.D., only to learn that capitalism had decayed and been transformed into a socialist utopia, a golden age of peace, cooperation, and plenty. Like Gronlund, whose influence on him is uncertain, Bellamy was a Marxist who rejected violent class struggle and appealed to the humanitarianism of those uncorrupted by either capitalist or union bureaucracies, that is, to America's middle class.[6] His socialist vision, also like Gronlund's, entailed a cooperative, nationalized economy that equalized wealth in order to reinforce a family-centered, individualist, democratic culture. The formula apparently worked. More copies of *Looking Backward* sold in America than of any other American novel since Harriet Beecher Stowe's *Uncle Tom's Cabin*, and dozens of similar utopian novels were published by 1900. Several small, and short-lived, political parties and experimental communities sprouted in and around Boston. In the early 1890s, Julius Augustus Wayland, a successful entrepreneur turned socialist, and publisher of the enormously popular journal *Appeal to Reason*, exhorted his many readers to peacefully abolish

capitalism and establish in its place a cooperative socialist commonw
His Ruskin Colony in central Tennessee, like the Bellamyite communities, was a step in this direction. Fabian socialists, nourished by this renaissance of utopianism, split from the SLP and propagandized a peaceful, flexible, idealistic socialism aimed primarily at the middle class. And, finally, Eugene Victor Debs, Gronlund's most famous disciple, composed, in 1897, the principles of Social Democracy, which combined a Fabian-like socialist idealism with a utopian commitment to establishing a cooperative commonwealth in the American West.

This late-nineteenth-century project of joining American ideals to Marxian critique was intellectually astute, but, in the context of America's ballooning economy, anachronistic. From 1880 to 1900, bituminous coal production in America grew from 43 to 212 million tons; anthracite from 30 to 57 million tons; pig iron from 4 to 14 million tons; steel from 1.25 to 10 million tons.[7] Technology grew apace: telephones, typewriters, adding machines, and increasingly sophisticated means of communication all lubricated the humming economy. Wealth became increasingly concentrated in huge trusts and monopolies owned by legendary financial moguls like Rockefeller, Morgan, Swift, Duke, Frick, Pillsbury, Ward, and Roebuck. In 1870, one American in four lived in cities; in 1900, two in five; by 1920, more than half. By 1900, America was the wealthiest industrial nation in the world, but almost one in four Americans earned below $700 annually, the official poverty line. Working conditions were appalling. Utopian leftism simply couldn't understand or alter these events. Along with the concentration of wealth went control of educational and news media, the arts, and government. Capitalists increasingly shaped America's cultural and political values, and of course reinforced liberal-democratic-capitalism. Workers, even those with secure jobs, were struggling to survive economically, lacked educations, and had little control over public-policy decisions and almost no leisure time. The middle class, caught in the American dream of financial success, sought wealth rather than cooperative commonwealths. Utopian socialists were left with neither a constituency nor an effective means of communicating their euphoric message. In touch with America's cultural nerve-pulse, they were nonetheless quarantined by the consequences of economic development.

The utopian left knew that materialist revolutionary formulas were useless in a nation that treasured its individualist heritage. They were, in this sense, more politically savvy than their orthodox comrades. However, they naively assumed that revolutionary acts would pour spontaneously from enlightened minds under any conditions, and thus they ignored the unbreakable link attaching values to conditions, will to surrounding environment. The cultural dislocations caused by America's expanding economy pushed working and middle class citizens further into an increasingly difficult struggle to survive and prosper. They would choose socialism only if convinced that

capitalism—so boldly reinforced in journals, films, churches, and schools—was neither inevitable nor just. But this conviction would follow, not precede, the futile struggle to improve living conditions. Having abandoned struggle as indecent and un-American, utopians quickly turned irrelevant. Orthodoxy acknowledged the importance of class struggle, but its intellectual baggage, imported from Europe, was dogmatically anti-individualist. America's indigenous left, faced with utopian irrelevance and materialist cant, had little room to maneuver. Some, like Gronlund, simply abandoned Marxism altogether. On the other hand, when Debs's hopes for a reformist workers movement and a communal commonwealth collapsed in 1898, he then established the orthodox Marxist Social Democratic Party (SDP) as a rival to the SLP. On the left, orthodoxy remained hegemonic because Americans such as Debs had nowhere else to go. However it lost precisely those people and ideas it needed to become a successful mass movement in the twentieth century.

Some of these dissatisfied native radicals who lived in the South and Midwest took matters into their own hands by forming the Populist Party. Populism, like Marxism, criticized capitalism as exploitative, elitist, and undemocratic. Its platform sought to abolish monopolies and special privileges, enfranchise all workers and farmers, and nationalize public utilities. Clearly, Populism and Marxism shared a broad spectrum of theoretical and practical positions.[8] Populism's potential electoral appeal among farmers, traditionally anti-Marxist, was enormous. Indeed, North Dakotan entrepreneur-turned-socialist Arthur C. Townley opportunistically campaigned as a Populist and managed, in 1910, to elect Lynn Frazier—his Non-Partisan League candidate—as Governor of the state. Nationwide, Populists attracted 8.5 percent of the 1892 Presidential vote, easily surpassing the highest percentage ever achieved by a Marxist candidate. Populist supporters in rural America, in league with Marxism's predominantly urban constituency, would have fused into a politically potent radical coalition. However, Populism's sin, from an orthodox point of view, was its relevance—what DeLeon called its petit-bourgeois mentality. It doggedly refused to abandon America's rural ideals of private family-owned farms, easy credit, and smashing bankers' economic power by abolishing the gold standard. DeLeon, on the other hand, believed that individualism and private property would disappear with the inevitable collectivist rebellion, and Populism's "curse of gold" theory confused symptom for cause. Rather than blending radical theory and practice, orthodoxy chose to fight a potential ally and preserve theoretical purity. Both orthodoxy and Populism suffered: the former moved even further from mainstream America, the latter wasted a rational foundation for its simmering outrage.

DeLeon's obstinance, in the end, was self-defeating. In 1901, dissatisfied SLP right-wingers known as "kangaroos," and led by Morris Hillquit, joined with Debs and many unaffiliated socialists to form the Socialist Party (SP),

which grew rapidly until 1912, and retained its basic character and strength until 1919. It was an open, contentious party that permitted a wide range of tactical points of view. Eventually these congealed into left and right factions. The former favored direct and immediate revolutionary action. The latter, trade unionism and limited cooperation with capitalist interests, including the state. With the SLP tightly controlled by DeLeon and the SP splintered into factions, Marxism in America prior to 1919 was shaped by key tactical questions (economic organizing or political activism, trade unionism or industrial unionism, peaceful or violent action) and rivoting personalities (DeLeon, Debs, Hillquit). Unquestioningly materialist,[9] these leftist parties were, in true frontier style, concerned with getting things done rather than theorizing abstractly.

These were the years of orthodoxy's greatest popularity. By 1911, 33 cities were run by socialists, including Milwaukee, Berkeley, Butte, Flint, and Jackson, Michigan. In 1914, the SP's membership reached 118,000, its candidates won over 1,200 public offices nationwide (including two elected Congressmen), and it published or financed over 300 periodicals. Debs garnered 897,011 votes in the 1912 Presidential election, 5.9 percent of the total.[10] This remains the highest percentage ever achieved by a Marxist party. Factors such as deteriorating factory conditions, the growth of trusts and decline of traditional crafts, worker dissatisfaction with the AFL's narrow craft unionism, the influx of European socialists, and the survival of a Populist tradition, all provided the SP an opportunity to expand its popular base. Its diluted historical materialism highlighted the polarizing of rich and poor, and tried to unite workers and sympathetic nonworkers into a politically powerful coalition for change. Owners of small family farms as well as tenant farmers, whose numbers were rapidly expanding particularly in the Midwest and Southwest, were pleased by a 1910 SP resolution permitting private ownership of farmland. By understating materialist dogma and, instead, debating apt revolutionary tactics, the SP attracted many dissatisfied Americans.

This early success, however, was short-lived. A widening schism between left and right versions of historical materialism gradually sapped the SP's internal resolve. Debs, Louis B. Boudin, and Louis C. Fraina condemned what they called the social democratic reformism of the Victor Berger and Morris Hillquit-led right, and suggested a more confrontational strategy. After 1914, patriotic intellectuals began exiting the SP to protest its war policies, and to support one of their own, President Woodrow Wilson. Espionage Acts passed in 1917 and 1918 heartened the Federal government to prosecute hundreds of socialists, further depleting SP ranks. Local vigilante groups harassed SP members and violently disrupted meetings. Rising farm prices and easy credit chased farmers back into mainstream politics. Government meliorative programs guaranteeing worker safety, the right to organize on the job, and a minimum wage, combined with Congressional passage of the

Clayton Act and the establishment of the Department of Labor, all clouded the SP's reputation as America's preeminent voice of labor. In brief, inept, factionalized leaders and changing perceptions exploded the SP's ballooning popularity.

Although SP rolls declined only fractionally by 1919, over half of its members were then foreigners, compared to 12 percent in 1912.[11] American workers no longer believed in America's working class party. In 1919, Fraina, Boudin, and the SP's left wing—including 7 language federations and the leftist state organizations of Michigan and Massachusetts—were precipitously expelled by the victorious right. Most subsequently united with elements of the SLP to form the Communist Party of America (CP), which henceforth would dominate the organized left. The SP survived, but only as a shadow party. Decimated by the loss of its left and unable to lure organized labor, the SP unraveled rapidly. In 1928, its presidential candidate, Norman Thomas, received only 267,835 votes, the lowest total since 1900, and its membership roll after 1930 vacillated between 7,000 and 24,000.[12] It was continually outsmarted and coopted by the CP on the left and the Democratic Party's New Deal on the right, loosing members to both. Those who remained jockeyed viciously for control. By 1936, at least six distinct factions were recognizable, from the left's "clarity" group to Thomas on the right. Eventually the opportunistic Norman Thomas emerged victorious. Thomas's decision, in 1940, to oppose America's entry into World War II eliminated what little popular support still existed. Thereafter, under Thomas's aloof custody, the SP spoke out only on specific issues, and emerged after the war as a reformist interest group. In 1950, Thomas himself, in effect conceding that F.D.R.'s New Deal was all workers could or should ask for, proposed abandoning political activity altogether. The motion was defeated by delegates to that year's SP convention.

Factionalism continued to plague the SP throughout the 1950s. In 1954, Michael Harrington took his Young People's Socialist League (YPSL)—the youth branch of the SP—into an alliance with remnants of the Trotskyite Independent Socialist League (ISL), and called the new organization the Young Socialists League (YSL). Both the ISL and YSL rejoined the SP in 1958, with Harrington as co-chair and leader of a faction favoring radical realignment of America's mainstream political parties. When the SP refused to endorse U.S. withdrawal from Viet Nam in 1972, Harrington formally resigned, leaving the SP to conservative ex-Trotskyites led by Max Shachtman. Later that year, after Shachtman died and his followers quit the SP to form the Social Democrats, USA (SDUSA), the leftist Debs Caucus—which had resigned angrily in 1971—resurfaced as SP leaders, where, as far as anyone knows, they remain today.[13] These convoluted internecine struggles belied the organization's actual political impotence.

The history of the Communist Party has been plagued by "a bewildering number of splits, amalgamations, and further schisms which, combined with

the semi-clandestine existence of most of the combatants, make . . . Communist history murky indeed."[14] Beyond all the tactical and personal disputes, name changes, internal disagreements, policy shifts, front organizations, and expulsions—all amply documented by others—four factors stand out.

First, from its origins in 1919 to the present, the CP has advocated a rigidly orthodox brand of Marxism. The blush of revolutionary success in Russia, the interventions of Bukharin and Trotsky into domestic CP affairs, and the early writings of its best theorists all set the CP in ideological cement. Theoretical twists and turns involving race, gender, and the state, which we will examine later, merely rationalized the preeminence of historical and dialectical materialism.

Second, beginning in 1921, the Soviet Union was the ultimate source of most significant CP policy in America. Membership was itself governed by Moscow's Twenty-One Points, and internal disputes were usually resolved "either by a cablegram from the Comintern or by a trip to Moscow."[15] Harvey Klehr, the CP's most recent biographer, is unequivocal: "Even when the Party's tracks are clear and seemingly autonomous one must search for their Soviet sources."[16]

Third, except for brief periods preceding the Nazi-Soviet Pact, immediately following World War II, and preceding the Hungarian intervention in 1956, the CP's popularity steadily declined. Even during the Depression its Presidential candidate, William Z. Foster, polled only 103,151 of almost 40 million votes cast, and the CP captured only one local office: a mayorality race in a tiny Minnesota hamlet. By 1935, almost two-thirds of its 25,000 members were foreign-born, and the rate of turnover was so high that it took 7 new recruits to gain 2 additional members. The CP's secret national membership rolls are difficult to estimate, but scholars agree they never exceeded 75,000 or 80,000 (which may have been reached in 1938–39 and again in 1944), and have plummeted to 3,000 (in 1958, following a period of intense government harassment that resembled the Palmer Raids of 1919–21, as well as the invasion of Hungary and Krushchev's denunciation of Stalin). Even in the 1930s, at the peak of its popularity, almost one-half its members were located in the New York City area, 40 percent were unemployed, 20 percent were Jewish, and fewer than 25 percent were women.[17] Hardly a cross-section of America. It currently claims 17,500 members, concentrated primarily in a few industrial states. In the 1984 Presidential election its candidate received 35,561 votes, .03 percent of the national total.

Finally, the CP's early failure to become a mass-based movement combined with the SP's escalating irrelevance to turn American Marxism from a political into a predominantly intellectual movement, encompassing a shrinking number of intellectuals at that, many of whom had been expelled or had voluntarily resigned from the CP.

Neither the SP nor the CP succeeded in mobilizing America's workers. Their failure, however, is shared by numerous orthodox splinter groups that have appeared and disappeared since 1919. The largest and most influential of these was the Trotskyists. Born as the Communist League of America in 1929, following Stalin's bloody purges of leftists in Moscow, American Trotskyism was continually reincarnated in organizations that appeared, splintered, and dissolved in dizzying order, "like an onion trying to commit suicide."[18] Trotskyists focused on esoteric tactical issues that were unintelligible to most workers and uninteresting to others. They believed that Russia's socialist revolution would evaporate unless simultaneous revolutions occurred throughout the industrialized world, and thus bolshevism had to be reinforced by unrelenting CP insurrectionism everywhere; that the Soviet workers' state had degenerated into a dictatorial bureacracy, but could be salvaged; that backward nations, governed by the theory of combined or uneven development and directed by the Party, needed to forcibly telescope the development process; that CPs should "bore from within" existing trade unions and parties rather than create parallel institutions, and steer any cooperative alliances leftward; and that CPs, if deemed necessary, must impose their proletarian will on peasants. In brief, Trotskyism took a hard-line or leftist revolutionary position on most political issues, but condemned Stalinism and socialist bureaucratization. Leftist Trotskyists emphasized confrontational revolutionary tactics; rightist Trotskyists (also known as "Third Camp Socialists" or the "Shachtman Tendency," after its leader, Max Shachtman), the critique of socialist bureaucracy. Left and right accepted the unimpeachable character of Marxism-Leninism.

These hairsplitting quarrels were internal disputes among true orthodox believers that most Americans neither heard nor cared about. National membership in Trotskyist organizations likely never exceeded 2,000, and is in the hundreds today. In 1984's national elections they were supported by barely .02 percent of the American electorate.[19] Nevertheless, particularly the rightist variation of Trotskyism unintentionally jostled some followers into questioning the unquestionable, that is, materialism. It therefore exerted an estimable intellectual force in the 1940s and 1950s by spawning creative radical thinkers such as James Burnham, Irving Howe, C.L.R. James, and Michael Harrington.

After the 1956 denunciation of Stalin, the Moscow-controlled American CP was purged of pro-Stalinist "left-sectarians," who then, led by former chairman William Z. Foster, predictably denounced the new leadership's "revisionism." Vicious internal struggles prompted John Gates, editor of the *Daily Worker* and a leader of the revisionists, to resign from the Party with most of his supporters. Membership fell from 20,000 in 1956 to about 3,000 in 1958. Disorder and controversey accelerated until Gus Hall became General Secretary in 1959, and consolidated revisionist control. This disintegration of what was the orthodox left's largest and most stable party, com-

bined with the proliferation of splinter parties loyal to victorious Third World revolutionary movements in China, Cuba, and Viet Nam, further ruptured orthodoxy's tiny constituency. Today's panorama of orthodox parties is still dominated by the CP (technically, the CPUSA), which remains loyal to Moscow and committed to proletarian revolution. Paradoxically, it now supports progressive non-communists when permitted to do so, and advocates a higher minimum wage, increased social spending, decreased military spending, a six-hour workday, and public works projects. In effect acknowledging its own failures, it has belatedly evolved into the most flexible of orthodox parties by permitting common-sense to at least temporarily replace dogma. The SLP survives, emphasizing the electoral component of De-Leonism, but still committed, like the master, to proletarian insurrection. There are about 500 enthusiastic members. The Socialist Workers' Party (SWP), founded by James P. Cannon in 1938 as successor to the Communist League of America, remains the oldest and largest of the Trotskyist organizations. Trotskyist splinter groups include the Workers' League (WL), Workers' World Party (WWP), and the Spartacist League (SL). Maoism is represented by the Revolutionary Communist Party (RCP) and the Communist Party (Marxist-Leninist) (CP,M-L). The largest unaffiliated orthodox parties are the Communist Labor Party (CLP) and the World Socialist Party of the United States (WSPUS). Finally, numerous orthodox terrorist organizations exist, the most well-known being the May 19th Communist Organization and the Weather Underground. Total membership in the entire spectrum of orthodox organizations is barely 25,000—enough people to fill one end-zone of a typical university arena on a breezy football Saturday in October.

II

"The history of American radicalism," lamented a disillusioned participant, "is largely a history of failure."[20] We have seen that Marxism only marginally influenced the U.S. and impacted even less on the worldwide history of socialism. Marxists, with few exceptions, have performed miserably as candidates for public office. Even in the 1930s, when the CP was fairly stable and unified, Federal government repression was minimal, the Soviet Union was perceived as a potential anti-fascist ally, and working class America was in the throes of economic and social upheaval, Marxism was politically impotent everywhere but in scattered immigrant communities and native-born sectors that had special needs, resources, and characteristics. Although Marxian radicalism, of course, did exist in America throughout the late nineteenth and twentieth centuries, its appeal was always negligible and insufficiently articulated. The salient question is "why?" and there are probably as many answers as questioners. It would, I think, be safe to say

that Americans generally, and most workers in particular, have simply ignored it.

The nature of an actor's relationship to external surroundings is at the heart of any methodology of social inquiry, and is a key issue for Marxists and non-Marxists alike. Empirical social science, which is hegemonic today in capitalist America, defines actors as enclosed, complete entities whose perceptions are determined by empirically verifiable objects encountered in everyday life. Consciousness, like a moving billiard ball, is guided by unilinear, causal links with external objects. Rather than beginning with one small, isolated part and then building empirical connections, dialectics, an alternative scientific method, begins with the whole and clarifies how each part fits and works. Empirical science presumes the autonomy of constituent parts; dialectics, the irreducible complexity of the whole. From the latter's point of view, objects are inseparably linked to, and defined by, the processes by which they were created, and the broader environmental contexts that generated the processes. Each separate thing therefore embodies a reality that transcends the immediate empirical and commonsensical: its history, its hidden links to other things and conditions, its unfolding but unrealized future. Nothing magical has been insinuated here. Dialecticians acknowledge the reality and importance of concrete specifics, and empiricists recognize interrelationships. The issue is one of emphasis, that is, of how best to organize reality and communicate knowledge. Dialecticians believe that they accurately reflect the actual quality of social life, and also explain the sources and consequences of empirical facts. As a method of social inquiry, dialectics is epistemologically valid and practically useful. It can elucidate problems and proffer pertinent solutions. Empirical science, valid and useful for natural scientists and technicians, inadequately conveys the complex overlay of realities experienced by social actors. As social science, it effects only mundane explanations of thoughtless behavior.

Analyzed dialectically, a perception is merely one component of a complex, dynamic social whole that embodies the perceiver's personal and social histories, world environment, socio-economic structures, dominant values, and everyday activities. Each level is defined by, and also partially defines, that whole. Consequently, Marxism's failure in America indicates, for dialecticians, both a collective unwillingness to accept it and also the immense power of American and world capitalism to inhibit certain kinds of perceptions from becoming too widespread.

Social reality, in sum, is irretrievably fractured into levels ranging from the psychological to the communal, and each level embodies the totality of intersecting parts that comprises the dynamic whole. Social scientists thus find themselves in a humbling position. Any single explanation of American Marxism, by definition, is partial and one-sided, illustrating some relevant phenomena and occluding others. A traditional orthodox emphasis on class clarifies objective economic factors from which personal decisions emerged,

even as it conceals such non-economic ingredients as race, gender, and religion. On the other hand, highlighting working class values accentuates the significance of ideas and free actions, but obscures the social role of impersonal structures. Alternatively, by accenting America's socialist movement itself, we clarify one institution's impact on socio-economic structures and personal values, but lose the panorama of relevant nonpolitical factors. No single approach, alone, suffices, because its subject matter is internally related to that which it ignores. Conversely, each explanation clearly illustrates one social aspect better than others. Distortion, it appears, is an unavoidable cost of social inquiry. We must select explanatory foci not on their correctness—they are all equally distorting—but rather on how well they isolate what we want to know about.

Scholars have, in fact, explained the failure of American socialism in four related but distinct ways, accenting either maladroit socialist institutions and personalities, unfavorable economic conditions, inopportune social and political factors, or the cultural hegemony of liberalism.[21] None of these explanations is patently false. Each highlights one important aspect of America's liberal-democratic-capitalist totality in order to illustrate its historical relevance. America's capitalist economic base, for example, buttressed originally by free market mechanisms and a laissez-faire state but more recently by state intervention, is an integral component of the liberal-democratic totality. It is internally, dialectically linked to American individualism as well as to America's political and social structures, reciprocally defining and being defined by these other social elements and the whole. Materialists isolate this economic factor and proceed from there, selecting this distortion in order to magnify objective, class-related phenomena that help explain socialism's forgettable past. Whether one isolates and magnifies class or, instead, socialist institutions, sociopolitical structures, or culture depends on what one wants to know about socialism in America. The danger lies in absolutizing any single factor. By ignoring class altogether, for example, we swallow bourgeois assumptions regarding the unqualified separation of civil society and politics, thereby rationalizing capitalist hegemony. Similarly, materialists overlook noneconomic factors, and by so doing limit their options in America to irrelevance or authoritarianism. Both alternatives misconstrue reality, turning distortion into dogma. Neither, alone, adequately explains American socialism.

In forthcoming chapters we will isolate the nonorthodox features of American Marxism, and for this the cultural paradigm is singularly pertinent. Socialism's weak American showing, in this view, is directly attributable to our compulsive, frontier-style individualism, which fluorished unsullied by significant ideological alternatives. The Constitution, still the signpost for America's liberal democracy, institutionalizes Locke's natural rights of life, liberty, and property, and divides power as a means of limiting it. American society is characterized by voluntarism, religious toleration,

and pluralism. Its legal system protects rights, liberties, and privacy. The athletic games Americans play, the films they enjoy, the philosophies they embrace, the values they teach youngsters, their native art forms, all are thoroughly conditioned by an unchallenged, rabid individualism. Socialism, in this context, appeared irrelevant, unnecessary, and dangerously unpatriotic. To those accepting this cultural paradigm, materialist socialism was doomed in America regardless of the internal character of its parties or personalities. Moreover, objective economic, social, and political factors inhibiting socialism merely bolstered hegemonic subjective attitudes.

While mainstream Marxists doggedly backed the SP, CP, or an orthodox faction, others on the left quietly began to reformulate Marxian theory and practice to accomodate America's idiosyncratic individualism. They have, in effect, molded Marxism to liberalism, producing a corpus of theory and strategy that constitutes American nonorthodox or neo-Marxism—the "Yankee Red" of our title. Predictably, the process unfolded in typically American style: as pragmatic reactions to particular problems experienced by orthodoxy, or to unanticipated changes in the liberal totality. Thus, there are no American Marxists comparable to those grand nonorthodox thinkers of twentieth century Europe. More importantly, American leftists lack a synthetic philosophy that can neatly package neo-Marxist ideas into one coherent, organic theory. Notwithstanding these deficiencies, however, a renaissance of creative ideas and tactics is brewing on the American left that could, potentially, augur liberalism's demise.

More specifically, nonorthodox Marxism in America has crystallized around four important components of the liberal worldview: the hegemony of conscious subjects; the state as impartial arbiter of diverse interests and politics as an apt means of transforming society; science as systematic empirical inquiry; and the pluralist belief that policy formulation is characterized by a conflict between multiple, competing social interests. Each of these unquestioned presuppositions of American life has been enthusiastically rejected by orthodox Marxists, who emphasize impersonal laws of history, the priority of economics, dialectical materialism, and dominant class hegemony. Acknowledging both the widespread popularity of these liberal tenets and the subtle, unanticipated, almost unnoticed changes in the way modern liberal institutions in America actually work, neo-Marxists have stretched radical theory to incorporate these subjective and objective factors. The result is an explosion of revolutionary socialist thought that falls smartly into these four categories, and constitutes an indigenous American brand of Marxism.

As we shall see, many neo-Marxists have been motivated by economic, social, political, and institutional phenomena, as well as by a desire to culturally assimilate Marxism. Contemporary leftist theory, therefore, is directly linked to economic events in America's capitalist base, the character of its parties, and recent sociopolitical events. The cultural paradigm's superior

value turns not only on its own usefulness in interpreting new and unexpected patterns of left theorizing, but also on its classifying potential: it meaningfully organizes and explains the entire range of nonorthodox literature. As a hermeneutic for understanding nonorthodox Marxism in America it is unsurpassed.

Conclusion

The left in early nineteenth century America was originally composed of disillusioned patriots seeking a more perfect, egalitarian union that was sanctified by the Constitution and the revolutionary spirit of 1776. European radicals landed on its shores to direct the revolutionary movement in the name of scientific socialism, an imported materialist doctrine which was received hesitantly by native radicals and fearfully by everyone else. By 1890, orthodoxy had won its fight with nonmaterialist socialists, and was on its way to losing the war with capitalism. Orthodoxy chose to ignore America's diverse labor force, its intense liberal traditions, its dynamic middle classes, and its complacent, fearful masses. Instead, they squeezed America's left into rigid economic categories that denied authenticity to everything but class, in effect trivializing the nation's most heartfelt beliefs and commitments. Marxists, the self-proclaimed voice of the masses, "found themselves strangers in a strange land."[22] They failed miserably in mobilizing discontent, which was real and widespread, and came to lead a movement without followers.

Marxism had to somehow reestablish its links with indigenous American values if it was to succeed. Orthodoxy couldn't accomplish this without sacrificing its raison d'être, that is, its materialist worldview. American neo-Marxists, on the other hand, were not burdoned by dogma. They interpreted cognition as important in itself, not mechanically shaped by matter, and perceived society as a multi-dimensional, interpenetrating totality, with the economic base only one of many reciprocally linked factors. Ideas are conditioned by the manner in which we live and work. But everyday lifestyles are also affected by subjective needs and expectations, which, in turn, are conditioned by everything from genetics to peer pressure, religion, gender roles, class, and the kind of food we eat. Life in society, in other words, is a complex interconnected whole, not merely a cause-effect relationship between base and superstructure. Class struggle is thus not simply a battle between owners and producers in the workplace. It is also a cultural, religious, political, and philosophical conflict over which beliefs will dominate a people's thoughts and behavior, and thus condition their economic activities. The goal of dialectics, from a nonorthodox perspective, is to reestablish life's internal relationships by reconstituting this dynamic whole.

Neo-Marxists have incrementally reformed Marxist theory by tapping heretofore neglected sources lying deep within the American psyche: un-

hindered subjectivity, political activism, empirical science, and pluralism. This new American Marxism is more complex and subtle than orthodoxy, but also more in tune with the actual cares of a variegated working class.

Notes

1. On this topic see Morris Hillquit, *History of Socialism in the United States* (Revised ed.: New York: Funk & Wagnalls, 1910), pp. 21–134; David Harris, *Socialist Origins in the United States* (Assen, Netherlands: Van Gorcum, 1966), pp. 1–7; Albert Fried (ed.), *Socialism in America* (New York: Doubleday, 1970), pp. 6–10; and Philip Foner, *American Socialism and Black Americans* (Westport, CT: Greenwood Press, 1977), pp. 3–4.
2. See Charles Sotheran, *Horace Greeley and Other Pioneers of American Socialism* (New York: Humboldt, 1892); H. S. Foxwell, "Introduction" to the English translation of Anton Menger, *The Right to the Whole Produce of Labor* (London: Macmillan, 1899); A. M. Simons, *Social Forces in American History* (New York: Macmillan, 1911); and Harold Laski, *The American Democracy* (New York: Viking, 1948).
3. See Paul Buhle, *Marxism in the U.S.A* (London: Verso, 1987), pp. 29–31; Howard H. Quint, *The Forging of American Socialism* (Columbia, SC: University of South Carolina Press, 1953), pp. 6–12; Theodore Draper, *The Roots of American Communism* (New York: Viking, 1957), pp. 11–14; Harris, pp. 8–13; and John P. Diggins, *The Left in the Twentieth Century* (New York: Harcourt Brace Jovanovich, 1973), pp. 54ff.
4. Patrick Renshaw, *The Wobblies* (New York: Doubleday, 1967), p. 53. See also L.Glenn Seretan, *Daniel DeLeon: The Odyssey of An American Marxist* (Cambridge, MA: Harvard University Press, 1979); Diggins, p. 66; and Harvey Klehr, "Daniel DeLeon," in Robert A. Gorman (ed.), *Biographical Dictionary of Marxism* (Westport, CT, and London: Greenwood Press, 1986), pp. 90–91.
5. Laurence Gronlund, *The Cooperative Commonwealth* (Cambridge, MA: Harvard University Press, 1965), p. 73.
6. Quint, pp. 28ff., contends Bellamy's radicalism was shaped by Gronlund's. Arthur E. Morgan, *Edward Bellamy* (New York: Columbia University Press, 1944), p. 388, claims that Bellamy never read Gronlund, who abandoned orthodox Marxism when he read Bellamy.
7. See Melvyn Dubofsky, *We Shall Be All* (New York: Quadrangle, 1969), pp. 6–7; and Renshaw, pp. 48–50.
8. See Stoughton Lynd, *Intellectual Origins of American Radicalism* (New York: Pantheon, 1968) and Norman Pollack, *The Populist Response to Industrialist America* (Cambridge, MA: Harvard University Press, 1962).
9. In 1904 the first national platform of the SP stated that socialism should not be "a theory imposed upon society for its acceptance or rejection." Instead, it is "the interpretation of what is, sooner or later, inevitable. Capitalism is already struggling to its destruction." Proceedings, National Convention of the Socialist Party, Chicago, Illinois, 1–6 May, 1904, p. 308.
10. See James Weinstein, *The Decline of Socialism in America* (New York: Vintage,

1967), p. 22; Bell, p. 99; Draper, p. 41; Diggins, p. 60; and David A. Shannon, *The Socialist Party of America* (New York: Macmillan, 1955), p. 5.

11. Harvey Klehr, *The Heyday of American Communism* (New York: Basic Books, 1984), p. 4.

12. Constance Ashton Meyers, *The Prophets Army* (Westport, CT: Greenwood Press, 1977), pp. 109–10; and Bell, p. 157.

13. Eric Thomas Chester, *Socialists and the Ballot Box* (New York: Praeger, 1985), p. 143.

14. Klehr, p. 4.

15. Diggins, p. 95.

16. Klehr, p. xi. See p. 540.

17. See *ibid.*, pp. 54–91, 153–66; Warren Lerner, *A History of Socialism and Communism in Modern Times* (Englewood Cliffs, NJ: Prentice-Hall, 1982), p. 230; Chester, pp. 58–9; Charles Hobday, *Communist and Marxist Parties of the World* (Essex, England: Longman, 1986), pp. 306–7; Maurice Isserman, "The Half Swept House: American Communism in 1956," *Socialist Review*, 12 (January–February 1982), pp. 73–87; Bell, p. 140; Irving Howe and Lewis Coser, *The American Communist Party: A Critical History 1919–57* (Boston: Beacon, 1957), pp. 437–99; Buhle, pp. 184–99; and Draper, pp. 213–20.

18. Max Eastman's words quoted in Constance Ashton Myers, *The Prophet's Army* (Westport, CT: Greenwood Press, 1957), p. 14. See also Max Shachtman, "Footnote for Historians," *New International*, 4 (December 1938), p. 377.

19. Myers, pp. 54f; and Hobday, p. 309.

20. Lasch, p. viii.

21. The first approach is illustrated by the pertinent work of Rossiter, Bell, Weinstein, Kipnis, and Kilko. The second, by orthodox materialists. The third, by Werner Sombart, Selig Perlman, Dahrendorf, Schumpeter, Boorstin, and Thernstrom. And the last by Hofstadter, O'Connor, Ariel, Becker, Diggins, Appleby, and particularly by Louis Hartz, whose *The Liberal Tradition in America* (New York: Harcourt Brace & World, 1955) crystallized the argument. A reaction to Hartz's thesis has recently formed around the republicans Bernard Bailyn, J. G. A. Pocock, and Gordon Wood.

22. Buhle, p. 59.

Radical Subjectivity

Marxism claims to be the theory and practice of human liberation; America, the home of freedom. We have seen, however, that orthodoxy believes objective historical laws determine the form and content of liberated social behavior. Americans, on the other hand, define freedom as self-determined, subjectively meaningful activity. They have, consequently, rejected materialism philosophically and politically, even as many of their own dreams of freedom turned into economic nightmares.

Some Marxists, influenced by the liberal tradition, see truly emancipatory social theory, that manifests liberating actions, arising only from a radical subjectivist critique of encrusted values and institutions. One disturbing fact, they argue, must be confronted by capitalists *and* Marxists: Thoughtful subjects decide for themselves what to believe. Truth lives only in consciousness, which impersonal social theory will inevitably mute. Orthodoxy, therefore, deceptively rationalizes the transferring of actual decision-making power from free subjects to an elite cadre. Its emancipatory rhetoric screens a real commitment to autonomous truth, which in appropriate conditions is crammed down the throats of unenlightened citizens, irrespective of numbers or working class credentials. Only by redesigning Marxism, eliminating "objective" factors that rationalize dictatorship, can it survive as a workers' movement and succeed in America. Marx's socialist utopia lives in the reflective experiences of its beneficiaries. As scientific theory and revolutionary praxis, Marxism is justifiable only through the radical self-consciousness of capitalism's dispossessed.

In this chapter we will outline the troubled history of liberalism and subjectivism, and then see how some nonorthodox Marxists have subjectively revitalized the American left—accommodating, rather than disregarding, its liberal heritage.

I

Subjectivist philosophy, based on the epistemological primacy of consciousness and the commitment to self-determining freedom, has roots in the ancient and medieval worlds but did not fully blossom until the Enlighten-

ment. Martin Luther's heretical theology situated divinity in the conscious perceptions of God's flock and advocated faith through personal fulfillment rather than an overbearing Church hierarchy. Individualism germinated in sixteenth and seventeenth century social theories. With the onset of liberalism, particularly Hobbes's bleak vision of a warring world of purely self-interested subjects, medieval spiritualism was decisively shattered by the radical notion of human autonomy. Hobbesian man is alone and isolated, living as a self-interested ego. The validity of everyday knowledge is measured solely by its practical utility in increasing the life chances of competitive subjects vying for society's limited resources. The implications, unintended by an author entrenched in seventeenth century rationalism, were revolutionary: Human nature was irretrievably cut from transcendental moorings, leaving truth at the mercy of self-interested subjects. Social, political, and ethical theory were no longer compelling in themselves. Their emptiness meant some cruder force kept us peacefully together, one whose rationale was the experiential need of each citizen daily threatened by death. Knowledge now meekly served subjectivity.

John Locke's reaction was unequivocal. Uncontrolled subjectivism served almost no one's needs, least of all the social class sponsoring the original break with spiritualism in the name of individual liberty. Though medievalism was irreparably shattered, the concrete needs of a growing middle class made some form of *a priorism* indispensible. Self-interest had somehow to be fused with objectivity in order better to protect bourgeois property, prestige, and liberty. The synthesis was manufactured by a natural truth, based on self-evident "reason," that guides egotistical individuals to peaceful, cooperative interaction while simultaneously safeguarding liberal political and economic rights. This ideal knowledge replaced the brute force of Hobbes's Leviathan, without sacrificing self-determining freedom. Lockians assumed, therefore, that experienced knowledge coincided with absolute truth, subjectivity and objectivity overlapped. Society existed objectively, reflecting the natural order of things, but also guaranteed each citizen the right to own property and determine privately how serious his participation and commitment would be.

This optimistic retreat from naked subjectivism progressed through the nineteenth and twentieth centuries, with phrases like "enlightened self-interest" and "basic rights" replacing the increasingly antiquated "natural laws." The design, however, was fixed: human autonomy tempered by a cool, inviolable truth protecting personality and property. This promethean task distinguished the evolution of philosophical liberalism from John Stuart Mill to T.H. Green, Leonard Hobhouse, John Dewey, and John Rawls. Liberals unhappy with this strained synthesis of subjectivity and absolute truth embraced empiricism, which impersonally, factually described the objective world while leaving liberal institutions untouched. By the second decade of this century, except for purists like Kierkegaard, Nietzsche, and Husserl,

subjectivism was known only in the mutilated forms of liberalism and empiricism.

Liberalism, in brief, remained trapped between consciousness and chaos. It aspired to universal self-determination but feared the potential consequences, which could topple liberalism's hegemonic class and restructure the political system. America exhibits this cultural schizophrenia. The commitment to individualism has always been widespread and intense among indigenous Americans, who, as a rule, cherish their privacy and resent government intrusions. On the other hand, the objective limits to free activity are carefully defined and enforced by knowledgeable, powerful elites, all of whom share a disproportionate vested interest in the status quo.

Orthodoxy has focused solely on capitalist class hegemony, disregarding the significance of common everyday attitudes. These, it argues, are determined by one's position in the base, that is, by class. Since matter unfolds predictably in history, dominant classes will come and go according to scientific laws. Moreover, each will stamp its own worldview on the entire cultural network. Consciousness is therefore epiphenomenal. In capitalist America, workers needed to disregard individualism, acknowledge their collective proletarian character, and fulfill history's socialist destiny. Orthodoxy will not dignify attitudes, regardless of their popularity, that are objectively false and transient.

II

Orthodoxy accepts unquestioningly the laws of historical and dialectical materialism. On the other hand, neo-Marxists reflectively evaluate leftist dogma from a nonmaterialist perspective, accepting only what can explain a world in which joy, suffering, love, and anxiety—not merely economic processes—touch workers' lives. Consciousness, in brief, is real and important. The price of ignoring subjectivity is irrelevance. Increasingly, American Marxists believe this is too high a price to pay.

The subjectivist reaction to orthodoxy appeared simultaneously in America and Europe at the turn of the century. Whereas Americans devised apt tactics, Europeans philosophically reformulated Marxist epistemology. This Marxist division of labor—Americans and Third World leftists concentrating on practical policy, Europeans on abstract theory—has, several notable exceptions notwithstanding, persisted throughout this century. In dealing with the thorny problem of subjectivity, European neo-Marxists relied on Hegel and Husserl to purge the left of objectivism.

For the Hegelian left,[1] all of Marx's scholarly work focused on the process by which capitalism engendered authentic proletarian self-consciousness. Until 1846, Marx emphasized capitalism's alienating qualities, its submersion of human authenticity in commodity fetishism and the injustices of the market. Afterwards, he stressed the empirical relationships by

which workers were first exploited and then radicalized. While Marx was progressively more attuned to concrete material factors, he also suggested that both alienation and exploitation are more than their material components. Capitalism's negation of human potential was conceptually measured against an idealized species-being. Marx believed alienation preceded capitalism and helped cause it, and humanity's essential quality is an openness to nature and society.[2] The former implies that self-perceptions mature in history and cause new social and economic forms. The latter interprets capitalism as blocking self-realization. Together, they express the Hegelian notion of Reason historically realizing itself in reflective self-consciousness. Materialists have neglected Marx's Hegelian dialectic, focusing entirely on the one-dimensional, nonspeculative terminology from the later work. Predictably, Hegelians contended, orthodoxy eventually lost its reflective revolutionary spark, descending first into Kautskyite reformism and then Stalinist totalitarianism.

Hegelian leftists believed that in appropriate conditions, which Marx studiously described after 1846, humanity would reflectively perceive the interpenetration of subject and object, particular and universal, and then rebel against capitalism's institutionalized inhumanity. History was therefore evolving toward human freedom, realized in the revolutionary praxis of reasonable actors. Its current tool was the working class, for their tragic suffering was the impetus to correct thinking and pertinent behavior. Freedom and necessity coalesced in an essential truth cognitively experienced by reasonable workers at a mature stage of capitalist development.

Husserlian leftists in Europe,[3] like the Hegelians, hoped to resurrect the subjective element of Marx's dialectic, but without Hegelian abstractions. They argued that Marxism, particularly its theory of alienation, could provide theoretical tools for creating radical social theory that also avoided *a priorism* and preserved the integrity of free subjects. Although Marx, of course, was neither a phenomenologist nor a philosopher intent on stretching the limits of subjectivity, he did, phenomenologists contended, believe in humanity's irreducible freedom. Marx's life work, even the later economic writings, was devoted to justifying and realizing a society of self-determined citizens, unencumbered by oppressive capitalist institutions. Human beings, for Marx, freely created the conditions that now alienated and enslaved them, and could, potentially, undo their creation. Economic exploitation and cultural alienation were neither inevitable nor irreversible.

Phenomenologists argued that although his strategy and style changed, all of Marx's writings presumed humanity's irreducible freedom. Prior to 1846, Marx philosophically measured everyday experiences in capitalism, finding them deformed and inauthentic. Later, he translated philosophical critique into a science that factually substantiated humanity's fall into inauthenticity. Here, economic phenomena were seen as crystallized forms of human praxis that eliminated the very possibility of praxis. The later scientific works thus

empirically demystified reified activities. They did to classical political economy precisely what Marx had earlier done to Hegel: purge it of abstractions that obscured the human origins of society and emasculated humanity's free potential. In brief, the early philosophical anthropology was implicit in the later scientific critique, despite the latter's factual, nonphilosophical style. History, for left phenomenologists, was made first in reflection and then in self-determining praxis. This was Marx's central, truly revolutionary insight.

Both Hegelian and phenomenological traditions offered nonorthodox Marxists in America philosophical reasons for taking subjectivity seriously. Where orthodoxy stamped its version of reality on the social world, subjectivist neo-Marxists acknowledged instead the irreducibility of consciousness and the importance of translating economic process into radical self-awareness. For Americans, the message from Europe was clear: the subjective component of human emancipation couldn't be imported from abroad. It had to be rooted in real problems and meaningful solutions.

III

In 1901—fourteen years after Antonio Labriola, in the "prelezione" of his *Problemi della filosofia della storia*, had first summoned an Hegelian revitalization of orthodoxy—the SP was founded in America. All of its leaders pledged allegiance to the Engelsian principles of scientific socialism. But in spite of this materialist consensus, SP members disagreed sharply when analyzing American conditions and formulating tactics. By its 1904 convention, the party had split into Left, Center, and Right factions, each with its own leaders and programs.[4]

The SP Center-Left

The Right was was lead by Victor Berger. It favored reformist tactics like those of European social democrats then mobilizing around Eduard Bernstein. Until 1907, Center and Left factions were, ideologically and tactically, virtually indistinguishable. Leftists, however, courted only blue-collar workers and spoke in simple, purely proletarian colloquialisms. The Center, led by Morris Hillquit, embraced intellectuals as well as workers, and fashioned abstract monographs that eluded most workers but kept several radical presses busy. A broad Center-Left coalition constituted a large majority of SP members and guided SP policy from the party's founding in 1901 until about 1907. It also produced the most popular SP leaders during this period, including Debs, William Haywood, and Algie Simons, a Phi Beta Kappa recipient and editor of the *International Socialist Review*.[5]

The Center-Left coalition, particularly its Left component, soon encountered a serious dilemma. Marx's materialist conception of history, in-

cluding the theory of economic determinism, accurately explained capitalist America, where the bourgeoisie used their economic might to shape government, morality, and all of social life. But materialism was superfluous in a land of immigrants and individualists. American workers neither understood nor appreciated *a priori* laws that ignored everyday problems. SP Leftists could not on the one hand claim to authentically represent real American workers, and on the other propound a foreign, incomprehensible ideology. Their solution was simply to disregard the theoretical problem: Marxism could be justified nonphilosophically because it adequately explained everyday reality and, in practice, improved proletarian living conditions. American Marxists would shun compulsive theorizing by neither confirming nor denying historical materialism. Since materialism in any case couldn't be convincingly defended in American factories, the SP sensibly sided with workers rather than philosophers.

Unhinged from materialism's deadweight, the SP during its early years tried to win proleterian hearts. America, it argued, embodied two distinct classes: capitalists and workers. After the rapid industrialization of the late 1800s, capital was split into large corporations and trusts, and small businesses. The Republican Party was controlled by the former, the Democratic Party by the latter. Both Republicans and Democrats hoped to strengthen capitalism by favoring their own loyal entrepreneurs. Socialists needed to stimulate workers into consciously realizing that their battle for higher wages and improved factory conditions was part of a broader struggle that pitted them against Democratic and Republican class enemies. A class-conscious proletariat would then join the SP and catalyze the final struggle. SP strategy thus turned on deemphasizing abstract theorizing while supporting projects that would eventually transform workers' into enlightened revolutionaries. In the SP's hands, Marxism was no longer a preordained plan. Instead, it sought to change reformist workers' attitudes by plugging into, and exascerbating, meaningful grassroots struggles. Revolutionary working class consciousness, heretofore taken for granted, was now worth fighting for.

This fresh concern for worker subjectivity meant that orthodoxy's revolutionary bromides needed reformulating. Factory insurrections could very well destroy those large corporations and trusts that provided workers their only means of livelihood. Rather than asking workers to sacrifice their economic interests for an orthodox abstraction, the SP concluded that only factory ownership, not the factories, should change. By transferring the economic struggle to politics, that is, having workers vote en masse for socialist candidates, a people's government could peacefully nationalize factories with a minimum of economic disruption. The Center - Left - controlled SP became the political voice of American workers, and ceded to unions the task of workplace organizing. The SP's vital job of awakening worker consciousness was facilitated by a strategy that workers, who had

struggled valiently for the right to vote, could believe in. Although the Right's reformist proposals, such as public ownership of utilities, might benefit workers in the short term, the Center-Left coalition favored worker struggle, emancipation, and self-goverment, all through socialist electoral activity. By voting for socialists, workers were, on their own initiative and in their own preferred manner, realizing historical necessity and completing a revolutionary process that capitalism's own internal contradictions had begun.

SP success would be measured by the size of the socialist vote and the number of SP candidates elected to office. Consequently, SP activities during these years were primarily in the areas of electioneering, public demonstrations, and lectures, and the publication of mass circulation socialist literature and journals. It hoped to build popularity among workers by sharing the experiences and indignities of proletarian life, and communicating information through everyday, neighborhood channels. Grassroots SP activism among farmers was also initiated, but not the Populist-Socialist alliance that might possibly have succeeded. Intellectuals, with their abstract theories and vague prescriptions, were uninvited. Debs, in 1912, actually suggested eliminating them from leadership positions in the party. The SP's goal, for which intellectuals were deemed unsuited, was the arousal of working class consciousness through thoughtful activism, rather than ideas. Authentic knowledge was rooted in that self-conscious, critical awareness one achieves when everyday problems are confronted and, through struggle, solved. This kind of critical knowledge could not be memorized.

By 1906, the Center-Left coalition showed signs of disintegrating, in spite of steady progress in increasing membership rolls. Orthodox SP leftists began reemphasizing the confrontational aspects of class struggle and the need for violent insurrections. It also wanted more energy spent on radical union organizing, and less on electioneering. The Right, on the other hand, perceived electoral activity as an end, rather than, as it was originally conceived, merely a means of inciting critical subjectivity. By 1906, the predominantly middle class, intellectual Center, already uncomfortable with the Left's anti-intellectualism, turned right. Power in the SP passed from the Center-Left to the Center-Right. Eventually, it would pass to the Right only, with the party's complexion becoming entirely reformist. Nonorthodox leftists, now alienated from the left and right of what was once their own party, began searching for an institutional home.

Wobblies

Their first stop was 122 Lake Street, Chicago. On 2 January 1905, twenty-one men and one woman ("Mother" Mary Jones), representing the Western Federation of Miners (WFM) and the American Labor Union (ALU), agreed

after three days of secret meetings to convene that spring in Chicago in order to establish a new, revolutionary workers organization. Two hundred and three national delegates came to Chicago. The WFM and ALU represented the largest bloc of workers, and were led by Vincent "The Saint" St. John; Father Thomas J. Hagerty, a maverick Catholic priest; and William E. Trautmann, editor of the Brewery Workers' newspaper, *Brauer Zeitung*. Sensing its ebbing influence in the SP, the Left faction sent, among others, three of its most prestigious members, Debs, Simons, and William Dudley "Big Bill" Haywood. Center and Right factions opposed this venture from the beginning. The opportunistic Daniel DeLeon headed a delegation of SLP members as well. These contentious, partisan leftists survived numerous personal and political quarrels to create the International Workers of the World, better known as the Wobblies, the first truly American national labor organization.

St. John and Haywood eventually left this distinguished pack behind and became the organization's preeminent leaders. St. John was a miner, prospector, and union organizer in Colorado, and eventually rose to the presidency of the Telluride Miners' Union in 1901. He was constantly hounded by Federal and State authorities for an assortment of alleged crimes, and was arrested several times, though not convicted. Formally uneducated, St. John drew on his earthy, occasionally violent mining experiences to achieve, in 1908, the rank of General Organizer. Much of the IWW's limited success during the 1908–1915 period was due to the no-nonsense organizational skills of St. John and his aide, Ben Williams, editor of the official IWW journal *Solidarity*. When his services were no longer appreciated, St. John returned to his beloved mountains and died in 1929, while prospecting for gold.

Born in a Salt Lake City boarding house in 1869, Haywood was big, bellicose, and bawdy, an uneducated "proletarian-intellectual" whose gritty courage and common sense turned him into a popular working class hero.[6] He joined the WFM in the late 1890s, and later the SP, where he became a spokesperson for the Left. Among colleagues, he acquired a reputation as an effective organizer and tactician. In 1905, during labor struggles in the Colorado coalfields, he and two others were kidnapped by Pinkerton agents, brought to Boise, and tried for complicity in the murder of Gov. Frank Staunnerberg of Idaho. Although successfully defended by Clarence Darrow, the by now notorious Haywood became untouchable. He roamed the country until 1912, an independent socialist with an enormous following. His important role as an IWW representative to the striking Lawrence, Massachusetts, textile workers catapulted Haywood back into the IWW hierarchy, where he eventually succeeded St. John as the single most powerful Wobbly figure, known for his efficient management techniques and spellbinding oratory. Haywood and other leftists were summarily imprisoned and tried during a Federal government crackdown in 1917. To the chagrin of his

many supporters, Haywood jumped bail in 1919 and escaped to Moscow. He was quickly disillusioned with the apparatchik mentality of the Bolshevik bureaucracy, turned again to excessive drinking, and died, unmourned and alone, in 1928.

The fact that independent, strong-willed, formally uneducated people like these gained power in the IWW is significant. They were common Americans blessed with the uncommon ability to powerfully communicate everyday working class experiences. They were, in this sense, educators who taught people in their own language what, based on their life experiences, they should already have known. Knowledge, for the Wobblies, was a state of mind rather than a body of doctrine: An enlightened, critical self-consciousness that could shock people into improving their own lives.

Wobblies, therefore, did not enjoy toeing the theoretical line. Actually, in the IWW there was hardly a theoretical line to toe. Wobbly leaders, like their successors in the New Left, would adopt almost any idea that helped organize and mobilize workers to act collectively. An unspoken and largely neglected foundation of Wobbly radicalism, from its beginning, was orthodox dialectical materialism. The famous Industrial Union Manifesto that concluded the first Chicago conference in 1905 explicitly endorsed Marx's materialist analysis of history. Later, the IWW Preamble iterated an orthodox version of America's class struggle and described the organization's role as "aiming steadily at the complete overthrow of the capitalist wage system."[7] Yet this almost precognitive orthodox mentality did not prevent Haywood, for example, from redefining America's class struggle into a tripartite battle between owners, skilled laborers, and workers. Or stop Wobbly leaders from enthusiastically supporting bourgeois workplace reforms that, by legislatively improving factory and living conditions, would, it was felt, empower workers.

Occasionally Wobbly leaders would rankle conservative American intellectuals by joining Darwin and Marx.[8] From this Wobbly perspective, social evolution mimicked organic evolution. Capitalism, which Marx accurately depicted as one moment of a natural historical cycle, was simultaneously the fittest survivor of medieval culture and the seedbed of proletarian hegemony. As empowered workers demonstrated their unique ability to right capitalism's wrongs, they would confirm both their own superiority over entrepreneurs and the biological necessity of socialism.

Finally, some Wobblies were syndicalists, who reduced proletarian struggle entirely to autonomous trade union activism.[9] These syndicalists, several of whom held leadership positions, believed the vanguard of proletarian struggle was the trade union, and its most formidable weapon the strike. They struggled to abolish skilled craft unions because these splintered workers into independent associations that negotiated from weakened, isolated positions. Invariably, craft unions became conservative, focusing on pay scales rather than power, and generating a simplistic faith in capitalist

legality. Syndicalists also felt that mechanization would eventually trivial-ize craft unions and all specialized industrial skills. Industrial unions, they argued, must organize instead around manufactured products, not tools or skills. To be effective, whole factories or, if possible, entire industries had to be targeted. Humanity's ultimate weapon in battling capital was the general strike, which, by empowering workers, would teach them to run factories and transform the industrial process. The syndicalist motto, eventually adopted by the IWW, was "One union of all workers in an industry; all in-dustries in one union."

Orthodoxy, Darwinism, and syndicalism were all abstractions created by European intellectuals in an alien environment. The IWW was an indigenous American workers' organization guided by organic representatives of com-mon people. Its ideology was always framed by the rough-hewn patina of American individualism, with its stress on common sense and citizen autonomy. Proletarian power, not ideological purity, was the Wobbly pot of gold; and IWW leaders, regardless of ideology, knew that Americans' affec-tions for family, land, and freedom had somehow to be transferred to class. Intellectually, revolution could well be inevitable, but from a practical, thoroughly Wobbly point of view, workers first had to consciously ex-perience their shared exploitation and then coalesce into a mobilized force powerful enough to challenge capital. In brief, history would be realized only when the power of capital could no longer match that of workers. And Wobblies believed that power required class solidarity, the bonding of self-conscious actors into a cohesive revolutionary group.

Wobbly ideological discourse, consequently, was more atuned to strategic or tactical problems than to theory. The question for Wobblies was never "Which theory is correct?" but "Which theory could best mobilize workers into a unified, critical social force?" Where the SP's Left simply ignored theory altogether, Wobblies decided to pick the most efficacious ideas from among the alternatives. Thus, orthodox Wobblies, for example, enthusiasti-cally supported grassroots-inspired reforms as a means of empowering workers. On the other hand, orthodoxy's impersonal laws of history, which ridiculed reformism, were also useful educational tools during workplace discussions, and in pamphlets, journals, and books. Putative logical con-tradictions were irrelevant. Logic was for intellectuals, not workers.

Wobbly syndicalists felt that the length and intensity of an average workday combined to dominate the lives of typical workers. Everyday reality for most Americans was thus the reality of paid labor. We identified first as workers, and then as citizens. Union membership was therefore a quintessentially personal and meaningful status. Moreover, union activism was singularly capable of mobilizing laborers into a powerful collective force. Syndicalists wanted the IWW to focus all its resources and energy into organizing workers on the job, creating radical unions where workers could emancipate themselves from the tyranny of everyday life.

The IWW's early years were marked by a fierce debate between those favoring unions as the only vehicle of proletarian interests, and those who would also organize politically. This was not really a debate between syndicalists and orthodox Marxists, although many of the former favored economic action only, and many of the latter political action as well. It was primarily a tactical dispute among revolutionaries all of whom strove to create critical, self-conscious proletarian solidarity. St. John led the anti-politics group. He felt proletarian political activism was futile and self-defeating in a state so tightly controlled by large corporate trusts. Capital wouldn't meekly roll over in the face of worker discontent by abandoning the state, its most important legitimizing tool. Even if progressive legislation somehow cleared the Congress, it was worthless without an organized working class to force compliance. St. John concluded that Wobblies should organize sympathetic industrial unions, from which inspired workers would emerge to challenge capitalist hegemony.

No Wobbly seriously disagreed with St. John's political analysis, but many rejected his tactical conclusions. Haywood and Frank Bohn, for example, conceded that the enormous cultural power of businesses and trusts precluded radical proletarian political activism.[10] For as long as American workers were powerless, they would continue suffering. Since political power belonged to capital, the anti-capitalist struggle had to be waged in factories by free and revolutionary unions. However, political tactics were nevertheless prerequisites for a successful workers movement, primarily because only a neutralized state—one where interclass conflict diluted the political power of capital—would allow workers to consolidate economically. Additionally, political activism could stir workers into realizing their collective electoral strength, just as union organizing aimed to empower workers economically. Although a union vote meant more to a worker than a vote for President or Senator, Americans esteemed the act of voting itself, and Haywood felt it was foolish to waste this opportunity for proletarian advancement. Hence he urged working people to "use the ballot at every opportunity," and was himself a candidate for Governor of Colorado in 1906.[11] In both instances, Haywood advanced the thesis that proletarian politics was a useful means of protecting and empowering workers when combined with union organizing. In sum, both economic *and* political activities were desirable.

Despite intense internal quarrels, actual Wobbly policy consistently reinforced Haywood's pragmatic line. The Preamble to the Wobbly constitution held a "political clause," which partially satisfied both sides by advocating industrial unionization and unaffiliated political activism. St. John managed to excise this provision in 1909, thereby shoving marginal Wobblies who favored political activism, like E.V. Debs, back into the SP. However, even during the 1909–16 years, immediately preceding Haywood's return to power, the IWW sponsored free speech campaigns in 26 western cities, most

in response to local ordinances that limited or forbade soapbox speaking in the streets; it struggled energetically to protect proletarian civil rights; it actively supported electoral campaigns on all levels to elect progressives and advocate socialism; and, finally, it vigorously supported public works and service programs that, it felt, by improving working class conditions would make the fight for socialism that much easier.[12] These practices, of course, continued under Haywood. Worker empowerment was always the Wobbly goal; doctrine, despite the rhetoric, a discardable means.

Wobbly tactics in the factory, the locus of revolutionary protest, aimed at reaching workers by plugging into subjectively meaningful events. Workers were prodded into what Wobblies called "direct action," which included any workplace activity that increased wages, reduced hours, or improved conditions. In practice, this meant engaging in both strikes and what Haywood called "passive sabotage."[13] The assumption here, as in Wobbly social theory generally, was that successful tactics would be theoretically justified retroactively. In the short term, workers undertook any potentially useful means of protest that they believed in and were committed to. Even violence was not ruled out. Nor, however, was it officially advocated, and American courts never did convict a single Wobbly of committing a violent act. Wobblies always attached their policies to real working class needs. They never told workers what to do or why they should do it. In Haywood's words, "any tactics" were acceptable in America's proletarian struggle against capitalism. Even the event Wobblies felt would finally annihilate capitalism, the "general strike," was theoretically undefined, at the mercy, so to speak, of rebelling workers themselves as they applied it to their own perceived needs.

The same self-governing unions that precipitated the general strike would, it was felt, evolve into grassroots political organizations. Post-revolutionary government would exist administratively, to coordinate production, but would not own factories. Instead, each industrial union would own and manage an industry, and democratically select representatives, preferably technically trained experts, to regional and national bodies that would coordinate national production. Socialist governments would exist, in Ben Williams's words, as "whatever central body they [workers] may find necessary."[14] Nor did Wobblies explain how socialism would be defended against internal and external opponents. These were questions that free workers, active members of self-governing unions, would answer. National authority would be somewhat centralized, but would consist of citizens representing local, mass-based, democratic organizations. Wobblies were anti-bureaucratic socialists before bureaucratic socialism even existed.

Although the Wobblies still occupy a national headquarters on the second floor of a shabby commercial building on North Halsted St. in Chicago, their influence in America had actually ceased by 1924. Their membership had peaked during 1919–23, when the Federal government estimated it at

250,000, and the IWW's own figures ranged from 58,000 to 100,000. But even during these good years IWW membership turned over at an average rate of 133 percent annually. Up to one million people, at one time or another, held IWW cards, but the organization never attracted more than 5 percent of American trade unionists in any year.[15]

One reason for this poor showing was government persecution, particularly in 1917, when Wobblies sought to organize workers in key industries. Almost every Wobbly official was arrested, and headquarters throughout the nation were raided. Wobblies were tarred and feathered in Oklahoma, packed into cattle cars and abandoned in the Arizona desert, and kidnapped and hanged in Montana. Those leaders who survived were repeatedly hauled into court on charges that often appeared incredulous. In addition, the early syndicalist-orthodox split, which had abated somewhat after 1912, recurred when Moscow persuaded the IWW, in 1924, to join the Red International of Labor Unions (Profintern). Wobblies immediately split into communist and anti-communist factions, and the latter attracted an anarcho-syndicalist fringe.[16]

Notwithstanding government persecution and internal discord, the Wobblies had more fundamental problems. They were established on a romantic belief in the wisdom of enlightened workers who, through struggle and education, would become socialist rebels. But this critical consciousness never appeared, at least among the masses, and the Wobbly belief in participatory democracy precluded central guidance. Wobby ideology became hopelessly imprecise, generating internal confusion at a time when capitalism was consolidating its economic and political power. It was continually challenged—by improving economic conditions, the CP, the AFL, the government—but could not coherently defend itself because of the unconditional pledge to self-determined proletarian action. Leaders such as Debs, Simons, DeLeon, Moyer, Trautmann, Foster, Flynn, Ettor, Tresca, Giovanniti, and Cannon eventually exited in search of a saving doctrine. Liberalism, in similar straits, created natural laws to track free actors onto acceptable avenues of social behavior. Similarly, orthodox historical materialism permitted a socialist vanguard to define proletarian freedom. Wobblies, on the other hand, were unalterably committed to preserving free and meaningful working class subjectivity. The days of reckoning, however, bypassed toiling Americans, unnoticed. And Wobblies, their faith still vibrating, could neither explain nor rectify the unanticipated silence. The Wobblies' star was stuck in the mucky *Lebenswelt*, and by 1924 its glow had subsided.

Although their political failure would be repeated by others, most recently the New Left, the brutality of both communist and capitalist regimes has preserved the Wobbly dream of reflective, participatory, community-based, self-governing socialist democracy. The Wobblies had inspired leftists

everywhere to re-think the delicate balance between democracy and objective truth.

"New Intellectuals"

In America, a group of wealthy, bohemian intellectuals praised the Wobblies' "pragmatic," "anthropocentric" socialism. William English Walling, Walter Lippmann, and Max Eastman were the nucleus of the Greenwich Village based "New Intellectuals," which eventually grew to include John Reed, Jack London, Upton Sinclair and others.[17] Their popular influence was primarily through the journals *New Review* and *The Masses*, both of which fluorished before 1916, especially among disenchanted Ivy Leaguers. This was a sentimental alliance of diverse intellectuals who were deeply disillusioned with American acquisitiveness. Through art and nontraditional lifestyles they hoped to transcend the *Lebenswelt* and provoke in others a spiritual radicalism that would have practical, revolutionary consequences. They were, in short, artistic Wobblies, radicalizing a privileged, highly educated constituency by means of spiritual direct action and artistic sabotage.

The informal association of New Intellectuals rapidly dissipated in 1914 over the controversial issue of whether or not to support SP pacifism. After 1919, several former members joined the CP, where they were muzzled by proletarian apparatchiks. Others cultivated successful literary careers, or, like Walling or Reed, forged reputations as nonaffiliated radicals. Authentic revolutionaries almost in spite of themselves, the New Intellectuals became important symbols among nonorthodox leftists. Productive workers, they implied, were also sensitive, intelligent people, who read, thought, and felt. Radical artists, the cultural avant-garde, nourished the seeds of reflective freedom in a manner that union organizers couldn't, and were thus irreplaceable. The New Intellectual's legacy was, in time, realized by radicals like Richard Wright and Harold Cruse, both of whom, we shall see, eloquently testified to the irrelevance of a totally scientific socialism.

Debs

This working class thirst for beauty as well as truth may have contributed to the widespread popularity of Eugene Victor Debs. Born in Terre Haute, Indiana in 1855, this former Democratic member of the Indiana Assembly, ex-leader of the American Railway Union, and five-time SP presidential candidate was a powerful orator with a romantic, even effusive style that audiences adored. While imprisoned in 1894 for his leadership role in the successful Pullman Strike, he began reading about utopian and scientific socialism. The ideas gelled when, after being released, he observed police breaking a strike: "In the gleam of every bayonet and the flash of every rifle the class struggle revealed itself."[18] Debs joined the utopian Brotherhood of

the Cooperative Commonwealth and established the Social Democracy of America (later the SDP) before joining the SP in 1901, completing his conversion to Marxism. Apparently Debs despised personal conflict.[19] In any case, he was an inept administrator who, until it was much too late, spurned the SP prerogatives that were his for the asking. Debs joined the IWW at its inception, but exited when St. John excised the "political clause" from its rules. Despite some personal feuds and tactical disagreements, Debs never repudiated the essence of Wobbly radicalism: its stress on enlightened, critical worker consciousness.

Like others in the SP's Left faction, Debs, after 1895, uncritically accepted Marx's laws of historical materialism. Neither interested in, nor apparently capable of, exegesis, Debs focused on the practical question of why, given the inevitability of socialism, it had not yet appeared in America. His answer, like the Wobblies', was direct and simple enough for even average Americans to grasp: individualist attitudes and selfish behavior had actually eroded American workers' Constitutional rights. The Founding Fathers' efforts to ensure everyone's freedom of speech, press, and assembly were, for Debs, of "everlasting benefit to mankind."[20] Unfortunately, the Constitution not only lacked the means of achieving these noble ends, it actually subverted them by deifying self-interest and thereby blocking the majority's collective power. Individual rights, narrowly conceived as a citizen's ability to do what he or she wants with whatever he or she owns, trivialized the idea of majority rule by creating a hegemonic class of wealthy entrepreneurs. Their wealth bought power, prestige, and the ability to effectively shape the nation's political agenda. On the other hand, workers, the overwhelming majority, passively condoned their own horrible exploitation because each "free" individual felt alone, isolated, and powerless. Alienation and inauthenticity comprised, for workers, America's liberal legacy.

Debs was translating Marxist theory into an American vernacular in order to touch the dispossessed emotionally, working through, rather than around, powerful patriotic sentiments. If workers could realize that exploitation was not only wrong but un-American, then their shame would turn to anger, their guilt to pride, and their isolation to a shared rebelliousness. In brief, workers needed to self-consciously experience their victimization and their collective, class power. This raised awareness, not knowledge of objective laws, was Marxism's "supreme demand," and Debs hoped his inspiring oratorical style would prove an apt means.[21]

Debs's point was that workers themselves, as individuals, had to "cultivate the habit of doing ... [their] own thinking."[22] Capitalism survived only because obsessive individualism shamed and immobilized workers, blocking genuine, mass-based democracy. As individuals gained a measure of self-respect, they would proudly acknowledge their personal contributions to society, and, paradoxically, realize their well-being was linked to that of all workers. Working class self-consciousness was a prerequisite for

democracy. "The working class are in an overwhelming majority. They have the numbers. They ought to have the power. And they would have the power if only they were conscious of their interests as a class." Until this happened, Debs presciently warned, socialism and democracy were merely dreams, which might turn into catastrophic nightmares if imposed on an unprepared populace. "The people are not yet ready. They must be further educated. They would not know what to do with their freedom if they had it."[23] Before campaigning for socialism, leftists needed to teach workers to think for themselves. When the latter task was successfully completed, the former would become unnecessary.

Since real knowledge was experienced rather than taught, Debs believed that the laws of historical materialism became manifest through proletarian struggle, not scientific theory. Whereas the Wobblies saw struggle as a practical means of improving conditions and hence empowering workers, for Debs, struggle was its own reward, regardless of the outcome. The act of resisting capitalist injustice explained, illustrated, and confirmed Marx's theses without even opening a book.

Like the Wobblies, Debs granted industrial unions the preeminent role in mobilizing proletarian workplace struggle.[24] However, Debs was tactically more flexible. Ideally, he favored industry-wide organizations to coordinate worker activities. But to court favor with existing unions, Debs added that any particular union's size and structure depended on factors such as the industry's level of technology and its workers' values. Moreover, unions needed to organize independently of political parties. Although Debs was on record as opposing reformist craft unions, he didn't support the Wobbly position of immediately annihilating the AFL. Worker loyalty to existing unions must, said Debs, be respected. Far from hindering progressive change, this loyalty bound workers, and was therefore a valuable weapon for mobilizing and coordinating worker protest. Of course, the weapon remained unloaded for so long as union leaders ignored members. Consequently, loyal workers needed to effectively control their unions, just as loyal Americans had to control public policy-making. Unions, like societies, must be experiences in self-management that generate class unity. "Too long have the workers of the world waited for some Moses to lead them out of bondage. He has not come; he will never come. I would not lead you out if I could; for if you could be let out, you could be led back in again."[25]

Any avenue of proletarian consciousness-raising was, for Debs, worth traveling. Although unions represented the economic interests of workers and catalyzed workplace struggles, the SP embodied their political interests. Since knowledge arose from struggle, the SP had to be run by and for workers whose political tool it was, not intellectuals or bureaucrats. It sponsored national policies, such as Proportional Representation and universal enfranchisement, that could facilitate democratic, grassroots struggle. Socialist electoral victories, for Debs, meant that an intensifying working

class consciousness was being reinforced by both the political struggle and its legislative reforms. Politics, in other words, was an educational tool whose reformist fruits nourished a growing sense of proletarian outrage. Successful political struggles engendered knowedgeable workers who pushed the political system to its limit, and then beyond. Knowledge, personally experienced in struggle, precipated rebellion. Although Debs felt struggle was its own reward, successful struggles were even better. By improving factories and reforming society, they reinforced workers' collective will to continue struggling. Eventually, knowledgeable workers would reach for nothing less than the truth: the inevitability of socialism.[26]

Debs was thus an indigenous revolutionary, "American enough for the most prejudiced cultural nationalist and red as flame." His working class appeal was as a defender of constitutional principles upon which the nation was founded. Not, however, because this Constitution was a desirable end, but because average Americans cherished it. Two decades before Gramsci wrote about "cultural hegemony," Debs was advocating an organic socialism of his own, self-consciously experienced by workers whose lifestyles and beliefs were worth more than volumes of socialist rhetoric. Socialism, for Debs, would be created by and for workers. If *they* valued electoral politics, socialist leaders needed to turn the ballot into a "powerful weapon" of progressive change that could transform the state into the political equivalent of industrial unions, capable of legislating proletarian hegemony. Except for the courts ("so notoriously in control of capital, and so shamelessly perverted to its base and sordid purposes . . . "), American institutions comprised for socialists an arena of contestation where workers fought to improve what they already valued, to rebel without mindlessly destroying. Violence, in this context, was dysfunctional rather than morally wrong. For defiant individuals, violence was a psychological safety valve. For the working class, however, individual acts of violence were disastrous. When successful, violence reinforced a cult of physical power and isolated action. If it failed, actors were physically punished and demoralized. Neither alternative empowered dispossessed workers. On the other hand, even Americans' desire to own property was a potential locus of anti-capitalist proletarian struggle (e.g., "We [socialists] are going to establish private property, all the private property necessary to house man, keep him in comfort and satisfy his wants"), as long as socialists acknowledged that real people—with irreducible aspirations—were more important than socialist dogma. Debs's quest to achieve life, liberty, and happiness in America was therefore "a question not of 'reform,' the mask of fraud, but of revolution."[27]

The anti-intellectual subjectivism of Debs and the Wobblies was noticed by two radical intellectuals, Louis B. Boudin and Louis C. Fraina, who hoped to justify it philosophically. Both men considered themselves Marxists and were colleagues of Debs in the left faction of the SP, both joined the CP in 1919, and neither could survive for long among historical materialists.

Their brief, ill-fated intellectual experiment, which was too esoteric for workers and too radical for orthodox Marxists, reinforced among leftists the belief that in America practical results, not theories, are what count.

Boudin

In 1912, at about the time George Lukács was writing the essays which would eventually comprise his monumental *History and Class Consciousness*, the American leftist Charles H. Kerr collected and published several of Boudin's essays under the title *The Theoretical System of Karl Marx*. This book, the first intellectually sophisticated commentary on Marxism published in America, tried to clarify, from a materialist point of view, Marx's basic ideas, and then to refute his critics. It opened with a materialist homily. The economics of a given epoch, Boudin assured us, the material means of production and distribution, comprise "the basis of every social order" and "the last cause of all social changes and political transformations."[28]

On tactical issues, Boudin demurred somewhat from standard orthodox rhetoric. First, he claimed that Marx and orthodox economists mistakenly ignored the important economic consequences of international wars and domestic waste, both of which permitted monopolies to consume excess capital and hence postpone the anticipated crisis of inadequate consumption. Socialists, some of whom later fine-tuned Boudin's analysis, were thus urged to oppose military and domestic spending policies whose consequences would, by aiding capital, hurt workers. And second, Boudin's *Socialism and War*, published, like Lenin's *Imperialism*, in 1916, related Western imperialism to the political and economic exigencies of late capitalism.[29] Like Lenin, Boudin interpreted imperialism and war as the final stage in capitalism's evolution, a desperate grabbing for new markets and cheap resources that foretold its imminent collapse.

Boudin's philosophical ambitions, however, are what set him apart. Anticipating Lukács, he interpreted each specific Marxian concept as part of a broader total system that conditioned its meaning. Marxists therefore needed to look "to the spirit pervading the whole of his [Marx's] work, for the explanation of any dark point or the solution of any problem encountered. . . . [Marxism's] separate parts or aspects must be considered with relation to each other and with a view to the whole, and cannot be understood unless so considered." On this crucial point, regarding the priority of dialectical textual interpretion over literal description, Boudin condemned orthodox Marxists as "vulgar materialists," unwilling to read Marx's seminal ideas, particularly his notion of subjectivity, in the dialectical spirit in which they were written.[30]

Orthodoxy's materialism, charged Boudin, was incomplete rather than mistaken, freezing only one element of Marx's complex and fluid presenta-

tion. Ideas are, indeed, economically determined, with each class intellectually rationalizing its practical interests. Once unleashed by economic
development, however, ideas became powerful class weapons that "play a
distinct and quite important role" in transforming society. This was because
the human mind, although embedded in physical and social conditions, was
nonetheless creative and free, utterly capable of assimilating unfamiliar
material and generating unanticipated behavior. A worker, for example,
struggling in capitalism, is "thrown on his own resources [and] . . . begins
to think for himself, to form his own ideology." These new ideas, born in
surrounding material conditions and expressed in activities that will alter
these conditions, are also "revolutionary factors in themselves and help
destroy the old order of things." Often even "neutral classes of society and
. . . people whose interests lie in the opposite direction are carried away by
the new ideas," and become unlikely revolutionaries.[31] By lucidly explaining and anticipating events, ideas, in effect, take on a life of their own,
generating concrete change even before economic conditions become untenable.

Orthodoxy's placid, nondialectical materialism ignored the context en-
veloping Marx's view of economic causation, especially Marx's subtle
theory of species-essence and the vital historical role he attached to self-
conscious class struggle. Boudin's Marx "is no fatalist. He does not believe
that society develops automatically, without the aid of the human beings
who compose it . . . "[32] Marx's laws of history, for Boudin, merely illustrate
that, at certain historical junctures, economic conditions, reflective consciousness, and actual social struggles crystallize into rebellions. By ignoring everything but economics, orthodoxy was neither historical nor
materialist, and therefore could not justifiably call itself Marxist. Its crippled notion of subjectivity insured socialist irrelevance rather than revolution. To realize history's potential, Marxists had to enter society's factories
and ghettos, and cultivate the kind of meaningful class struggle that would
unite thoughtful workers into a powerful revolutionary force. Economic factors would determine when and where socialism was born, but only workers
willing to fight and die for a cause they believed in could deliver it.

Boudin's synthesis of reflective subjectivity and materialist science was
overdue but shallow, particularly when compared to *History and Class Consciousness*. The logical difficulty of reconciling free actors and *a priori*
material laws was eliminated by simply redefining freedom to include
necessity, rather than, as Lukács had done, replacing materialism with a
philosophy that carefully wove cognition into the fabric of history. Boudin's
dialectic doesn't really tell us what happens if reflective workers choose not
to rebel, or act precipitously at the wrong moment. Should historical
materialists accede to popular opinion, or loose faith in the masses? When
the Leninist American CP chose the latter path, Boudin, always an unrepentant materialist, had, philosophically, nowhere to go. In order to remain a

democrat *and* a materialist he relinquished the core of his Marxism: the priority of working class consciousness. By 1924, Boudin had retreated into Kautskyism, with its passive materialist optimism.[33] He had successfully evaded orthodoxy's Party dictatorship, without sacrificing principle. But the price, that is, abandoning the commitment to reflective proletarian hegemony, was terribly high.

Fraina

Louis C. Fraina was an Italian immigrant raised on Manhattan's Lower East Side, an SLP activist at the age of 15, a Wobbly at 18, and a colleague of Boudin's in the SP's Left faction and the CP. An ex-DeLeonite and admirer of Lenin, Fraina's writings are more practical than Boudin's, geared more toward mobilizing proletarian struggle and raising consciousness than justifying these goals philosophically. Nevertheless, Fraina's subjectivist brand of Marxism, and its reconstruction after colliding with CP orthodoxy, closely resemble his colleague's.

In *Revolutionary Socialism* (1918) as well as his numerous essays in *New Review*, Fraina applied the science of historical materialism to understanding the monopolistic, imperialistic character of American state capitalism.[34] He outlined the economic forces that systematically transformed a competitive, laissez-faire society into one regulated by a behemoth capitalist state that employed its military and financial weapons to maximize private profit. Fraina believed that the state had overtaken large trusts and corporations in consolidating capitalist hegemony, primarily by buying the loyalty of the newly emerging middle classes with growth stimulating social, military, and educational policies. In short, the state in modern capitalism had become so vital to the system's survival, and its enormous resources so tightly controlled by business, that it could deliver nothing of value to workers.

Fraina accused the SP's ascendent Right Wing of having embraced a self-defeating strategy. Its goals of government ownership of industry and socialist electoral victories, even if realized, would strengthen the capitalist state, not workers, and would thereby diffuse America's socialist movement. By opting for reformism and Statism, the SP elevated the narrow self-interest of power hungry politicians over real proletarian needs. Fraina located the source of this ideological pollution in SP determinism.[35] Historical inevitability, in the official SP version, promoted a naive optimism, a passive calmness among workers, who were told that, since socialism was a foregone conclusion, reformism was defensible. Working class revolutionary potential thus remained neglected and untapped, while conditions worsened. The SP had sold out America's workers and abandoned its own radical legacy.

Contrary to orthodox opinion, this legacy embodied subjective as well as

objective factors. Potentially creative workers, for Marx, were inhibited by oppressive capitalist conditions. Orthodoxy's obsession with economics, on the other hand, turned workers into puppets, dancing mechanically to the tune of historical materialism. Fraina hoped, like Boudin, to invigorate the subjective aspect of Marx's dialectic by concentrating on the process by which objective historical laws were integrated into workers' actual experiences. Socialists, as Fraina saw it, had to elevate and intensify the "moral, intellectual, and class consciousness of the proletariat," instead of reiterating scientific platitudes. As it was, "The brilliant concept of the materialist conception of history, with its full-orbed recognition of the non-economic factors involved in the social process, has in some quarters been distorted into a rigid and preposterous 'economic determinism.'" Orthodoxy, in sum, was wrong not in believing that capitalism was self-destructing but in naively concluding that socialism was inevitable. Its objectivity, in fact, remained abstract until concretely expressed in working class subjectivity. Thinking rebels, not scientific laws, would actually transform society.[36]

What Marxism lacked, argued Fraina in 1915, was a psychology of human potential, to supplement its economic analysis of social potential. By "humanizing" socialism in this manner, historical materialism would be verified in workers' actual intellectual, emotional, and spiritual experiences.[37] Prior to 1919, Fraina saw popular culture as the bridge to this psychology, connecting economic laws and proletarian consciousness. Religion, music, sports, dance, avant-garde theater, and other popular leisure activities represented, for Fraina, creative, spontaneous, and liberating proletarian behavior. Rather than emphasizing the reactionary, decadent features of pop culture, as orthodoxy did, socialists needed to tap its enormous energy and use it to generate proletarian solidarity. By engaging capital in these popular arenas socialists could write, sing, choreograph, and play their way directly into mass consciousness. Political revolution would fall naturally, like a plump fruit, from these cultural roots. In this spirit, Fraina, in 1917, joined the staff of *Modern Dance* magazine to explain how bourgeois repression was being contested by joyous men and women moving freely in America's dance halls.[38]

By 1919, Fraina had become disenchanted with both the SP and the slow pace of working class cultural progress. The Russian Revolution convinced Fraina that proletarian discontent and anger, which in Europe had burst into violence and in America was intensifying, simply couldn't fit into available cultural outlets. Socialism had to provide workers a new program and theory that would translate their anger directly into revolutionary activism.

With one eye on Moscow, Fraina saw that only mass rebellion by a mobilized proletariat could prevent "the collapse of all civilization." "Mass Action," that is, "the instinctive action of the proletariat, gradually developing more conscious and organized forms . . . . [T]he proletariat itself in action,

dispensing with bureaucrats and intellectuals, acting through its own initiative," became Fraina's means for getting workers to coalesce subjectively in order to realize history's objective truth. This revolutionary process began with industrial unions organizing exploited workers and, as objective conditions matured, accelerated into a kind of national general strike first against large businesses and then the entire social and political edifice of capitalism. The initial strikes would feed upon both the psychological consequences of success and capitalism's intensifying objective contradictions, turning, finally, into a full-fledged revolution. "Mass action is dynamic, pliable, creative. . . . [It] is equally a process of revolution and the Revolution itself in operation."[39]

On the other, post-revolutionary side of mass action lay socialist democracy, characterized by self-governing productive units or councils, what Fraina called a "communism of the organized producers." Each industrial unit (e.g., coal, steel, textiles, agriculture, etc.) comprised a department of the Industrial State. Workers in each industry would organize into Local Councils, and these would, in turn, unite into General Industrial Councils that would coordinate with other General Industrial Councils into a central administrative organ for the entire production process. "The central administration is directive, and not repressive," coordinating production by directing and regulating local units. The latter, however, formulated economic policy and remained sovereign. Fraina's socialism was built on factory-based, self-governing workers' councils in which "employees become free, creative workers in the community of labor."[40]

Lenin's success in Russia convinced an ebullient Fraina that spontaneous, creative subjectivity could be squeezed into economic history without diluting either its spontaneity or creativeness. Thus, while he sincerely believed that "the subjective factor of a revolutionary proletariat alone will convert the objective conditions of Capitalism into Socialism," he also warned that subjectivity "must be directed" away from "proletarian suicide."[41] Directed, of course, by the Leninist Party, which Fraina, flushed with its success in Russia, unequivocally advocated. Needless to say, Fraina's elitist Party was only temporary. It would organize workers' mass action and guide the post-revolutionary dictatorship that would eliminate capitalism. Although Fraina's early and late writings were profoundly non-hierarchical and democratic, from 1918 until the early 1920s he hitched his cart to Lenin's rising star, apparently unaware that theoretically and practically he was left with nothing to stand on.

Even though Fraina led many Left faction members into the CP, orthodox officials were, from the very beginning in 1919, suspicious. In 1920, Santeri Nuorteva, a Soviet official in New York City, accused Fraina of spying for the U.S. Department of Justice. Tried and acquitted by the CP, Fraina nevertheless couldn't completely lift the veil of hostility his comrades bore. Two years after the trial, Fraina was again reproached, this time for embezzling

Third International funds and organizing a left opposition in Mexico. The Party overruled Fraina's denials and expelled him. Humiliated and poor, Fraina returned to the Lower East Side, where he changed his name to Lewis Corey and turned quietly into a scholar.

The putative contradiction between Fraina's subjectivism and materialism, which had also proved Boudin's undoing, festered during the 1930s. *The Decline of American Capitalism* (1930) and *The Crisis of the Middle Class* (1935) both confirmed empirically Marx's predictions regarding capitalism, but neither followed the orthodox line. The first book was indebted to the liberal Charles Beard, and implied that America's economic problems could be solved from within, rather than as part of a worldwide socialist movement. In the second, Fraina depicted an American middle class with distinct nonproletarian interests, and was inclined toward a pluralist democratic view of politics. The CP excoriated both books. By 1942, in *The Unfinished Task*, Fraina's subjectivism finally overwhelmed his materialism.[42] A nonmaterialist Marxism was inconceivable to Fraina. Because he had now explicitly rejected materialism, he was compelled also to expunge the socialist utopia. His new "functional democracy" was administered not by workers, but instead by educated middle class professionals. Sovereignty was now located in the balanced cooperation of management, labor unions, and the State, not in self-governing workers' councils. Finally, monopolies were to be turned into public corporations, not taken over by workers. Marxism, materialism, and totalitarianism had congealed into a single entity. Ignoring the proliferating body of neo-Marxist European literature, Corey in effect conceded that the attempt to subjectively revitalize Marxism had failed.

In one sense, Fraina was correct. The *theoretical* synthesis of Marxism and subjectivism, the unrealized project of both Boudin and Fraina, had failed dismally. Marxism had first to be philosophically redefined in nonmaterialist terms, and this neither Boudin nor Fraina could do. Orthodoxy systematically and logically reduced subjectivity to economics. Any economistic attempt at reconstituting reflective subjects was doomed from the beginning. When Boudin and Fraina belatedly realized this, one deserted subjectivity and the other discarded the Marxist baby with the materialist bath water. The lesson for nonorthodox American Marxists was crystal clear: The nontheoretical project of Debs and the Wobblies to raise proletarian consciousness solved the logical dilemma by avoiding it, but also preserved their Marxist credentials and provided an institutional base to work from. Given the immature state of American radical theorizing, anti-intellectualism was theoretically justifiable.

Hook

Sidney Hook, one might say, was the exception who proved the rule. A brilliant intellectual who had studied phenomenology in Germany, a student

of John Dewey, and for many years an engaged Marxian radical, Hook knew that Lukàcs and Karl Korsch were invaluable to the project of subjectively reinvigorating Marxist theory.[43] Orthodoxy, he argued, was incorrectly steered toward determinism by Engels and the Lenin of *Materialism and Empiriocriticism*, and had destroyed Marx's delicate balance of fact and value, object and subject. Hook saw in Marx's early theory of praxis the vital function consciousness played in history. By ignoring this early work, and in effect obliterating the context of Marx's later theory of historical materialism, orthodoxy had vulgarized Marx's dialectic. Marxism was turned into yet another tired, distorted, hyper-deductive social science.

Hook anchored his critique in the pragmatist claim that science, "naturalistic, historical and empirical throughout," is objectively true, regardless of personal values or society's class character.[44] Authentic Marxism, which dialectically blends object *and* subject, was therefore not a science. By reifying Marxism, transforming it from a critical theory of social change into an objective science, orthodoxy erased consciousness from history and buried the subjective needs and experiences of workers.

Real science, for Hook, invalidated orthodoxy by disclosing empirically that mature economic conditions alone will not necessarily cause a revolution. Other, non-quantifiable factors are needed, such as class consciousness and a people's critical openness to anti-capitalist propaganda. Marxism, "neither a science nor a myth, but a realistic method of social action," directs us to act reflectively in order to satisfy real needs, rather than to depend on theory or wait for history's laws to unfold mechanically.[45] Consciousness is the foundation of authentic Marxism, and social change, not knowledge, its goal. Hook accepted most of Marx's economic theories *not* because they were scientific, but because they expressed theoretically workers' practical interests and activities. Workers must make the appropriate value judgments themselves and take the personal risks of rebelling. Science could verify the empirical accuracy of these judgments and the actual utility of revolutionary activism. It could not, however, determine the beliefs or actions of reflective workers.

Hook's *Toward the Understanding of Karl Marx* (1933) was the most important work of philosophy yet produced on the American left. It took the critical first step of deconstructing orthodox materialism, thereby opening the door to a meaningful theory of subjectivity. But rather than entering a room filled with the difficulties of working class inauthenticity, Party organization and tactics, and post-revolutionary socialism, Hook suddenly stopped. Perhaps it was the orthodox establishment's unusually hostile rejection of *Toward the Understanding of Karl Marx*. Perhaps the warped, factionalized reality of the American orthodox left disengaged Hook's razor-sharp intellect. Certainly, the left's fear of opposing Stalinism outraged the irrepressible professor. In any case, after 1936 Hook withdrew into Dewey's pragmatism.[46] The task of formulating a democratic Marxism was

abandoned entirely. Like Fraina, Hook equated materialism, Marxism, and totalitarianism, and urged scientists and democrats to reject them all. Capitalism, despite its evils, permitted empirical experimentation, and hence encouraged scholars to uninhibitedly verify the anticipated consequences of social action. The mature, pragmatic Hook believed science was the prerequisite for democracy. Marxism, despite noble intentions, generated a closed society where materialist dogma replaced science, where the democratic spirit was purged by Party bureaucrats. The task of defining philosophically an open, contentious, egalitarian society, which Hook had enthusiastically tackled as a Marxist, was left to the Europeans.

Mattick

One continental Marxist, Paul Mattick, came to America from Germany in 1926, hoping that frontier individualism would provide a fertile background for his subjectivist leftism. He was immediately submerged in radical activities, first as a tool and die worker, and then as a Wobbly, a founder of the United Workers Party (eventually renamed the Group of Council Communists), and an author of several notable monographs. For over half a century Mattick impressed American workers and academics as an eloquent proponent of nonorthodox Marxism. His intellectual ties to Europe's radical tradition meant, however, that for many on the American left Mattick would always remain an outsider.

Mattick's Marxism was rooted in the early twentieth century Council Communist movement that was led by the Dutchmen Antonie Pannekoek and Herman Gorter. Council communists believed that socialism would originate as spontaneous, popular insurrections of angry workers struggling to improve factory conditions. These would be institutionalized in self-governing workers' councils that directed production and promulgated public policy. In this vein, Mattick traced the history of authentic socialism from Luxemburg, through the prerevolutionary Lenin, to Sorel, the Wobblies, the 1905 Revolution in Russia, the February Revolution in 1917, and the German Revolution in 1918. All of these Marxian thinkers and movements advocated spontaneous activism, a council system of self-government, and democratic organizations that lasted.[47] On the other hand, the orthodox Russian and Chinese revolutions were, as Mattick saw them, not socialist at all. Rather than empowering workers, as Marx had intended, they disingenuously abolished the bourgeoisie without touching capital as a social relationship. Workers and peasants in these two socialist states were still exploited. Only the exploiters changed. Now, argued Mattick, the authoritarian, Party-controlled state, by regulating the market—i.e., centrally controlling production, consumption, and distribution—has stabilized capitalism's wage-labor system. Capital and labor remain separate, and the

former, the workers' state, still rules the latter. Communist state capitalism thus differs from bourgeois capitalism only in form, not substance. Orthodox ideology cosmetically adapted capitalism to its own contradictions, and coopted workers with words rather than deeds.

In *Anti-Bolshevik Communism*, Mattick concluded that, popular misconceptions notwithstanding, orthodoxy, social democracy, Keynesianism, and fascism were merely variations of one theme: how best to keep workers producing at minimum costs and maximum output. All these social systems deprived workers of their "self-initiative" and subjected them "to the control of a leadership which did not share their living and working conditions."[48] Workers, today, had to either accept exploitation by adopting one of these stop-gap alternatives, or refuse it by abolishing anti-worker systems, wherever they appeared on the ideological spectrum.

Mattick was confident that capitalism's objective economic crises would soon place the subjective moment of decision at hand. Whereas most Marxists concentrated on how commodities were circulated and surplus value realized, Mattick emphasized the process by which surplus value was produced, and argued that, over time, capitalist production led to a decline in the rate of profit on total capital. For as long as capital and labor remained separate, therefore, continuing economic crises, some resembling the 1929 debacle, were inevitable. Keynesianism, fascism, and bogus socialism, by expanding the state's economic functions, could slow but not stop the process.

This economic certainty, however, only meant that, periodically, workers' everyday lives would be disrupted and the legitimacy of nonworker ideologies questioned. At these times in history, workers either struggled and took control, or passively accepted leftist or rightist economic tricks. Worker subjectivity, in brief, determined the actual consequences of objective economic processes. If workers self-consciously rebelled, socialism was likely. If not, then capitalism, as it has since 1929, would survive in several ideological costumes. To Mattick, inevitable economic crises don't necessarily elicit revolutions.

America's Keynesian consensus, argued Mattick, would be continually tested by economic disasters of varying intensity. Admittedly, past socialist movements "have faded, and ... new ones may fail again." Success was possible, however, if workers experienced their exploitation, struggled collectively, and politically institutionalized their sovereignty. Mattick felt strongly that only workers' councils—self-governing, factory-based, revolutionary organizations—could mobilize and coordinate this struggle, and offer workers the opportunity to live democratically. Their mere survival would teach workers self-sufficiency. Small victories would feed proletarian confidence and ambition. And coordinated national campaigns would quickly strip capitalism to its hierarchical, nondemocratic core. "It is only through the experiences of self-determination, in whatever limited ways at first, that

the working class will be enabled to develop toward its own emancipation."[49]

In the tradition of Debs and the Wobblies, Mattick's nonorthodox Marxism cultivated worker consciousness by directly confronting real life experiences. His goal, like theirs, was to promote self-conscious critique, not dogma. Socialism would rise spontaneously from the depths of worker discontent.

Johnson Forest Tendency

During the 1940s and 1950s, Mattick's subjectivist neo-Marxism was shared by several significant groups and thinkers. Foremost among these was the Johnson Forest Tendency (JFT), which culled its unusual name from the pseudonyms J.R. Johnson and F. Forest, taken by C. L. R. James and Raya Dunayevskaya, respectively, during the 1941–51 period. The JFT first emerged in 1941, from within the Trotskyist Workers Party (WP), which had split from the Socialist Workers Party (SWP). In 1947, the JFT left the WP, and again joined the SWP, where it remained until 1950, when it abandoned Trotskyism altogether and renamed itself the Correspondence Publishing Committee (CPC). Dunayevskaya, one of two JFT founders and spokespersons, exited the CPC in 1955 to establish the News and Letters Committee. The other, James, left in 1962. Confronted with the loss of its major theorists, the CPC changed its name to Facing Reality before fading into obscurity in the early 1960s. Although the movement had failed politically, more than any other single individual or organization in the 1940s and 1950s, it had epitomized the Wobbly spirit of subjectivist radicalism. Culturally, therefore, the JFT performed the important role of educating left-leaning students and labor leaders in the 1950s to the theory and practice of democratic Marxism. In a liberal environment already enamored of local autonomy and self-initiative, the JFT thus helped Americanize Marxism for an entire generation of New Left radicals.

Reflecting its subjectivist radical tradition, the JFT advocated workers' autonomy as the means by which capitalism would be transformed. Workers, therefore, were potentially independent of both capital and their own official organizations, including the CP and labor unions. James, Dunayevskaya, Grace Lee (later Boggs), Martin Glaberman, and others in the movement produced numerous studies in the 1940s and early 1950s equating the Soviet Union, Nazi Germany, and America as modern anti-worker totalitarian systems, in effect verifying empirically Mattick's accusations. *State Capitalism and World Revolution* (1950), the most significant of these early manuscripts, argued that Taylorism and Fordism characterized commodity production throughout the industrialized West, regardless of a regime's stated ideology. The anti-worker principles of profit, efficiency, and labor rationalization were hegemonic throughout the West, uniting fascism,

capitalism, and Stalinism. Orthodoxy had mistakenly identified socialism with the form of a state's ownership of capital rather than the quality of its social relations. "Russian Communism rests on the mainspring of capitalism—paying the worker the minimum and extracting from him the maximum."[50] Marxist regimes thus turned naturally toward state-controlled, profit-oriented economies, which quickly evolved into Party dictatorships. Liberal Americans abhorred centralization of any kind. No wonder, then, that socialism in America had faired so poorly. On the other hand, workplace and neighborhood democracy, where citizens actually ran political and economic institutions, was authentically Marxist without being foreign. The JFT thus cast its lot with a nonorthodox Marxism that fit nicely with America's tradition of self-government.

JFT argued that spontaneous and free actions could liberate workers, ending forever the hegemony of both capital and hierarchical CPs, the unsuspecting agents of capital. New grassroots workers' organizations resembling Lilburne's Leveller Party, the 1871 Commune, and the Soviets of 1905, would emerge to institutionalize revolutionary justice. As supporting evidence, members of the JFT compiled and analyzed instances of factory insurrections where workers angrily confronted management and unions, and then organized spontaneously into self-governing councils.[51] Written in a nonacademic vernacular, often through first-hand participant accounts, these monographs compiled twigs of data to feed an eagerly awaited firestorm of worker discontent. They would, contended the JFT, be concretely verified by new proletarian insurrections, and intellectually rationalized much later, in post-revolutionary serenity.

This anti-intellectualism was a calculated tactical decision, particularly by the movement's preeminent representative, C. L. R. James. Born in Trinidad in 1901, James came to America from England on a lecture tour in 1938, and stayed until his expulsion 15 years later. James, like Hook, was a first-rate intellectual and a sophisticated philosopher, in addition to being an engaged activist whose efforts on behalf of blacks, we shall see later, would help change the course of radical theorizing in America. His *Notes on Dialectics* (1948) superimposed Hegel's dialectical method on a history of Europe's revolutionary labor movement, in order to justify the JFT intellectually. In this carefully researched and argued work, James concluded that proletarian self-consciousness was inextricably part of history's objective process. Trotsky and Stalin were therefore unreasonable as well as dangerous, obliterating real worker subjectivity in the cause of some mythical objective truth. By opposing dictatorships, capitalist and socialist, workers would experience their own potentials as well as history's telos, and in so doing verify the accuracy of Hegel's dialectic. "The proletariat will decide. The thing is to tell the proletariat to decide."[52]

James knew that this revolutionary message needed to bellow spontaneously from the sleeping proletarian giant. His research for the JFT

revealed numerous examples of revolutionary workers motivated solely by their own immediate needs rather than the plans of Party officials. "Workers ... know more than any vanguard party can tell them." Political theory therefore needed to be founded on what workers themselves were thinking, doing, and hoping. Hegel's and Marx's ideas, he concluded, would be verified by ordinary people—like those living in Hungary, Poland, and South Africa, as well as in America—self-consciously struggling to be free and happy. They *are* the synthesis of history and subjectivity. Marxism's great task, for James, was to nurture proletarian democracy from the bottom up instead of speculating abstractly about absolute truth. This included not only the nuts and bolts of factory organizing, but also writing books about proletarian passions such as cricket, and novels depicting the everyday worlds of oppressed people. A radical working class culture would stimulate both critical thinking and revolutionary politics. Indeed, one JFT legacy was the organizations and journals members established to democratize human relationships as a means of empowering common citizens. Disadvantaged groups like women, blacks, gays, and environmentalists were encouraged to form nonhierarchical, self-governing interest groups to control policy-making on pertinent issues. The resulting decentralization, it was hoped, would spread to factories and neighborhoods, and eventually to the entire nation. "Our task is to help in making the workers *aware* by precept and organization of their great task of emancipation in a society which increasingly shoves the whole of humanity down the road to barbarism."[53]

Highlander Center

This Gramscian tactic of radicalizing workers by nonintrusively injecting the class struggle into popular proletarian culture did not originate with the JFT or the New Left. On 1 November 1932, a former theology student and admirer of Reinhold Neibuhr's Christian Marxism, Miles Horton, founded the Highlander Folk Center in the foothills of East Tennessee. Highlander was, and still is, an educational institution that helps people struggle with real problems that grow from local conflict situations. It tackles only endemic regional concerns, and encourages local communities to decide for themselves what these are. Envisioning a classless, egalitarian, nonhierarchical society, Highlander has directed its educational techniques to creating class-conscious workers prepared to govern themselves. Beyond these vague generalities, however, have lain specific people, problems, and solutions. Highlander has always adamantly refused the role of scientist or seer. The powerless need to define their problems, ask Highlander for help, live and work with others sharing similar problems, discover apt solutions, and then return home to do whatever they believe appropriate. Highlander has provided needed conceptual tools and instilled confidence, but has not been

a vanguard organization. Confused people searching for truth have quickly learned that it grows naturally from living and struggling together.

Highlander's distinctive contributions to American subjectivist neo-Marxism were the educational techniques it employed to alter worker consciousness. Participants from different communities who shared a common set of problems converged on Highlander for workshops that lasted from a weekend to two weeks. During their stays they lived simply in a communal atmosphere, sharing experiences and slowly bonding into a unified, coherent group. The workshops were neither hierarchically structured nor taught. Participants listened, talked, and gradually developed a sense of shared suffering and solidarity. Those who had already successfully struggled communicated the strategies they found useful, without advocating them. Answers materialized almost imperceptibly, from the bottom up, through collective efforts. The democratic *process* of learning became an important lesson. In Horton's words, "our efforts to live out our ideals makes possible the development of a bit of proletarian culture as an essential part of our program of workers' education."[54]

Native music and folk arts, "bits of proletarian culture" that often accompanied or symbolized human suffering, were seamlessly knit into the Highlander experience. They entertained participants, but also unforgettably communicated the shared suffering of the powerless and, especially, fused every single individual into an active, creative group. Popular culture, in brief, was used to educate and empower. In an anti-intellectual, nonideological environment like Highlander's, the music of Pete Seeger or the Carawans, not *Das Kapital*, mobilized workers to think critically and struggle. Highlander perceived the theoretical ambiguity of protest songs as their greatest strength: they generated a radical consciousness without supplying recipes that would deny workers the freedom of self-actualizing choice. At Highlander, ideology was considered undemocratic when severed from the objective reality of struggling, reflective people. When it wasn't, Highlanders often called it music.

Cued by workers' actual concerns, Highlander has always been on the cutting edge of America's progressive social movements. In the 1930s and 1940s, until the scourge of McCarthyism made even the CIO fear the democratic potential of its members, it trained hundreds of local union activists to organize factory workers and mobilize them politically to influence local elections. During the 1950s and 1960s, Highlander worked with civil rights activists, including at one time Martin Luther King Jr. and Rosa Parks. Blacks' civil rights had always concerned Highlander, but usually in the context of desegregating unions. As local Southern communities actively challenged racist institutions, Highlander responded by teaching black and white protesters to work effectively together to achieve integrationist goals by using tactics they felt most comfortable with. By 1964, Highlander began responding to regional problems in Appalachia such as poverty, strip

mining, dependency, welfare, powerlessness, and nonindigenous land ownership. As always, workshops used popular cultural artifacts in training people to think critically, act effectively, and assume responsibility for their lives. This, not thousands of volumes of cryptic Marxist commentary, embodied Highlander's homegrown radicalism.

The New Left

The history of subjectivist American Marxism, we have now seen, is long and rich, encompassing philosophers, politicians, artists and activists, all of whom believed that Marxism could and should adapt to its individualist environment. The events that began in the early 1960s, and have since been called "New Left," have been outrageously mislabeled. Very little is "new" in the New Left. We shall now see that its subjectivist radicalism and even its nontraditional tactics were embedded in a past that stretched back to the SP's Left Wing faction. What was "new" in the early 1960s was the cultural context in which these venerable nonorthodox ideas flourished.

The 1950s initiated a period of unprecedented economic growth and prosperity in America. For the majority of Americans living outside traditionally depressed areas, unemployment and inflation were low, economic mobility high, and consumerism blossoming. Students, entering universities in record numbers, confidently prepared for the many lucrative managerial and professional positions that, for them, were the pot of gold at an expanding economic rainbow's end. Unlike the years that preceded and would follow, these were open-ended, optimistic times for middle class students. Times of learning and leisure, when ideals could be digested intellectually and then dispassionately measured in the real world. They often came up short. Michael Harrington's *The Other America* debunked "the land of freedom and plenty" thesis. Persistant racism and sexism, incomprehensible assassinations, an unjustifiable war in Southeast Asia, and the moral vacuousness of upscale suburban living, all pushed many young people over the edge of cynicism into a pit of despair and guilt.

Those who decided against simply dropping out altogether often sought political answers. For them, mainstream liberal-democratic-capitalism was the source of, not the solution to, America's problems. The political right, in this time of wasted rather than scarce resources and despised vestigial traditions, was irrelevant. The orthodox left had accurately predicted a national crisis, but apparently for the wrong reasons. Capitalism was thriving, employed workers were fat and content, and our de-Stalinized Soviet saviors were systematically brutalizing their neighbors. At an impasse, many students turned to nasty, mind-altering drugs in part to protest the dearth of viable political alternatives.

At this point in the late 1950s and early 1960s, the unlikely actually happened: subjectivist neo-Marxism, gestating for over fifty years, began leak-

ing into mainstream American culture through several unexpectedly popular leftist sources. Leo Huberman's *We The People* (1932)—lively, accessible, and written from the perspective of America's "little" people—seemed to pierce the pompous elitism of both capitalists and bureaucratic socialists. It appealed particularly to young historians in the late 1950s, who were disillusioned with their staid, apologetic, hierarchical discipline. F. O. Matthiessen's *American Renaissance* and C. L. R. James's *Moby Dick* similarly jolted American literary critics. Several widely read radical but nonorthodox journals (e.g., *Partisan Review* in the 1940s, *Politics, Liberation, Dissent, Studies on the Left*) openly condemned economism and called for a new democratic radicalism nurtured on meaningful proletarian struggle and realized in grassroots democratic institutions. Some popular contributors to these journals, for instance, C. Wright Mills, Paul Goodman, and Irving Howe, became role models for an entire generation of young radicals. They were energetic, nondogmatic, intellectually sophisticated, radical, and uninhibitedly American. Their nontraditional socialism was funneled by student leaders and sympathetic professors to a student body thirsting for progressive new ideas.

These propelled radical Americans headlong into an unfamiliar past. While people like Haywood, Debs, Fraina, Boudin, James, Mattick, et al, were not exactly household names, their ideas, appropriately packaged and exchanged by student leaders at numerous anti-war demonstrations, soon were. New Leftism, like the neo-Marxist tradition that spawned it, hoped to create among average people a consciousness of their shared exploitation in capitalism, the potential power inherent in collective activity, and the necessity to use that power while struggling for democracy. It wrapped these familiar goals in several distinct proposals which, because of the movement's decenteredness, were not always universally accepted.

First, New Leftists believed that successful revolutions were self-justifying, and could occur wherever and whenever a carefully organized group of revolutionaries destroyed extant elites. Anti-intellectualism, we have seen, is an integral component of subjectivist neo-Marxism. By emphasizing the positive, that is, praising successful activism rather than criticizing abstract thought, New Leftists fully appreciated the contributions of Third World revolutionaries such as Che Guevara, Regis Debray, Frantz Fanon, and Mao Zedong. Since successful revolutions answered all the hypothetical questions that Marxists traditionally debated, New Leftists believed that Marx's dialectical legacy was bequeathed to these activists, not to intellectuals imprisoned in abstractions.

Second, because capitalist domination was reinforced in all sectors of capitalist society—from T.V. commercials to factory conditions, electoral politics, sexual mores, and organized religion—New Leftists concluded that revolutions had to totally transform the entire network of bourgeois values and institutions. Reformism, which separated these sectors and worked

piecemeal, could alter government policies but not the overall quality of capitalist exploitation. Meaningful social change occurred simultaneously on all social levels, or survived in none at all. Revolutions, therefore, could not, as for syndicalists, focus only on factories. Admittedly, work was particularly important because it directly supported capitalist relationships of production. The bourgeois work ethic—discipline, honesty, frugality, and forebearance—generated a passive, pliant work force that was easily manipulated by capital. New Leftists proffered the concept of self-fulfilling praxis, or "play," to replace the drudgery of capitalist factories. This higher standard, if accepted by workers now serving the false gods of profit and efficiency, would fundamentally humanize social production and distribution, eventually substituting cooperation and love for exploitation. But proletarian lives encompass far more than factories. Authentic New Left revolutionaries had to simultaneously alter noneconomic bourgeois attitudes regarding such things as sex, drugs, education, family, and marriage. In brief, New Leftists, like their unacknowledged mentors Fraina, James, and Horton, equated real democracy with proletarian cultural hegemony, and advocated an alternative, grassroots pop culture to reflectively enliven workers.

Finally, New Leftists blissfully discovered what subjectivist neo-Marxists had been preaching for over five decades, that authentically democratic revolutions must permit men and women to determine their own fates. This meant that proletarian rebellion needed to be consciously chosen by outraged citizens struggling to improve their lives. Successful collective struggles would empower rebels to create rather than obey public policy, thereby eliminating leadership hierarchies. New Leftists therefore argued that revolutions had to be spontaneous collective outbursts, not premeditated or externally directed by a self-appointed vanguard. They were to be non-supervised, community-based, nonhierarchical, self-governing, and participatory: the crystallizing of critical, free subjects into sovereign collectivities of neighbors and friends. New Leftists were thus outraged by what they perceived as the "old" orthodox Left's false claims. Its hegemonic revolutionary parties brutally enslaved workers while professing to emancipate them. It ruled in the name of workers but in the interests of a bureaucratic elite that, like its entrepreneurial comrades in the West, sought only wealth and power. Its fate, finally, would be determined by the same New Left revolutionary forces now wrecking capitalism.

"Participatory Democracy" emerged as the movement's slogan. The governing New Left presupposition, which was of course as old as the Wobblies, was that groups of people must be educated by struggling collectively to improve living conditions. Subjectively meaningful knowledge would then pass into and through mass experiences, which encompassed an inarticulate egalitarianism that participatory democracy would bring to the surface. The struggle for political and economic decentralization—i.e.,

communities controlling their own schools, enacting their own laws, and regulating their own neighborhoods; and workers regulating factory conditions as well as planning, with their neighbors, production and distribution—would thus emancipate and radicalize participants. New Left art, music, dance, and theater would relate to local concerns, communicate in shared cultural idioms, and seek to actively involve, not merely entertain, audiences. Radical aesthetics found beauty in free collective action. Even bourgeois law, appropriately purged of idealist abstractions, became for New Leftists a potential means of empowering the masses.

This entire multidimensional educational process, involving common people on every level of social activity, would fulfill the age-old American dream of establishing government by and for all the people. Indeed, one New Leftist argued that participatory democracy, by returning America to its most cherished tradition of autonomous self-government, would finally realize that oldest of indigenous political documents: the Articles of Confederation. Patriotic American workers, by means of legitimate forms of political, economic, and cultural struggle, would thus learn that subjective freedom is concretized only in collective class action leading to revolutionary socialism.[55] New Leftists, in their theory and praxis of participatory democracy, tried to redeem in socialist tender the American Revolution's unfulfilled promises of personal liberty and social justice.

Conclusion

In retrospect, the plight of New Leftism indicates both the strengths and weaknesses of subjectivist neo-Marxism. By humanizing historical materialism, keying it to the real beliefs of average people living in typical circumstances, it turned Marxism away from totalitarianism and toward the reflective acquiescence of mass public opinion. Sympathetic observers could, with clear consciences, grab onto Marxism *because* they were democrats, knowing that their movement's success depended not on secretive Party maneuvers but on its grassroots appeal. Especially in liberal America, these subjectivist, democratic credentials were tickets into the political arena. Consequently, in appropriate social conditions such as occurred in the late 1950s and 1960s, subjectivist Marxism could captivate a wide spectrum of nonpropertied Americans who were fed up with capitalist hypocrisy but afraid of orthodox socialism.

But, in an unanticipated dialectical twist, its short-term appeal, in time, turned fatal. The New Left's flexible, usually legal, and very popular tactics, combined with their nondogmatic speeches, attracted a heterogeneous variety of what Weinstein called "militant interest-group activists," people

who supported social activities like rent strikes, marches, demonstrations, boycotts, and occupations, not for their revolutionary value, but as useful means of reforming social inequities.[56] In liberal America, New Left "revolutionaries" were often fellow travelers laboring to replace inept officials, change the law, or establish liberal freedoms for political nonparticipants. Their goals left capitalism untouched, so in this sense they were using, as well as being used by, authentic New Leftism. It was a marriage of convenience with one partner unaware of its own liberal bias and the other unwilling to discuss such esoteric nonsense. New Leftism was thus transformed, in practice, into a nebulous, unfocused social movement, encompassing liberal activists as well as hard-core revolutionaries who rejected liberalism entirely.

By subsuming theory in practice, New Leftism, and the older brand of subjectivist neo-Marxism it represented, received both more and less than it bargained for. The turbulent 1960s, with its protest movements, riots, and civil disorders, were at least partially conditioned by New Left activists organizing young people in America's streets. New Leftists felt that theory inhibits subjectively meaningful action. And action is what they got, often among elite social groups and in nonurban areas even they could not have anticipated. New Leftism was a success. But its popularity among dissatisfied people was at least in part due to its anti-intellectual courting of popular opinion. By welcoming anyone willing to disrupt the status quo, New Leftism transformed itself into a nonrevolutionary movement, composed of such unlikely comrades as hippies, ecologists, students, potheads, naturalists, vegetarians, black activists, feminists, avant-garde artists, neo-conservatives, revolutionaries . . . the list stretched almost endlessly. Each mobilized around perceived issues of immediate concern, issues prompting anti-"establishment" protest. But very few harbored anti-system ulterior motives, and even fewer were transformed into socialists. With anti-intellectualism rampant, however, basic differences separating revolutionaries and nonrevolutionaries never surfaced. New Leftism thus failed dismally if we judge it by its original criteria. While instigating social action, from their revolutionary perspective this action in general was insubstantial. "Not since the forties had so much effort and expectation . . . ended in so little." As capitalism reformed, the war in Viet Nam ended, and economic insecurity, for students and workers, intensified, most New Leftists were defused, and the coalition was disbanded. Former members drifted into corporate and professional positions or sought emotional fulfillment elsewhere, perhaps in religious or cult groups. Radicals, on the other hand, inflated subtle doctrinal disagreements into dozens of hostile, irreconcilable parties. New Leftism, once thought to be a beacon of revolutionary democracy, disintegrated into "a mood in search of a movement."[57]

It appears that, in America at least, the subjectivist version of Marxism is a necessary but not sufficient component of successful leftist movements.

By bending to popular beliefs and empowering masses of people, its potential appeal encompasses a wide range of blue-and white-collar workers, students, professionals, and nonhegemonic special interest groups. Its intriguing, nonintellectual blend of subjectivism and Marxism, however, in appropriate conditions will attract a following but not sustain it. This is because liberal Americans want to be free without being arbitrary. They want to knowledgeably determine their own lives while remaining inwardly confident that what they are doing is intellectually justifiable. Subjectivist neo-Marxism didn't proffer intellectual guidelines. It reinforced liberalism's autonomous spirit without ever explaining why or how, when universally realized, empowered, free actors would generate socialism. If autonomous freedom is neo-Marxism's final goal, then perhaps anything that empowers any group is justified. This, apparently, was Staughton Lynd's view when he supported the right to nonviolent civil disobedience, even when applied to "the white Southerner who might wish to disobey a federal civil rights law in a way that would at least immediately harm no one else."[58] On the other hand, some in the Wobbly, JFT, and New Left terrorist fringes felt that radicals should unthinkingly annihilate reactionary persons and institutions. Neo-Marxism must somehow transcend such extremes by explaining how the meaningful subjectivity of empowered actors blooms in the collective goals of a united, mobilized, hegemonic working class. In the process, it needs to describe how racial, sexual, class, religious, ethnic, occupational, and psychological components of consciousness are fully realized only in socialism. And what role government plays in gaining and maintaining those freedoms mobilized communities have struggled, sometimes painfully, to achieve. How, in short, individual freedom and self-government for America's majority sustain, and are sustained by, socialism.

These abstract ideas would have concrete results. Their voluntary acceptance will indicate participants are subjectively committed to socialism; their rejection, a willingness to continue in capitalism. They become the left's intellectual nourishment, without which mass-based political movements will internally fracture. Moreover, such theory would complement rather than replace the community-oriented appeals which in the 1960s proved so popular, augmenting with solid principle the intense emotional bonds uniting capitalism's victims.

The history of subjectivist neo-Marxism indicates that creative thinking is desperately needed. When political movements, regardless of their popularity, lack intellectual substance, when they nonreflectively unite heterogeneous activists, they likely will dissolve as quickly as coalesce. The radical tradition that began early in this century in the SP and the Wobblies, and culminated in New Leftism, has shown the democratic potential of nonorthodox Marxism. Unfortunately, it could never translate its powerful emotional message into a reflective, widespread subjective commitment to socialism.

Notes

1. E.g., Labriola, Lukács, Korsch, Gramsci, Luxemburg, Pannekoek, Gorter, Jaurès, and more recently, Marcuse, and the mid-career Kolakowski.
2. See Marx, *Economic and Philosophical Manuscripts* in *Karl Marx: Early Writings* (New York: Vintage, 1975), p. 352.
3. E.g., Paci, Tran Duc Thao, Sartre, Merleau-Ponty, and others.
4. See Ira Kipnis, *The American Socialist Movement, 1897–1912* (Westport, CT: Greenwood, 1968), pp. 107–125, 171–79.
5. Other notables of the SP's Left included Kate O'Hare, Louis Boudin, Charles Ruthenberg, Emil Herman, Ella Reeve Bloor, and Rose Pastor Stokes.
6. The phrase is from John P. Diggins, *The Left in the Twentieth Century* (New York: Harcourt Brace Jovanovich, 1973), p. 67.
7. *The Preamble to the Constitution of the IWW*, in Paul F. Brissenden, *The IWW* (New York: Russell & Russell, 1919), p. 353.
8. See, for example, Ben H. Williams, "Trends Toward Industrial Freedom," *American Journal of Sociology*, XX (March 1915), p. 627.
9. Including St. John, William Traubmann, and Frank Bohn. See Frank Bohn and William D. Haywood, *Industrial Socialism* (Chicago: Kerr, 1910), pp. 36 and 43–46; and Vincent St. John, *The IWW: Its History, Structure and Methods* (rev. ed.: Chicago: IWW, 1919), p. 19.
10. See Bohn and Haywood, esp. pp. 36–39 and 49; and William E. Bohn, "Reformer and Revolutionist," *International Socialist Review*, X (September 1909), pp. 204–9.
11. Haywood, "What Haywood Says on Political Action," *International Socialist Review*, XIII, 8 (February 1913), p. 622.
12. See Joseph R. Conlin, *Bread and Roses Too* (Westport, CT: Greenwood, 1969), p. 100; Kipnis, pp. 319–21; Bohn and Haywood, pp. 58–59.
13. See Elizabeth Gurley Flynn, *Sabotage* (Cleveland: IWW, 1916), unpaginated.
14. In Melvin Dubofsky, *We Shall Be All* (Chicago: Quadrangle, 1969), p. 167. See also Bohn and Haywood, pp. 45–51; and Haywood "Socialism—The Hope of the Workers," *International Socialist Review*, XII (February 1912), p. 462.
15. See Patrick Renshaw, *The Wobblies* (New York: Doubleday, 1967), pp. 245–71; Brissenden, p. 350; Diggins, pp. 84–85; and Dubofsky, pp. 398–444.
16. On this final split, see John S. Gambs, *The Decline of the IWW* (New York: Cambridge University Press, 1932), esp. p. 206.
17. The quoted term is from Robert Rives LaMonte, "The New Intellectuals," *New Review*, II (January 1914), pp. 35–53.
18. *Debs: His Life, Writings, and Speeches* (Chicago: Kerr, 1908), p. 82.
19. See Nick Salvatore, *Eugene V. Debs* (Urbana, IL: University of Illinois Press, 1982), pp. 220–61.
20. Arthur Schlesinger (ed.), *Writings and Speeches of Eugene V. Debs* (New York: Heritage, 1948), p. 111.
21. Debs, "Unionism and Socialism," in *Debs: His Life, Writings and Speeches*, p. 138.
22. *Ibid.*, p. 136.
23. Debs, "Craft Unionism," in Harold W. Curry, *E.V. Debs* (Boston: Hall, 1976), p. 67.

24. See *ibid.*; "Class Unionism," in *Debs: His Life, Writings and Speeches*, pp. 401–25; "Revolutionary Unionism," in *ibid.*, pp. 427–43; and "Industrial Unionism," in *ibid.*, pp. 445–66.

25. Schlesinger (ed.), p. 225.

26. Debs, "The Socialist Party's Appeal" (1904), in Gene Tussey (ed.), *Eugene V. Debs Speaks* (New York: Pathfinder, 1970), p. 106 and "Unionism and Socialism," in *Debs: His Life, Writings and Speeches*, pp. 19–55.

27. David Shannon, *The Socialist Party of America* (Chicago: Quadrangle, 1967), p. 12; Debs, "Liberty's Anniversary," *Twentieth Century* (4 July 1895), quoted in Currie, p. 128; Debs, "Unionism and Socialism," in *Debs: His Life, Writings and Speeches*, p. 131; Debs, "The Issue," (23 May 1908), in *ibid.*, p. 489; and Debs, "Outlook For Socialism in the U.S." (1900), in *ibid.*, p. 90.

28. Louis B. Boudin, *The Theoretical System of Karl Marx in the Light of Recent Criticism* (Chicago: Kerr, 1912), pp. 23–26.

29. Boudin, *Socialism and War* (New York: New Review, 1916), pp. 44–80.

30. Boudin, *Theoretical System*, pp. iv, 186, 216–17.

31. *Ibid.*, pp. 39, 228–29, 30, 30.

32. *Ibid.*, p. 180.

33. See Boudin, "Exit the Socialist Party," n.d., Louis Boudin Papers, Columbia University.

34. Louis C. Fraina, *Revolutionary Socialism: A Study in Socialist Reconstruction* (New York: Communist Press, 1918), pp. 13–74.

35. See Fraina, "Problems of American Socialism," *The Class Struggle* 2 (February 1919), pp. 46–47.

36. Fraina, *Revolutionary Socialism*, p. 76; "Revolution by Reaction," *New Review*, 3 (October 1915), p. 257.

37. See Fraina, "The Future of Socialism," *New Review* 3 (January 1915), pp. 7–20; and "Socialism and Psychology," *New Review* 3 (May 1915), p. 12.

38. Fraina's editorials are reprinted in "The Modern Dance," *Cultural Correspondence*, 6–7 (Spring 1978).

39. Fraina, *Revolutionary Socialism*, pp. 165, 196–97, 202–3.

40. *Ibid.*, pp. 81–82 and 220; Lewis Corey (aka Fraina), *Crisis of the Middle Class* (New York: Civici, Friede, 1935), p. 352.

41. Fraina, *Revolutionary Socialism*, pp. 210, 210.

42. Lewis Corey, *The Unfinished Task: Economic Reconstruction for Democracy* (New York: Viking, 1942), pp. 5–6, 127–36, 205ff.

43. Sidney Hook, *Toward the Understanding of Karl Marx: A Revolutionary Interpretation* (New York: John Day, 1933), p. 5.

44. *Ibid.*, p. 6. See also pp. 7–32.

45. *Ibid.*, p. 114. See also Hook, "The Meaning of Marxism," *The Modern Quarterly*, 4 (1930), pp. 430–35; and *From Hegel to Marx—Studies in the Intellectual Development of Karl Marx* (New York: Reynal & Hitchcock, 1936), p. 33.

46. See Hook, "The Scope of Marxian Theory," *American Socialist Monthly*, V, 7 (1936), p. 30. The passage to pragmatism is traced in Hook's later works, *The Hero in History* (1943), *Marx and the Marxists* (1955), and *Reason, Social Myths and Democracy* (1966).

47. Paul Mattick, "Workers' Control," in Priscilla Long (ed.), *The New Left* (Boston:

Porter Sargent, 1969), pp. 376–98. See also *Anti-Bolshevik Communism* (New York: Sharpe, 1978), p. xi.

48. Mattick, "Workers' Control," in Long (ed.), p. 383. See also *Anti-Bolshevik Communism*, pp. 80–81.

49. *Ibid.*, pp. 230, 230.

50. Raya Dunayevskaya, *Marxism and Freedom* (New York: Bookman, 1958), p. 22.

51. See the JFT's monographs *The American Worker* (1947), *Punching Out* (1952), *Union Committeemen and Wild Cat Strikes* (1955).

52. C. L. R. James, *Notes on Dialectics* (London: Allison & Busby, 1980), p. 181.

53. James, *At The Rendezvous of Victory* (London: Allison & Busby, 1984), p. 211; *The Future in the Present* (Westport, CT: Lawrence Hill & Co., 1977), p. 105.

54. Interview with Miles Horton, in Frank Adams and Miles Horton, *Unearthing Seeds of Fire: The Idea of Highlander* (Winston-Salem, NC: John F. Blair, 1975), pp. 35–36.

55. See William A. Williams, "Radicals and Regionalism," *Democracy*, 1 no.4 (October 1981), p. 93.

56. James Weinstein, *Ambiguous Legacy* (New York: Franklin Watts, 1975), p. 117.

57. Buhle, p. 253; Diggins, p. 176.

58. Quoted in James Finn, *Protest: Pacifism and Politics* (New York: Vintage, 1968), p. 241.

Proletarian Politics

The burden of intellectually substantiating neo-Marxism was far too heavy for American radicals, who were interested primarily in getting things done and realized that their constituency cared little about abstractions. In any case, radical intellectuals in Europe, beginning with Lukács, had preempted whatever lingering philosophical pretensions may have existed. America, consequently, never produced a Marxian masterpiece or master thinker to match the task it faced. Still, theory did emerge incrementally as the residue of several pragmatic attempts to Americanize Marxism.

This chapter outlines a neo-Marxian political theory that captured and institutionalized the collectivist impulse that had flickered among America's workers. Subjectivist leftists bet everything on this spontaneous action, and won very little. Orthodoxy, on the other hand, condemned bourgeois politics solely on the basis of a crude economism. They, too, failed politically. The task for nonorthodox Marxists was to carefully examine the nature of capitalist politics to see if the state's expanded social role, as well as workers' swelling dependency and loyalty, created an unforeseen arena for working class struggle.

I

In liberalism, self-interested actors live peacefully together by agreeing on a set of limits on subjectivity, originally called natural rights. Within these guidelines, citizens can join with others in order to more effectively compete for available goods and services. Government originated to enforce these guidelines, that is, to protect the self-interest and natural rights of all citizens. To eliminate a potentially chaotic struggle between self-interested groups that might destroy the guidelines, public decisions became sovereign with respect to all individuals. However, a government that was too powerful could threaten subjectivity. Hence, government was weakened somewhat by separating its powers into competing institutions, each of which could check the others. Governmental power was thus divided into legislative, executive, and judicial branches, and the policy-making process became a complicated affair that wound slowly through each branch. Public decisions

grew incrementally through this institutional tug-of-war, with each branch reflecting the relative strengths of mobilized groups seeking to maximize their own interests.

A second role for liberal government, therefore, is to impersonally coordinate and legitimize the endless struggle between competing individuals and groups. Government decisions, in this view, had to reflect a general tolerance of diverse interests, and the decision processes also had to provide an opportunity for all interests, new or old, to be heard—provided, of course, these interests fell within the guidelines. Fairness, impartiality, and justice were the systemic values to be sought and encouraged, and these things were best assured through protection of basic individual rights and procedures, primarily the rights of free speech, press, association, and due process of law. Both rights and fair procedures were held to be essential to participants who sought to achieve their goals within the public arena. Implicitly and explicitly, therefore, liberal theory perceived the institutions of government as a "neutral" field of conflict. That is, the political system was to be judged by its ability to achieve equilibrium through the balance of competing interests. It need not be judged by the moral content of the participants' demands. Regime stability was therefore a value in itself.

Given these goals, the pluralist system stressed the advantages to be derived by all interests in observing the procedural "rules of the game" and in "staying within the system" when resolving conflicts. In this regard, protest and demands for change were encouraged only so long as the interested participants were willing to accept the resolutions of conflict—laws, court decisions, administrative rulings, electoral outcomes—determined by a policy process of bargains and compromises within and between the institutions of government. In sum, once the guidelines were accepted, participants were free to pursue their own interests in society and in government.

Even liberals acknowledged imperfections in their assumptions and in the manner by which liberal government actually worked. The all-important guidelines, the government's commitment to protect individual life, liberty, and particularly property, assured the total separation of economics and politics. This effectively precluded public control of private corporations and businesses. It also meant that the enormous financial disparity between winners and losers in capitalism became part of its unquestioned "rules." The liberal assertion that the system provided relatively equal access to a multitude of interests was thus qualified by long-standing evidence that the unequal distribution of resources affects participants' access to decision-makers. Poor people could neither influence decision-makers nor benefit from public policy to the extent that rich people could. The imbalanced nature of liberal competition assured that a wealthy, prestigious elite maintained effective control of the political system, and thus was its principal beneficiary.

Particularly during times of economic duress, liberalism's losers, who comprised a majority of the population but played a minor role in decision-making, often questioned the game's rules and sought to destabilize the system. In response, elites modified the guidelines somewhat by injecting government, through policies aimed at minimizing the likelihood of economic downturns and their painful consequences, into the heretofore private economic sphere. To protect liberalism from system-threatening dislocations, what was originally a "laissez-faire" government expanded into society and economy in ways its liberal founders never anticipated.

Although a whole new set of economic and ideological problems accompanied this transformation, on the whole it effectively blunted the potentially disruptive cry for systemic change without fundamentally altering power relationships. The canons of liberal politics remained the consensual core of what most Americans perceived as their "system of government." They were seen not only as an empirically accurate description of the structure and processes of American politics but also as the morally preferred standard for determining the legitimacy of governmental action. Liberal government and politics, popularly perceived, resolved all conflictual issues through an institutional structure dominated by persuasion, compromise, and accommodation among a multitude of competing interests.

Orthodox Marxists see the truth of liberal government in the bowels of capitalist exploitation. The rhetoric of American constitutionalism purposely obscured a central fact of political life: the state's primary purpose is to protect and reproduce class relations. In capitalism, where workers' labor enriched property owners, the state, that is, the entire scope of governmental institutions, was a tool or instrument by which this wealthy class preserved its power. As expressed in Marx's and Engels's *Communist Manifesto*, it was "the organized power of one class for oppressing another . . . a committee for managing the common affairs of the whole bourgeoisie." Liberalism's complex formula for dividing power and protecting rights intellectually rationalized capital's hegemony as well as the administrative means by which capital could govern. This was the source of its popularity among the rich, who then "spread the word" to others through their control over education and culture. When liberalism inadequately protected their interests, capital quickly substituted more efficacious ideas and institutions, as it did in Nazi Germany or, on a lesser scale, in post-Depression America.

Since the liberal state was an instrument of proletarian exploitation, orthodoxy insisted that workers destroy it. Except for the United Front years, when Earl Browder joined the anti-fascist New Deal coalition, employing the 1938 electoral slogan "Communism is Twentieth Century Americanism," America's CP has consistently used electoral politics as a forum for revolutionary propaganda. Even today's diluted Party Program, which tactically supports certain progressive reforms, aims primarily at inciting workers to smash the capitalist state. As a tool of the bourgeoisie,

workers had to carefully take what the state offered, and then quickly destroy what remained.

II

Orthodoxy's materialist theory of the state simplified what Marx knew was a very complicated issue. Marx and Engels, in fact, offered several theories of the state which coexist in an uneasy and unstable relation. Neo-Marxists took this plurality of viewpoints to indicate that even Marx was uncertain regarding the bourgeois state's precise nature, and the role politics would play in working class rebellion.

The recent expansion of capitalist state power, they argued, significantly altered power relationships and provided workers an unanticipated opportunity for meaningful political activity. Liberal government was certainly a mechanism of social control, but had gradually become labyrinthine and was no longer in capital's hip pocket. Marx's own ambiguity indicated, perhaps, that he at least didn't rule out such events, or their tactical consequences. In America, where workers have traditionally trusted government at least as much as unions, the left could no longer rely on orthodoxy's pat anti-state formulas.

In letters to Lassalle (22 February 1858) and Engels (2 April 1858), Marx promised to outline a systematic theory of the state.[1] He never delivered, although his scathing condemnation of bourgeois politics, particularly in the *Communist Manifesto*, has reinforced orthodox instrumentalism. Marx also suggested, however, that under certain conditions the state can be independent from and even superior to all social classes, becoming, in effect, the dominant social force rather than the instrument of the dominant class. In the *Eighteenth Brumaire of Louis Bonaparte*, for example, the Bonapartist state, which "represented" a disorganized peasantry and petite bourgeoisie that were incapable of governing, was also autonomous and absolute: independent of any specific class and superior to them all. Marx left us the distinct impression that a politically independent state may, when it chooses, protect an economically and socially dominant class, without ever becoming its predetermined instrument.

By "independent" Marx meant that the capitalist state was, technically, separate from ruling class institutions (e.g., employers associations, chambers of commerce, etc.) and class-oriented political parties. Thus, although public officials often governed on behalf of capitalists, they didn't hold office simply by virtue of being capitalists. The interests of the capitalist state somehow surpassed or transcended the interests of the capitalist class. The former represented a public or common interest; the latter, narrow private interests. In capitalism, as distinct from pre-capitalist economic formations,

the state was established to represent the entire community, even though its programs may have benefited some more than others.

Winners and losers are determined by who actually defines what the "public interest" is, and thereby determines the quality of public policy. Marx knew that society's most powerful class, the bourgeoisie, defined the public interest in light of its private interests. This did not, however, automatically turn the state into capital's instrument for dominating society. Many documented examples exist, including some that Marx cited in *Capital*,[2] of capitalist states enacting and enforcing policies that favored workers rather than capital. In fact, the extent to which a state is dominated by capitalists is determined by the relative strength of contending classes. If classes are relatively equal in strength, in effect neutralizing each other politically, the state is free to operate independently, defining the public interest as it sees fit. This structural independence legitimized the capitalist state, allowing it "objectively," "neutrally" to enforce laws, such as protecting private property, that empowered a small class of owners at the public's expense.

Marx thus distinguished state power—that is, the political power of a dominant class, based on the balance of class forces in society, to protect its private interests—from the structural nature of the state, i.e., its independence from the economy. The latter, by assuring that accumulation of private wealth remained outside the public realm, also assured capital a dominant position in the class struggle. Marx thus recognized that state power could be won by mobilized workers lobbying successfully for political reforms such as enfranchisement and free mandatory public education. And Marx actively supported and campaigned for the entire range of worker-supported reforms.[3] But these reforms wouldn't effect the nature of the state itself, which remained structurally independent of the economy and thus reinforced capitalist hegemony. In other words, reforms left the nature of the capitalist state unchanged, even as it altered the manner in which public power was used. To Marx, only proletarian revolution could change the structure of the capitalist state. Even the most progressive reforms are, by definition, non-structural and hence incapable of ending exploitation. When organized workers gained sufficient political power, they would smash the bourgeois state, reattach politics and economics, and establish "a community of free individuals, carrying on their work with the means of production in common."[4] In a famous letter to J. Weydemeyer in March, 1852, Marx termed the ensuing social formation a "dictatorship of the proletariat." Despite praising the Paris Commune and anticipating the withering of both classes and the state, Marx never actually described what type of state this short-term dictatorship would be.

Neo-Marxists blend this nontraditional Marxian political theory with the consequences of recent events, such as the state's massive expansion into

the economy and the enormous increase of public employees whose livelihoods depend on the state. These have structurally changed the capitalist state by openly linking government policy to the careers, health, and well-being of millions of workers, as well as to the private accumulation of wealth. Political power can now be legitimately employed to regulate the economy, which means reforms could conceivably end exploitation. The struggle among classes for state control could, if workers were so inclined, be transformed into a struggle for socialism.

Even though orthodoxy viewed the state as capital's instrument, it also recognized that by ignoring electoral politics altogether workers risked isolating themselves from mainstream America and forfeiting the chance "to influence . . . [their] state."[5] This fuzziness pushed the CP into contesting national elections even while disclaiming their usefulness, mouthing the principle of electoral majoritarianism without really believing it possible. Such irresolution helped factionalize the orthodox movement around the electoral question. It also antagonized workers who fared badly economically but never lost faith in the liberal electoral process.

Their innovative theory of the state encouraged neo-Marxists to tap this enormous, politically active proletarian constituency. With state power up for grabs and public policy, since 1929, legitimately regulating private enterprise, a progressive electoral majority could, conceivably, significantly alter the system. Orthodoxy's anti-political stance was quietly abandoned. Neo-Marxists aimed to underline the state's contradictions by gaining political power or by winning meaningful economic reforms. With a progressive civil program to emancipate workers culturally, this new political tactic, it was hoped, could turn Marx's enigmatic "dictatorship of the proletariat" into a majoritarian, popularly elected socialist workers' state. Proletarian faith in liberal politics would be dialectically fulfilled in socialism.

III

The legacy of the Lassalleans—electoral socialists who, by 1890, had been routed by materialists in the struggle for leftist hegemony—survived amidst the victorious Marxists. Even Engels realized that it made good political sense to electorally contest America's bourgeoisie. Electoral campaigns mobilized workers, popularized socialism, and stimulated needed reforms that socialists quickly claimed credit for. Theoretically, the state remained an exploitative capitalist tool, but political activism was a tactic that, paradoxically, could destroy bourgeois politics. What occurred on the orthodox left during the years from 1890 until 1920 was the gradual transformation of political activism from an economistic tactic to an integral component of an evolving, nonmaterialist political theory. Neo-Marxian politics thus grew from, and resolved, a contradiction between theory and practice that even today fractures the orthodox movement.

DeLeon

After engineering the orthodox victory over Lasalleanism, SLP leader Daniel DeLeon anticipated American workers smashing the capitalist state. Unfortunately, orthodoxy's formulaic prescriptions didn't work. Searching the substructure for a working class constituency, DeLeon failed miserably in taking over the dying Knights of Labor, and failed again in efforts to coopt the AFL. After his own Socialist Trades and Labor Alliance lasted a mere five years before succumbing to proletarian apathy in 1900, DeLeon concluded that new tactics were needed in a liberal America that lacked class-conscious workers. At least until 1905, when he abandoned the new strategy in order to infiltrate and control the IWW, electoral, not economic, activism became DeLeon's most direct route to revolution.[6] Properly educated by the SLP, DeLeon believed that American workers would elect socialists to both legislate needed reforms and also destroy the irredeemably evil bourgeois government. Industrial unions, guided by the SLP as well, would militarily defend workers' political gains and eventually become the organs of a new, socialist industrial democracy. DeLeon hoped to verify historical materialism through nontraditional, uniquely American tactics. Clearly, however, his view of the state remained solidly materialist.

The SP Right

The SLP's successor on the orthodox left, the SP, was split into Right, Center, and Left factions, and until about 1907 was controlled by a Center-Left coalition. In its first decade, all three factions agreed with DeLeon on the electoral question. The SP's primary role during these years was to mobilize workers into a class-conscious electoral force that could elect socialists in order to control public policy-making and eventually abolish the capitalist state.

In time, however, as the factions hardened into intractable enemies, the political consensus waned. The Left, with poor, mostly urban constituents, favored political activism only as one tactic in a larger scheme of inciting struggle and raising consciousness. The bourgeois state remained capital's instrument of repression. It had to be destroyed by enlightened workers rather than reformed. The Right, on the other hand, appealed to a better educated, wealthier group, and sought to calmly reconceptualize a Marxian theory of the state in order to account for the improving conditions of middle class life in America.

Socialism, it argued, had silently arrived in the form of public programs that alleviated the horrendous factory and living conditions of American workers. This so-called "police department socialism"—which in 1905 encompassed publicly financed and regulated police, post office, and transportation systems, as well as legislated restrictions on the dividends of public

service corporations—had fundamentally altered the state's role, transforming it from capital's weapon into a potential ally of workers. The missing link, in the Right's view, was proletarian political power, that is, the placing of socialists into public office. By electorally conquering the bourgeois state, workers could stretch government intervention into heretofore unregulated economic and social activities. Each new public program would then further socialize America—hence the popular SP aphorism "step-at-a-time socialism"—until the bourgeois state was entirely transformed into a workers' state. At that point, large trusts would be peacefully nationalized, and workers, through duly elected representatives, would become the dominant class.

Nationally, the Right supported reformist legislation—e.g., sick benefits, pensions, accident and unemployment insurance, maximum legal interest rates, and factory regulations—that would both improve workers' conditions and inject the state further into society. Both objectives were politically feasible if workers voted for either progressive liberals or, preferably, SP candidates for public office. Union-led strikes were perceived as too costly (financially and personally) for the limited benefits that unions could actually win for their workers. Moreover, they were unnecessary. A state could deliver more, in a shorter time period and with much less disruption, than even the most militant union. The Right was armed only with a promise to teach workers to register, vote, and peacefully execute Marx's scientific predictions.

Since most American socialists lived in cities, the Right concentrated primarily on organizing locally and contesting municipal elections. Its platform mirrored the problems and concerns of the Midwestern city (Milwaukee) that was home to several key Right leaders, especially by advocating home rule, public ownership of existing and new utilities, better schools and hospitals, civil service reform, and fighting municipal corruption. These were also popular issues in other municipalities, and the SP Right hoped to ride them into City Halls throughout the country. By incrementally socializing municipalities, a politically and financially empowered working class would be mobilized to electorally conquer state and national offices as well. The march of socialism in America would slowly, peacefully, and legitimately subject private enterprise to public control.

By 1907, the balance of power in the SP had shifted from the Center-Left to the Center-Right faction. After Debs, Haywood, Simons, Fraina, Boudin, and other distinguished Left veterans turned first toward the Wobblies and later the CP, the void was filled by three men who came to symbolize SP Marxism until the mid-1920s: Morris Hillquit, John Spargo, and Victor L. Berger. Hillquit and Spargo emerged from the Center faction, Berger led the Right.

When compared to most other leftists of the day, who were usually poor, unskilled, foreign born, and uneducated, all three men qualify as "insiders."

A Russian immigrant at 16 who joined and then bolted the SLP after feuding with DeLeon, Hillquit was a charter member of the "kangaroo" faction of dissident SLPers and later, with Debs, a founder of the SP. A very successful and wealthy attorney—in 1931 he was counsel for Standard Oil and Vacuum Oil in their attempts to reclaim nationalized property in the Soviet Union—Hillquit split his professional time between the ILGWU, which he legally represented, and well-heeled clients whose fees supported his yen for fine wines and food. Trotsky cynically observed that Hillquit was eminently qualified to lead successful dentists. John Spargo was an American scholar and intellectual whose radicalism somehow grew from a reverence for the English liberal tradition. And the Austrian-born Berger, a former school teacher and journalist who exited the SLP to help Debs establish first the Social Democracy of America Party and later the SP, was the most successful of American socialist politicians, with a hard-core Milwaukee union constituency that in 1910, 1918, and 1919 elected him to Congress.[7] All three men were Marxists knee-deep in middle class culture, more concerned with fine-tuning an improving capitalist system than annihilating it, and willing to bend orthodox dogma to empirical reality. Their political theories reflect this pragmatic radicalism.

Hillquit, Spargo, and Berger epitomized a uniquely American kind of historical materialist: in theoretical midstream, with the socialist ship barely afloat in America's liberal waters, invariably they jettisoned logic rather than plot a new course. All three claimed to be loyal Marxists, fully committed to the veracity and utility of materialism.[8] It is important to remember that at this time in America only Marxists fought against capitalist brutality, and nonmaterialist alternatives to orthodoxy just didn't exist. The SP was, and wished to remain, a Marxist party. Consequently, its leaders paid their theoretical dues by pledging allegiance to historical materialism. They realized, however, that pledging allegiance in America, particularly for growing numbers of employed workers and professionals, meant respecting liberal—not materialist—values and institutions. Tempted by their own middle class lifestyles, as well as their wish to succeed politically, Hillquit, Spargo, and Berger had it both ways. Their materialism was spiked with numerous incongruities that would nevertheless play well in liberal America.

Thus Hillquit's was a theory of society's evolution rather than a philosophical worldview, as if these could exist independently. Historical materialists predicting the inevitability of socialism, in Hillquit's opinion, were not fatalists. Nor did economic determinists presuppose the nature or function of the human mind. Orthodoxy, which Hillquit pointedly chose over any "revisionist" deviations, "is not committed to any school of philosophy and still less does it seek to advance a philosophic system of its own."[9] Spargo, on the other hand, was a self-described "liberal Marxian Socialist," which apparently meant that his brand of orthodoxy was some-

how "interpreted in a liberal spirit, such as Marx himself would approve."[10] This liberal interpretation convinced Spargo that the "inevitable and irresistible" nature of Marxism did not turn men into "mere puppets" or "automatons." "What is inevitable and irresistible is the constant development of conditions culminating in crises which compel men to struggle for relief from exploitation and misery and for a larger measure of happiness." Capitalist economic conditions inevitably will turn this struggle toward socialism, but "ideals, patriotism, religion, and love" will somehow influence us as well.[11]

Spargo's worst problem was not his indefensible argument, but orthodoxy's crudely exaggerated emphasis on theory and economics, its two weakest components. Paradoxically, the materialist Spargo criticized Marx's and Engels's materialism as utopian and false.[12] Although intriguing to leftist intellectuals, in practice Spargo claimed it created a dogmatic cult eager to subjugate nonbelievers and destroy democratic procedure. Moreover, Marx's economics misunderstood the true nature of value, which to Spargo (and Germany's Eduard Bernstein) consisted of some indefinite combination of a commodity's socially necessary labor time *and* its marginal utility for the consumer. Marx had ignored the latter.[13] Marx's theory of surplus value was thus economically false, even though its "sociological aspects"—i.e., its utility in explaining capitalist development, worker exploitation, and class struggle—were valid.[14] Spargo was impatient with purists who questioned whether Marx's theory of value could be both true and false. Absorbed by "the mere letter," rather than "the spirit," of Marx's teaching, these intellectuals were stained by "dry-rot and political decadence."[15] The mature, post-1848 Marx had rejected theoretical utopianism, with its attendant "raw, crude radicalism," and had in fact become "a good deal of an opportunist," interested in tactics and leadership, not logical theory. This practical, opportunistic trait, Marx's "most important teaching," Spargo termed "Applied Socialism." Concerned "not with abstract philosophy, but with the concrete problems of directing social movements," Applied Socialism, not historical materialism, bore the "scientific, evolutionary" marks of authentic Marxism.[16]

Whereas Hillquit and Spargo tried, lamely, to Americanize materialism, Victor Berger simply chose whatever Marxian theories best served his political needs. Thus it was not unusual for Berger to sanction Marx, Engels, Labriola, Darwin, Rauschenbusch, Debs, and Haywood—and, if necessary, distort pertinent texts—to appease Milwaukee voters. Interestingly, he selected one of the few European socialist scholars he had never communicated with, Eduard Bernstein, as patron, boasting that he was "rather proud of being called the 'American Bernstein.'"[17] Berger had crudely formulated a revisionist Marxism prior to 1899, but it was largely ignored. Bernstein's *Evolutionary Socialism*, published in that year, legitimized a heretofore unacceptable pragmatic leftism. Berger found Bernstein's critique of

materialism as well as his support for proletarian nationalism and peaceful, electoral strategies politically useful rather than philosophically correct. Since American elections probably couldn't be won by unrepentant revolutionaries, Berger argued in his *Social Democratic Herald* that socialism was the electoral fulfillment of liberalism, and thus part of America's political tradition. Some modified version of Bernsteinian revisionism was apparently required if the SP was to survive electorally in America. Berger's commitment to Bernstein was based solely on this political reality. During political crises, when reformism appeared tactically inappropriate, Berger, in speeches and articles, explicitly advocated violence and proletarian solidarity.

As philosophers, members of the SP Right faction obviously didn't measure up to even minimal standards of competency. Orthodox materialists in a liberal society, they feared irrelevance as much as dictatorship but were immobilized philosophically by their pragmatic middle class backgrounds and culture. They piled layer upon layer of irreconcilable liberal and materialist principles, and remained unable or unwilling to synthesize. These crude theories would eventually help transform SP Marxism into reductivist, nondialectical reformism, a political analogue of economism. But Hillquit, Spargo, and Berger nonetheless stumbled illogically into a Marxian theory of the state that was both richer and more useful than anything orthodox Marxists could visualize. It clearly disclosed the political dimension of proletarian struggle, and thereby fundamentally transformed Marxist political theory in America.

The modern state, Hillquit acknowledged, was the tool of the dominant economic class. But as modernizing social and economic conditions engendered new classes to challenge old ones, the state, mirroring the base, also changed. During such transition periods "the state reflects the indefinite character of the social and economic conditions, and while in the main it always serves the interests of the class temporarily in power, it frequently makes important concessions to the rebellious classes."[18] A "transitional state" therefore served both old and new classes, with the relative power of each class determined by the pressure it exerted on government officials. Hillquit felt that the American state had already been penetrated by workers, and hence was a "most potent instrument" of reforms that could significantly upgrade the quality of proletarian life. The state, in other words, had evolved from a negative instrument of bourgeois class domination to a neutral mechanism of reform vulnerable to whatever group or class that could control it.[19] Hillquit admitted that capitalists often backed reformist legislation in order to repress and pacify workers. However, new laws that protected workers and prevented capitalists from accumulating excessive wealth convinced him that the balance of public power was steadily shifting toward workers. At this crucial juncture Hillquit felt workers could finally transform the state into a positive force for progressive change that would

complete America's evolution from capitalism to socialism. Hillquit's state, like Hegel's, thus embodied the collective will of citizens past and present.[20] However, Marx had proven that citizens also join into classes, which struggle with other classes and use the state as an instrument of oppression. Since class struggle in history leads inevitably to proletarian hegemony, the modern transitional state had become the workers' best weapon for ushering in the socialist future.

Spargo, an avowed materialist with a scholarly affection for liberalism, combined both in his own surprising theory of the state. Human nature, he felt, is marked by a Hobbesian-like instinct for self-preservation. In conditions of scarcity, however, the survival instinct drove humanity into communities, where economic and social cooperation kept them alive. Because selfish actors could survive only in communities, each aspect of life—the individual and the social—now coexisted in the human psyche. "Life is an oscillation between these two motives."[21] By serving either one at the expense of the other we destroyed the unity of life and inhibited creative behavior. Capitalism elevated the self-interest of each citizen far above its concern for social justice. Consequently, it disregarded humanity's communal instinct and thereby generated exploitation, class war, and social upheaval. A collectivist system that denied the psyche's individuality would be equally unjust, disruptive, and inhumane. Only democratic socialism could uphold individual liberty and also the human need to strengthen the community by eliminating injustice. For Spargo, the psyche fluorished only in a vibrant, nonexploitative community.

The state, like human nature, was a combination of opposites. On the one hand, it was, as liberals knew, an independent institution mediating conflicts between competing actors and interests. By protecting individuals from each other the state could also preserve and strengthen the community. In practice, however, Marx had shown how the state succumbs to the most powerful class and becomes its instrument of self-preservation. The state, consequently, is both a neutral, independent guarantor of freedom and justice as well as a tool of the dominant class.[22]

Politics decides which state function—coercively protecting a dominant class or eliminating injustice via legitimate democratic procedures actually survives. Only if American workers replace capitalists in Congress can state coercion begin to protect democracy rather than privilege. When workers control the state, coercion will eventually cease. The state will then represent a cooperative, just society where individuality can grow unhindered by economic or social exploitation. The capitalist state, in short, will have evolved politically into a socialist state that preserved freedom and enforced justice. Like Hillquit, Spargo detected movement toward socialism in the modern state's proliferating social programs for workers. "In place of the old 'laissez-faire' spirit we have an increasing recognition and ac-

ceptance of social responsibility."[23] The state, then, was slowly being humanized.

The pragmatic Berger had a more mechanistic theory of the state. Capitalism, he argued, was evolving inexorably from a competitive, free market economy to one dominated by bloated monopolies and trusts that were increasingly inefficient. The state, formerly a tool of the dominant capitalist class, was now using government contracts, loans, political favoritism, and military force abroad to economically salvage big business. In the short run, workers were victimized by this state-sponsored corporate network of economic and political power. In the long run, however, as growing numbers of enfranchised workers mobilized electorally and the state responded to their demands, the concentration of economic and political power would accelerate rather than hinder change. Each fully monopolized industry could be quickly and efficiently nationalized merely by one Congressional act. With a politically aroused electorate in power, reinforced by an armed proletarian guard, major industries would be cleanly and smoothly nationalized. As capitalism inevitably consolidated its productive capacity in monopolies, just as inevitably it paved the road to socialism.[24] The capitalist state, in brief, was increasingly vulnerable to the concerted efforts of a united block of proletarian voters. It would be transformed electorally as the political dimensions of capitalist economics surfaced.

Seventy years before the term became voguish, all three SP leaders foresaw the "relative autonomy" of the modern capitalist state, that is, its transformation from merely a tool of capital into an institution that reflected and, potentially, influenced the relative power of competing classes. Later we will see how contemporary social scientists are, unknowingly, empirically verifying this insight rather than, as claimed, stretching Marxism into unchartered territory.

Hillquit, Spargo, and Berger agreed on the practical consequences of their innovative theories: the transition from capitalism to socialism would be slow and complicated, and characterized by reforms that gradually divested capitalists of excess wealth in order to finance programs for workers. Through this peaceful, legitimate procedure proletarian political hegemony would be secured, social relations slowly transformed, class divisions abolished, and exploitation ended. Marx's revolution will have been realized, in Spargo's words, "with as little friction and pain as possible."[25] Even without orthodoxy's "stupid phrases and senseless catchwords"[26] and bolshevism's violence, however, America's "revolutionary evolution" to socialism will have fulfilled the promise of historical materialism.

The immediate, what Hillquit termed "transitional," demands of socialism embodied a wide range of legislative proposals that would significantly better the lot of workers. They included universal suffrage and equal rights for women, the initiative and referendum, proportional representation in legislative bodies, the right of recall, greater autonomy for municipalities, abolish-

ing standing armies, reducing working hours and increasing salaries, public works for the unemployed, public medical and accident insurance, old-age pensions, public care for orphans and invalids, abolishing indirect taxes, instituting progressive taxes on property and income, municipal ownership of utilities, federal ownership of communications and transportation systems as well as all monopolies and trusts, and public (state or federal) ownership of all industries "as soon as they reach a stage where they become susceptible of socialization."[27] By limiting and redistributing excessive wealth, these were practical, and potentially enormously popular, proposals. More importantly, however, they expressed history's logic and spirit by expanding state activities into heretofore prohibited social and economic realms. Cumulatively, these piecemeal reforms would structurally transform capitalism. They were the evolutionary means by which Marx's socialist revolution would be fought in America.

Like most materialists, those in the SP Right faction doubted the capabilities of workers and didn't trust them to act rationally. If, as they believed, history was both objective and predictable, then the value of proletarian consciousness could be accurately measured: it was either authentic or inauthentic. The former qualified one for Party membership. The latter indicated a person was irrational and possibly dangerous, certainly in need of authoritative guidance. Proletarian struggle was valuable only if it generated authentic consciousness, but was otherwise worthless. Since the subjective outcome of spontaneous activism was problematic, SP leaders concluded that education, not struggle, was an appropriate means to radicalize the masses. The vital function of educating workers fell to the Party, which would efficaciously marshall the working class to its historical destiny.

Educators funneled workers' irrational, inauthentic impulses into channels that would ultimately lead to socialism. The nature of these channels was conditioned by a wide range of cultural factors. In Russia, for example, they led through military training toward armed insurrection. On the other hand, America's liberal and reformist mentality mandated nontraditional revolutionary tactics. Hillquit, Spargo, and Berger wanted to teach workers to pressure the state for needed reforms that would have short- and long-term consequences. In the short term, by redistributing wealth the reforms would strengthen workers in their struggle with capitalists for control of the state, and lessen their exploitation. In the long term, they would empower workers politically for the task of transforming capitalism into socialism. Practically, the SP therefore needed to popularize its reformist program and get its candidates elected locally and nationally; where and when appropriate, cooperate electorally with other parties without sacrificing its identity as the only mainline electoral party that was also revolutionary and socialist; and countenance the efforts of existing unions (including the AFL) to upgrade salaries and working conditions. When workers and unions final-

ly were enlightened, the SP would then be favorably positioned to socialize the means of production and govern democratically.

Class struggle and exploitation was, of course, a fact of life in capitalist America. But this reality needn't predetermine the working class response. The antagonism between workers and capitalists represented an unconscious law of social development that, in Spargo's imaginative view, resembled the law of gravity. Socialists needed to be conscious of class struggle to mitigate its worst consequences and, eventually, control it.[28] This was accomplished, however, only by realistically examining its form and content, not by blindly employing scientific formulas. By this nondogmatic standard, Marx was mistaken in assuming that capitalism would polarize into two classes only: manual workers and capitalists. A broad spectrum of intermediate groups, which identified with neither workers nor capitalists and comprised a majority of America's population, had arisen unexpectedly. Socialists courting only blue-collar workers could neither win national elections nor, if given the chance, govern effectively. Since electoral competition, not violence, was the correct revolutionary strategy in America, the SP Right had to redefine America's class composition.

This was accomplished, first, by acknowledging a vast middle sector in America consisting of skilled workers and craftspeople, small producers and merchants, professionals and intellectuals, and small farmers; and, second, positing the unbreakable interdependence of this middle group and blue collar workers. The argument, once again, hinged on the notion of authenticity. Empirically, the class affiliation of middle groups vacillated, "conforming now to the interest of the wage workers, now to the interest of the employers."[29] Preempting people like Eric Olin Wright, SP leaders concluded that these middle groups were, so to speak, up for grabs, that is, vulnerable to whichever class—workers or capitalists—that could prevail. Coopted by consumerism, middle groups currently emulated their capitalist patrons by accepting an individual form of production and seeking only higher salaries and more possessions. However, revolutionary classes throughout history have always attracted the allegiance of a section of the ruling class. As workers displaced capitalists in Congress, these middle groups, sensing their own best, authentic interests, would gradually switch sides.

This was not just wishful thinking. Concrete shared interests united workers and their middle class brothers and sisters. Petty bourgeoisie, for instance, rarely earned more than ordinary wage earners, and were constantly threatened economically by more efficient and profitable corporations. A worker-petty bourgeoisie alliance would be beneficial to both partners.[30] Skilled workers, like manual laborers and unlike capitalists, executed society's irreplaceable, system-preserving tasks. A natural economic partnership of all productive workers would thus lead to political and social alliances as well, and eventually bring down capitalism. Professionals and

intellectuals were, on the one hand, salaried workers, and, on the other, uniquely trained and equipped to testify on behalf of workers. Manual laborers understood neither their historical function nor the complicated science of historical materialism. The former needed workers' energy, productive skills, and numbers. The latter begged for intellectual leadership. Thus "a working class movement which deliberately refused to avail itself of all the gifts of intellect and education at its command, would be doomed to pursue forever the futile task of plowing sand."[31] Finally, like factory workers, most farmers were victimized by economic circumstances that benefited only the wealthy. Berger in particular sought a labor-small farmer alliance of equal partners, where both would survive and prosper in socialist harmony.[32] Some SP Rightists even included progressive, intelligent capitalists as members of the proletarian class.[33] Fair compensation for their nationalized properties might, in this view, turn them from enemies into allies. In any case, it was "wild nonsense" for Marxism to encompass only blue-collar workers. Socialism was for everyone, even smart capitalists. Moreover, it was tactically necessary and correct for Marxists to stretch their appeal beyond manual workers to the vast majority of middle class voters.

This new and politically powerful multi-class electoral coalition would nudge the transitional state toward socialism. SP Marxism in liberal America, in other words, sought to overthrow capitalism, not the state. The latter would always exist, regardless of ideology. In socialism, however, it would administer the economy rather than coerce people, and directly represent the majority of working class citizens. As a modification of, rather than departure from, the existing transitional state, "the socialist state will assume such concrete form, powers, and functions as the majority of citizens, unbiased by conflicting class interests, will freely choose to confer on it."[34] All three SP leaders, each with an ear to the political ground, foresaw few such changes. Wealth, including commodities and means of production, that did not exploit the labor of those other than the owner would likely remain private. What remained would be publically owned and managed. Similarly, existing political institutions—Congress, the Executive, the Courts, Federalism—would probably stay, with public enterprises coexisting on national, state, and local levels. Berger, for obvious political reasons, favored municipal ownership wherever possible. Hillquit and Spargo wanted semi-autonomous cooperative associations to supervise production that was too large for individuals but not suitable for governmental ownership. Within these broad guidelines, nonexploitative constitutional rights and freedoms would, it was felt, surely be preserved. The SP hoped, through socialism, to complete American democracy, not destroy it.

The distance between dialectics and dogmatism is terrifyingly small. SP Rightists had accurately detected the former in Marx and the latter in orthodox historical materialism. Their theory of the state reestablished both

the turbulent ebb and flow of political economy and the authenticity of American liberalism, which Bolsheviks had relegated to history's rubble. This message was sorely needed by an orthodox left submerged in personal, factional, and tactical disputes that neglected its central problem: the escalating irrelevance of materialism. SP electoral success during the years preceding World War I, when the Right faction ruled, substantiated their vision and turned socialism from a dream into a real possibility.

Even this modest victory was sweet, particularly after those lonely and bitter internecine quarrels. Furthermore, it troubled the bourgeoisie, and strengthened their reformist sectors. Public programs then meliorated salaries and working conditions, mollified employed workers, and legitimized bourgeois politics. This cycle—political activism generating economic growth and security, which justified and encouraged more political activism—turned the SP and its leaders toward the concerns of growing numbers of politically sophisticated, affluent workers and professionals. Lacking a foundational dialectical theory by which to measure their short-term gains, each increment of political power begat the dream of more power. Hillquit, Spargo, and Berger, all of whom had condemned orthodoxy's reductivism, eventually sanctified politics in place of economics, duplicating the evil that had inspired their own innovative theory of the state. From one of many arenas—economic, social, cultural, personal—where workers could contest bourgeois hegemony, the state became the sole dispenser of justice, and reformism the only appropriate tactic. Worker exploitation was reduced entirely to insufficient representation in government.

Hillquit was the only SP leader who believed that socialism would abolish the social division of labor and eliminate financial incentives as a means of allocating work, and even he waffled somewhat in asking higher salaries for those with "skill, diligence and general merit."[35] Generally speaking, SP socialism superimposed a state dominated by workers' representatives onto a bourgeois society that would remain largely intact. "The collectivity," in Berger's words, "will closely follow along the lines of what people have already long been doing, only they will do so from a socialist standpoint."[36] Capitalist means and relationships of production, in effect, would survive even in socialism. Labor and capital would stay divided as workers continued producing surplus value for owners, who then reinvested and decided how to use excess profit. Granted, capitalists would be replaced by the socialist state, but the hierarchical nature of bourgeois social relationships as well as the principle of unequal compensation for work performed would not substantively change, and always "the State must be superior to the employee and the employee subordinate to the State."[37] In sum, the causal priority of politics in shaping social life meant that, after the SP's electoral victory, nonpolitical aspects of social life could be left untouched.

Of course, the media had already turned bourgeois culture into the flesh and blood of American patriotism. The SP could therefore reap the political rewards of appearing both compassionate and ethnocentric. As part of a Protocol his ILGWU negotiated with capitalists in 1915, for example, Hillquit acceded to public opinion by disavowing the strike as a bargaining weapon. Spargo, who apparently shared the popular stereotype depicting most workers as both unenlightened and brutish, explicitly warned against the dangers of unlimited proletarian hegemony. While Spargo's socialist state would be legitimate and representative, it would also be controlled by intellectuals and bureaucrats, not workers. Guided by their constituents' working class interests the governing elite would likely establish a republic. But, if so inclined, they could even create a "constitutional monarchy," that would, of course, represent workers. Similarly, factories would be run by skilled managers and technicians who were supervised by the state, rather than by workers themselves.[38] And, finally, all three SP leaders, motivated by either personal conviction or, more likely, a wish to pander to the hideous but common passions of American voters, were outright bigots. Hillquit advocated universal suffrage and equal pay for women, but also inexplicably condemned what he saw as their natural passivity, which made them "better objects of capitalist exploitation than men." Both he and Spargo relegated women to the margins of public life.[39] Berger, in spite of his energetic support in Congress for measures aimed at improving the lot of the poor and powerless, was nevertheless the most egregious culprit. He is on record as defending American imperialism, and ridiculing blacks, Asians, women, Latins, Slavs, and Catholics. Himself a Jew, he occasionally employed anti-Semitic attacks to cudgel opponents during heated electoral campaigns. The SP was neck deep in the same gummy reductivism, in this case political rather than economic, that would later breed the Nazi-Soviet Alliance.

The passage of SP political activism from its being one means of achieving total cultural emancipation to its becoming mere reformism was completed in the 1930s. By then, the hegemonic Right faction, now called the "Old Guard," was being challenged from the left by a small, vocal, doctrinaire group of Marxist-Leninist "Militants"; and challenged from the right by the so-called "Progressives," a heterogeneous congregation of predominantly middle class, idealistic reformers, few of whom considered themselves Marxists. They favored an electoral strategy that would legislate an end to capitalism's grossest inequities without fundamentally altering the capitalist system. Right faction leaders, especially Spargo and Berger but also Algernon Lee, James O'Neal, and the membership of most state SP committees, had already spurned proletarian radicalism. Consequently, they were at home with Progressives rather than Militants. The final victory of the Old Guard-Progressive coalition accompanied the meteoric rise to power of Norman Thomas, an attractive, crusading orator who unfortunately lacked intellectual stature among leftists, not least because, as one biographer

has commented, he probably never studied Marx "with quite the ardor with which he read Wodehouse."[40]

The ex-clergyman son of a Presbyterian minister, Thomas expertly manipulated SP factionalism to his own advantage. During the 1920s and 1930s, he tendered and withdrew his support from various factions in order to further his own career, even supporting the Militants for a short time in the 1930s. It is likely that this opportunism, rather than any firm Marxian convictions, flavored his early thoughts on SP ideology. These were sporadic, contradictory, and often incoherent. Thomas, for example, believed that society's means of production shaped all social relationships and that economic determinism was "enormously useful as a positive guide to social thinking and social programs."[41] Nevertheless, "old-fashioned materialism" had turned into an "absolute scientific law" that "modern science," which apparently embodied pertinent psychological and moral variables, had already disproved.[42] In the 1930s, therefore, Thomas believed materialism was exegetically useful but, due to strong moral convictions, he was not, personally, a materialist. He thus courted, successfully as it turned out, the SP's left *and* right factions.

Thomas received his party's presidential nomination in 1928, and by the mid-1930s he had effectively consolidated a custody that would last until 1968. Once internal political pressures diminished it became clear that the moralist Thomas could comfortably adopt the SP's neo-Marxist theory of the state but would not formulate those dialectical principles that, alone, could block his own and his party's slide into reformism. Thus for a period of over 20 years, until 1953, Thomas gradually purged SP ideology of whatever residual radicalism had survived the 1920s. By the time *Democratic Socialism: A New Appraisal* was published in 1953, Thomas, now on record as supporting McCarthy's witchhunts against public school teachers and some government employees, was more concerned with fighting communism than attaining socialism.

Aside from reminding people of the occasional greediness of capitalism, Marx's ideas were now seen as either irrelevant or, employed unscrupulously, dangerous. Even in the early years, Thomas had rejected orthodoxy's class struggle thesis and had insisted that workers were primarily consumers rather than producers. This line of thought led straight to his later contention that regulatory legislation, by itself, could alleviate the worst evils of capitalism. Similarly, rational, bureaucratic state planning, by steadying the unpredictable free market, could increase wages, lower productive costs, and thus insure continued economic growth. Thomas's brand of socialism would therefore raise workers' salaries while simultaneously buttressing existing divisions of labor and social hierarchies. Capitalism, legislatively regulated only where and when necessary, would remain essentially intact. Thus the eloquent, attractive Thomas spoke compassionately about legislatively treatable social ills like war, extreme poverty, ignorance, waste, and

bigotry, but silently disregarded the left's traditional commitment to sweeping egalitarian change. By the mid-1950s, Thomas's SP became a haven for pacifists, anarchists, civil libertarians, socially conscious theologians, issue-oriented interest groups, and isolated pockets of unionized auto and textile workers. Political activism, the linchpin of a reductivist SP worldview, had become both means and end. Of course, the popular New Deal had already coopted its reformist legislative agenda in the 1930s, leaving the deradicalized SP without a cause or constituency. In retrospect, its evolution under Thomas was politically and intellectually superfluous.

Harrington

As the Aquarian age dawned in the early 1960s, the SP, with the aging Thomas still its titular head, was an anachronism: neither socialist nor a viable political party, only its name and the defrocked Trotskyists it attracted evoked its Marxian heritage. Michael Harrington, whose socialism incubated in the late 1940s with Dorothy Day and the Catholic Worker Movement, had read Marx and was painfully aware of orthodoxy's flat, reductivist dialectic. Until 1958, swallowing his intellectual pride, he adopted the Right faction's unsatisfactory formula of rhetorically backing materialism while hacking it to death with practical criticisms. During this period he led his Young People's Socialist League (YPSL), the youth branch of the SP, into the Independent Socialist League (ISL) of his mentor, Max Shachtman, where it merged with the ISL's youth wing to form the Young Socialists League (YSL). When the ISL joined the SP in 1958, Harrington was back where he had started, but with a new awareness that materialism was irrelevant to "mainstream American liberalism."[43] Realistic radicalism needed to integrate American beliefs, not, like orthodoxy, reject them.

Unfortunately, most of his colleagues in the SP, including Shachtman, were conscientiously realistic in reappraising American capitalism, but their fading radicalism had almost disappeared. Until the mid-1960s, Harrington acquiesced by concentrating on what he knew to be the SP's seminal contribution to American radicalism: its novel view of the capitalist state. His enormously influential first book, *The Other America* (1963), itemized the pervasive suffering of America's forgotten poor and urged interclass cooperation in legislating an end to poverty. Harrington correctly perceived the capitalist state as, potentially, a tool for progressive change. But by emphasizing suffering rather than inequality, class cooperation rather than conflict, reform rather than structural change, Harrington opted for SP reductivism, that is, the belief that legislation alone could extirpate the evils of capitalism.

By the mid-1960s, with the war in Asia escalating and domestic ferment intensifying, Harrington reevaluated SP reformism, and, more generally, the sterile distinction between the reductivist SP and the reductivist CP. In

November 1971, seeking a nontraditional alternative, Harrington assembled a caucus within the SP that became the core of what would later be called the Democratic Socialist Organizing Committee (DSOC). When the SP, in October 1972, refused to advocate withdrawal of U.S. troops from Viet Nam or endorse the liberal George McGovern's Democratic presidential nomination (the first proposal was called pro-Soviet, the second too radical), Harrington finally resigned as co-chair, and his DSOC bolted the SP. In 1982, after merging with the majority tendency of the New America Movement (NAM), the DSOC was renamed the Democratic Socialists of America (DSA). With Harrington its leading spokesperson and ideologue, the DSA became the largest, and also probably the most influential, leftist party in the country.

Harrington saved SP political theory from an ignominious fate by rediscovering the "forgotten genius of Karl Marx," that "foe of every dogma, champion of human freedom and democratic socialist."[44] Harrington detected what had preoccupied the best minds on Europe's left, and was the missing soul of SP Marxism: the dialectic. Marx, in the concept of "species-being," had defined man as both subjectively free and self-conscious, and conditioned by an objective world he had freely created. Man, in other words, was both free and determined, the creator and creature of circumstances. Subject and object, actor and world, spirit and matter, all interpenetrate in the totality we call life. Harrington called Marx's dynamic, multidimensional perspective "spiritual materialism," and distinguished it from non-dialectical idealism and materialism. It combined the romanticized ideals of Marx's youth with his mature economic writings, and thus accurately depicted Marx's entire lifework. Isolated, empirically verified social facts, viewed dialectically, were artificial and profoundly conservative products of the status quo, designed to obscure rather than illuminate interrelationships that might cause social change. Marxian dialectics penetrated these empirical deceptions by reconstructing the web of relationships embodying each social fact. Capitalism's empirical scientific paradigm thereby sustained bourgeois hegemony, while Marx's open and nondogmatic dialectical paradigm rationalized and realized worker emancipation.

From a broader perspective, Marx, argued Harrington, had clearly defined society as a dynamic totality where separate parts interpenetrated. Consequently, while his "magnificent insight" into the conflict between means and relationships of production "is one of the most usable truths of the twentieth, and the twenty-first, century,"[45] the economic base where this contradiction originated is organically related to social, political, and cultural phenomena. It simultaneously defines and is defined by both the collective whole and its particular components. What Marx called "economics" actually embodied consciousness, social classes, human interaction, and creative human artifacts, as well as means and relationships of commodity production. His mode of production is our mode of life.

Society is thus fluid rather than static. Economism and reformism, the poles of leftist theory, were equally mistaken: the former for absolutizing economics, the latter politics. Both are "one-sided categories which abstract from the living totality." Harrington admitted that Marx did view "the organic whole of capitalism from the perspective of its economic relationships," and orthodoxy had indeed accurately depicted the economic component of capitalist life. "There was, and is, a class struggle in the United States, and indeed it has been bloodier and more violent here than in Europe."[46] However, by obscuring historical materialism's actual noneconomic substance it trivialized everything but class and justified a dictatorship of those few who had deciphered history's objective, static economic formula. This betrayed Marx by encouraging "antisocialist socialism," where workers were enslaved by their liberators.[47] In fact, the intensifying contradiction in society's base unfolded only in concert with similarly intensifying contradictions in the superstructure. Political activism, therefore, was progressive only when part of a broader campaign of economic, social, and cultural emancipation, that is, only when dialectically linked to the real world. By severing this link, the SP had transformed a profound insight into the historical role of bourgeois politics into an inconsequential truism.

Capitalism has survived in America because, given its level of technological development, it best facilitated the production and distribution of commodities. Orthodoxy deduced from this and similar facts an *a priori* historical law. Harrington, on the other hand, knew the subjective parameters of economics. Conscious, reflective workers were tending the plows and pliers, and selling the commodities. Their commitment to capitalism was provisional, related to economic development but not entirely dependent on it. Today, for example, relatively backward Third World economies, seemingly ripe for capitalist modernization, are filled with brutally exploited peasants yearning for socialist justice. Their subjective beliefs are not synchronized with the level of their objective economic development, and a radical elite will likely emerge to dominate those unprepared to govern themselves.[48] Social change requires objective and subjective conditions to be at complementary levels of maturity. Neither is epiphenomenal. Socialism is based on cooperative, not competitive, production and distribution. It depends on there being enough material goods, when equally distributed, to keep everyone living comfortably. No amount of wishful thinking can eliminate the need for these objective conditions of material abundance. Conversely, however, capitalist economic abundance, like a cocked gun, will realize its potential only when there are citizens willing to pull the revolutionary trigger.

In economically developed America, Harrington believed the marriage of material wealth to revolutionary commitment was still unsettled. America lacked a citizenry that reflectively understood both the need for socialism

and the socialist possibilities inherent in capitalism. Subjectivists, we have seen, assumed that poverty, suffering, and especially struggle would create authentic workers. For Harrington, on the other hand, a mass-based socialist consciousness would grow as conditions improved. A rising standard of living, "that mood of rising enjoyments and declining satisfactions," outperformed poverty in stimulating workers into acknowledging their own best interests. Even Marx, Harrington noted, realized that effective Communist Parties needed to gently stroke industrial workers with improved conditions rather than hammer them with deepening poverty.[49] Restraint and moderation were Harrington's revolutionary catchwords. And the state, which was capable of raising living standards by incrementally redistributing social goods and services, became a vital arena of working class struggle. Meliorative public programs could effectively raise worker subjectivity to the level of capitalism's objective productive capacity. Only then would history's fateful coupling finally be consummated.

Orthodoxy had already decided this was impossible. As capital's most important tool, the state could perhaps tolerate socialist legislators but could never be adapted to workers' ultimate needs. Even progressive legislative programs only mollified workers without altering productive relationships. One way or another, workers had to destroy the capitalist state. For the SP Right, on the other hand, the state only temporarily served capitalists. It was politically vulnerable, and, potentially, fully adaptable to workers' needs. After capitalists were electorally vanquished, the state would become an instrument of socialist revolution. Disregarding class altogether, Norman Thomas's state was a neutral arbiter of diverse social interests that could be controlled merely by electing sympathetic politicians.

Harrington claimed to have dialectically synthesized the entire spectrum of leftist theories of the state. Each of these, he argued, was partially correct but neglected the interdependence and interpenetration of all social activities. Neither fully autonomous nor determined, the state is what Harrington called "co-determined,"[50] that is, subject to the constellation of reciprocally linked forces that defined its multidimensional reality. The state passively crystallized this turbulent environment and also actively sculpted it; it was both determined and determining, depending on the pattern of events one focused on.

For example, when examining the political function of classes, Harrington agreed with orthodox instrumentalists: the welfare state was indeed the "executive committee" of the bourgeoisie, defending the long-range interests of the capitalist system as a whole, although not always the immediate interests of specific capitalists. The modern capitalist state had turned into what Harrington called "socialist capitalism,"[51] a system that reinforced bourgeois hegemony through state economic intervention on behalf of capitalists. Welfare state progressivism, which initially seemed to empower the masses at the expense of the rich, was eventually coopted by the state and used to rein-

force the capitalist system. The state and its capitalist benefactors, in America, emerged from the New Deal stronger than ever, despite some short-term economic and political sacrifices.

However, instrumentalists didn't anticipate the surprising consequences of welfare state reformism. Millions of workers were more economically secure, particularly in times of crisis, than ever before; their influence on public officials was greater than they had ever dreamed it could be; and their multiplying opportunities for educational and cultural enrichment meant that life could be more fully enjoyed. Political reforms had empowered workers economically, socially, and culturally, without affecting the structures of capitalist domination. Reformism had transformed the capitalist state from a mere instrument of bourgeois interests into a semiautonomous agent of profound cultural change. Since capitalist hegemony embodies a blend of objective and subjective factors, an active, reformist capitalist state paradoxically subverts itself in the process of surviving politically.[52] By empowering the poor politically, introducing minimal working class economic security, and instituting mass cultural education, bourgeois reformism unintentionally cultivates an enlightened, potentially revolutionary subjectivity that can take root in America's economically rich soil.

The state, then, was an integral part of a bourgeois-dominated American system, and could never be fully adapted to proletarian needs. But the dialectical nature of this system, with its dynamic flow of social events that determined the meaning and functions of specific institutions, meant that government activity, for example, although it couldn't unilinearly cause rebellion, could impact the whole and incrementally alter its quality. Thomas, then, was partially correct: who governs does really matter, at least as much as what children learn in school or the economic demands of unionized workers. When the totality changes qualitatively, so will the political, educational, and economic systems. Ironically, it is through political, educational, and economic activism that the totality will be qualitatively changed. The many-faceted, agitated, incessant fusing and splintering of the social whole with its separate parts legitimated left political activism even in an undemocratic system.

Harrington's political agenda thus lay, in his own words, "midway between immediate feasibility and ultimate utopia."[53] While socialism was clearly democratic and revolutionary, socialist tactics needed to carefully nurture a mass-based, enlightened consciousness without shrinking America's impressive economic capacity. They had to be both progressive and practical. These goals could be accomplished, argued Harrington, by supporting and extending the political reforms initially begun by FDR in 1929 and continued by the Kennedy and Johnson administrations. A "third New Deal"[54] would, of course, nest safely within America's mainstream political tradition, and hence be feasible without working class violence.

Moreover, it could be as radical today as were, in their days, the first and second New Deals.

Its centerpiece, which Harrington felt had incubated on the old New Deals' ideological fringes, was the proposal to democratize the investment function, that is, to separate ownership and control of American business.[55] By placing the planning and investment decisions of private corporate enterprises in the hands of tripartite commissions representing government, labor, and capitalists, Harrington believed that a corner will have been turned in the struggle for socialism. Without annihilating any persons or classes, this legislatively achievable reform would, for the first time in America, empower workers to at least begin controlling the workplace. Corporate decisions on pricing, production, technology, plant locations, wages, and capital investment would reflect social needs rather than merely personal pecuniary interests, and would be partially determined by those most affected: workers.

Harrington's legislative agenda also included proposals to nationalize large companies that are major government suppliers or are financially distressed; to establish federal corporations to regulate and develop energy technology, transporation, health, and housing; to establish worker and consumer cooperatives that would run other large industries that produce irreplaceable goods or services; to utilize progressive tax reforms to redistribute income and wealth, and gradually abolish unearned income and inheritance; and, finally, to organize an "Office of the Future" to formulate and submit to local planning commissions long-range national planning agendas. All these reforms, Harrington believed, would blend into a decidedly mixed economy of nationalized, private, and cooperative factories. Consumers could democratically choose which factories go unregulated, and then willingly pay the price. And ever so slowly, raised living standards, democratic empowerment, and moral suasion from nongovernmental sources would raise workers' consciousness to a level matching their productive capacity. Eventually, the social totality will have been incrementally transformed through the progressive changes of its fused parts. At that point, subject and object crystallize into democratic socialism, a new totality that will both determine and be determined by new economic, political, social, and cultural institutions.

Because he solicits dramatic social change through prosaic activism, Harrington is probably best known in America as a tactician. Opposed by almost everyone on the left, he favored realigning America's two party system over establishing a competitive third party.[56] A progressive coalition of traditional New Deal allies such as unionized workers, minorities, the poor, and students already existed on the left fringe of the Democratic Party. Harrington felt that the likelihood of pulling this old coalition left and expanding it into a majority movement was far greater than beginning essentially from scratch in a socialist third party that, history had demonstrated, lacked a constituen-

cy. He focused, therefore, on purging its conservative wing in order to reconstitute the Democratic Party as a progressive coalition capable of winning elections and passing his reformist legislative agenda.

Obviously, this was feasible only by expanding the Democratic Party's electoral base far beyond its predominantly blue-collar New Deal constituency. Harrington responded, as his predecessors in the SP also had, by redefining America's class structure as a means of projecting a leftist electoral majority.

The mature Marx, Harrington claimed, had already foreseen unanticipated twists in European economic development, and was dissatisfied with orthodoxy's simplistic worker-capitalist dichotomy. Had he lived longer, Harrington believed Marx would have discovered an emerging new class of nontraditional workers who mitigated the worst aspects of the class struggle by mediating blue-collar workers and capitalists. Consisting of professionals, technicians, teachers, nurses, artists, and communications specialists—but not personnel managers, who were wedded to capital—members of Harrington's New Working Class shared several unique attributes. In general, they were employed in public and semi-public sectors of the economy. Their economic well-being was therefore keyed to federal policy, especially regarding the funding of public services. Education and work experiences predisposed them toward planning. Finally, they were salaried employees playing an increasingly vital role in production but lacking decision-making power on pertinent economic issues. Harrington believed, in short, that their self-interest overlapped with that of the Old Working Class. Both would benefit from expanded federal programs, higher salaries, improved working conditions, a cleaner environment, better public education, expanded cultural opportunities, and, especially, democratizing the workplace. Moreover, capitalism's worsening economic and fiscal crises, which threatened to eliminate jobs and deflate lifestyles, could unite old and new workers in a shared vision of full employment through planned social investment. The issues, people, and economic potential were there. Only the subjective commitment to improving life through meaningful social change was missing.

By eliminating objective laws, Harrington also eliminated certainty. The new class has traditionally been fully employed and secure, and is currently infatuated with corporate values. Reeducation will not come easily or quickly. There is also, of course, the possibility that an economic downturn will generate working class fratricide, with everyone frantically protecting her own scarce resources rather than working collectively to produce more. Industrialists could unglue the coalition by reducing their own short-term profits with higher salaries for significant new class members, who might then support a capital-dominated authoritarian remedy. Frightened blue collar workers and small farmers could also be manipulated into such right wing escapades. In brief, workers are necessarily neither left nor right politi-

cally. They have already exhibited both ideological tendencies. Where they go in the future will be determined by what they think is desirable and feasible.

By making the Democratic Party a home for traditional as well as new workers, and establishing therein a progressive, reformist platform upon which to campaign, Harrington hoped to create an attractive, legitimate working class alternative to capitalism. Almost alone among American leftists, Harrington is continually heard, seen, and read in mainstream communications media, gently squeezing his radicalism into the day's breaking news events and offering practical advice on who should be backed or opposed on key legislative issues. His DSA also works closely with the liberal wing of the Democratic Party and with several unions, primarily on building electoral support for progressive measures being debated in Congress. Such behavior has been roundly condemned by other leftists, who cannot distinguish it from mainstream liberal activism. Harrington nonetheless believes that small political and economic successes will reverberate on all levels of social life and eventually propel America into its socialist future.

Conclusion

Marxian political theory in America has evolved to the point where, as one pundit remarked, it has raised human suffering from a fate to a tragedy. Faced with liberalism's neutral state impartially mediating diverse interests, orthodox Marxists accurately reported the state's class nature and then foretold its inevitable destruction at the hands of victorious workers. The capitalist state was inherently evil for workers, and socialist political activism neither ethically nor historically justifiable. DeLeon contested elections in order to achieve popularity among workers, many of whom voted, and also as a way of gaining the power needed to dismember the bourgeois state. Basically, however, the state remained useless to workers already neck deep in an economic struggle.

The SP Right sensibly emphasized the disparity between materialist dogma and what actually was happening in America: the state had become a bourgeois class instrument *and* a means of raising proletarian living standards. The welfare state was an arena where workers could contest bourgeois hegemony. Political activism became, for the SP, an integral part of a rounded, realistic revolutionary strategy. Its goal was to control the state electorally, not destroy it, in order to legislatively complete the transition from capitalism to socialism.

Without a solid theoretical foundation, however, short-term electoral conquests and the growth of a privileged, electorally powerful middle class turned reformism from a revolutionary means into the SP's sole *raison d'etre*. Political activism became the only acceptable revolutionary tactic, and state power the only measure of democracy. Like orthodoxy's critique

of liberalism, the SP's theory of the state had turned reductivist. Neither had fulfilled its original revolutionary goal, although both advanced the left's critique of capitalism.

Harrington blended orthodoxy's radicalism with the SP's realism, and dialectically surpassed both. Socialism, for Harrington, meant changing production relationships by eliminating the social division of labor and democratizing significant decision-making processes, not merely redistributing wealth or nationalizing factories. Consequently, it required political emancipation—which was important and necessary—but also economic, social, and cultural emancipation as well. In short, people had to think and act differently in order to translate their newly acquired political power into socialism. This enlightened proletarian subjectivity was generated by contesting bourgeois hegemony in every social dimension. Harrington believed Congressional power was an indispensable weapon for such ideologically engaged workers.

The enormity of this revolutionary task often turned Marxists into visionaries neither aware of nor concerned with workers' real life experiences. Such messianism ignored what Harrington saw as humanity's innate imperfection. Conflict, the state, even classes will all survive interminably. Socialism will merely improve, not perfect, the quality of social living. Harrington's revolutionary pragmatism thus set Marxism in an America pulsing with all of life's bittersweet passions. It testified to both the capitalist state's power to improve proletarian lives and the mass appeal of reformism. And it banked everything on the belief that raised living standards and increased political power will, in concert with other struggles, fortify a democratic socialist impulse among workers.

Notes

1. *Selected Correspondence* (Moscow: International, n.d.), pp. 125 , 126.
2. Marx, *Capital* (Moscow: International, 1975), I, pp. 278–79.
3. See Marx, *On Revolution,* Saul K. Padover (ed.) (New York: McGraw-Hill, 1971), pp. 34, 116–17, 235, 343, and 350; *The Poverty of Philosophy* (New York: International, 1963), p. 172; and Marx and Engels, *The Civil War in the U.S.* (New York: International, 1961), pp. 139–40.
4. *Capital*, I, p. 326.
5. Marx and Engels, *Letters to Americans* (New York: International, 1953), p. 258. See also Marx's "From a Letter to Engels," in *On America and the Civil War*, Saul K. Padover (ed.) (New York: McGraw-Hill, 1972), p. 42.
6. DeLeon's political ideas can be traced in *What Means This Strike?* (New York: Socialist Labor Party, 1916); *Reform or Revolution* (New York: SLP, 1918); and *As To Politics* (Brooklyn, NY: New York Labor News, 1966).
7. Congress, reacting to rampant post-World War I anti-Red hysteria, twice refused to seat Berger, in 1918 and again in 1919.

8. See Morris Hillquit, *Socialism in Theory and Practice* (New York: Macmillan, 1919), pp. 1–9; *Socialism Summed Up* (New York: Fly, 1912), p. 34; and with John Ryan, *Socialism—Promise or Menace?* (New York: Macmillan, 1917), pp. 88–102, 133. John Spargo, *Applied Socialism* (New York: Huebsch, 1912), p. 18; *Karl Marx: His Life and Work* (New York: Huebsch, 1910), p. 325–26; *Sidelights on Contemporary Socialism* (New York: Huebsch, 1911), p. 52. Victor Berger, "Real Social Democracy," in *Berger's Broadsides* (Milwaukee: Social Democratic Publishers, 1912), p. 3.

9. Hillquit and Ryan, p. 237.

10. Spargo, *Sidelights on Contemporary Socialism*, p. 10.

11. Spargo, *Applied Socialism*, p. 31, and *Sidelights on Contemporary Socialism*, p. 55.

12. *Ibid.*, p. 127; and Spargo, *Bolshevism* (New York: Harper & Bros., 1919), p. 262.

13. Spargo, *Sidelights on Contemporary Socialism*, p. 148; *Karl Marx: His Life and Work*, pp. 337–45; and "The Influence of Karl Marx on Contemporary Socialism," *American Journal of Sociology*, XVI (July 1910), p. 37.

14. Spargo, *Karl Marx: His Life and Work*, pp. 328, 346; and Hillquit and Ryan, pp. 201–35.

15. Spargo, *Sidelights on Contemporary Socialism*, pp. 30, 22.

16. Spargo, *Karl Marx: His Life and Work*, pp. 331 , 333; *Sidelights on Contemporary Socialism*, p. 138; *Applied Socialism*, p.20.

17. Berger, "Not 'Revolutionary' Humbug," *Social Democratic Herald* (22 April 1905), p. 1.

18. Hillquit, *Socialism in Theory and Practice*, p. 93. See also pp. 93–98, from which the following short quotes are taken.

19. *Ibid.*, pp. 21–26, 86–98.

20. For the Hegelian influence on Hillquit, see *ibid.*, p. 24.

21. Spargo, *Applied Socialism*, p. 155. See also *Socialism* (New York: Macmillan, 1909), pp. 213–14.

22. Spargo, *Applied Socialism*, p. 50.

23. *Ibid.*, p. 59.

24. See in Sally M. Miller, *Victor Berger and the Promise of Constructive Socialism* (Westport, CT: Greenwood, 1973), p. 26.

25. Spargo, *Socialism*, p. 337.

26. Berger's words in Joseph R. Conlin, *Big Bill Haywood and the Radical Union Movement* (Syracuse: Syracuse University Press, 1969), p. 35.

27. Hillquit, *Theory and Practice of Socialism*, p. 102.

28. Spargo, *Socialism*, p. 152.

29. Spargo, *Socialism*, p. 164.

30. See Spargo, *Karl Marx: His Life and Work*, pp. 351–52; Berger, "We Did Not Create Classes," in *Broadsides*, p. 8; Hillquit, *Socialism in Theory and Practice*, pp. 160–61, 169; and *Socialism Summed Up*, pp. 20 and 91.

31. Spargo, *Sidelights on Contemporary Socialism*, p. 106. See also *Substance of Socialism* (New York: Huebsch, 1909), pp. 112–14, 140–42.

32. See Miller, p. 29.

33. See Carl D. Thompson, "Who Constitute the Proletariat?" *International Socialist Review*, IX (February 1909), pp. 603–11.

34. Hillquit, *Theory and Practice of Socialism*, p. 32.

35. Hillquit and Ryan, *Socialism—Promise or Menace?*, p. 81.

36. Berger, "Socialism and Communism," in *Broadsides*, p. 35.

37. Spargo, *Applied Socialism*, p. 22.

38. *Ibid.*, pp. 73, 125.

39. Hillquit, *Theory and Practice of Socialism*, pp. 232–34; and Spargo, "Women and the Socialist Movement," *International Socialist Review*, 8 (February 1908), pp. 449–55.

40. W. A. Swanberg, *Norman Thomas—The Last Idealist* (New York: Scribners, 1976), p. 106.

41. Norman Thomas, *America's Way Out* (New York: Macmillan, 1931), p. 137.

42. The first quotation is in Bernard K. Johnpoll, *Pacifists Progress* (New York: Quadrangle, 1970), p. 144. The second and third in Thomas, *America's Way Out*, p. 137.

43. Michael Harrington, *Fragments of the Century* (New York: Simon & Schuster, 1972), p. 91. See also p. 177.

44. From Harrington's dedication in *Twilight of Capitalism* (New York: Simon & Schuster, 1976). The following argument is in *ibid*, pp. 14–23, 162–95, 346–47; and *Socialism* (New York: Saturday Review Press, 1972), p. 65.

45. Harrington, *Socialism*, p. 108.

46. *Ibid.*, pp. 82, 83; "Comment," in John H. M. Laslett and Seymour Martin Lipset (eds.), *Failure of a Dream?* (Berkeley, CA: University of California Press, rev. ed., 1984), p. 525.

47. Harrington, *Socialism*, p. 4.

48. *Ibid.*, p. 236.

49. See Harrington and Deborah Meir, *Theory, Life and Politics* (New York: Institute For Democratic Socialism, 1977), p. 9. The earlier quote is in *Socialism*, p. 355.

50. Harrington, "Why We Need Socialism in America," *Dissent*, 17, 3 (May-June 1970), p. 265.

51. Harrington, *Socialism*, p. 187. See also "Soaking the Poor," *Commonwealth*, 97, 3 (20 October 1972), p. 57.

52. See Harrington, *Twilight of Capitalism*, pp. 206–7.

53. Harrington, *Toward a Democratic Left*, (Baltimore: Pelican, 1969), p. 14.

54. The term is introduced in Harrington, "The Politics of Poverty," in Irving Howe (ed.), *The Radical Papers* (New York: Doubleday, 1966), p. 135.

55. See especially Harrington, *Decade of Decision* (New York: Simon & Schuster, 1980), pp. 320–452 passim. The following proposals are found in Harrington, "What Socialists Would Do In America," in *Taking Sides* (New York: Holt, Rinehart & Winston, 1985), pp. 199–222; "Our Proposals For the Crisis," *Dissent*, 22, 2 (Spring 1975), pp. 103–4; "Full Employment and Social Investment," *Dissent*, 25, 1 (Winter 1978), p. 130; *The Accidental Century* (New York: Macmillan, 1965), pp. 279ff; *The Politics at God's Funeral* (New York: Holt, Rhinehart, & Winston, 1983), p. 217; and *Socialism*, p. 307.

56. Harrington, *Toward a Democratic Left*, pp. 247, 295–302.

4

Emancipatory Empirical Science

By the late 1960s, the skeleton of a nonorthodox Marxism was becoming increasingly visible in America. New Leftists had reassured radicals that personal growth was a necessary correlate of economic progress. One could, in short, do one's own thing and simultaneously serve the common good. Harrington, almost singlehandedly, had legitimized for bereft leftists America's romantic infatuation with political heroes like the Kennedys, Martin Luther King, Eugene McCarthy, and George McGovern. If, as Harrington implied, politics really did matter in America, than hitching onto rising liberal stars could brighten the prospects for America's eventual move leftward. Political engagement became radical as well as chic. The feeling grew that capitalism could be contested through leftist rear guard actions that incrementally eviscerated the pecuniary bourgeois soul.

These new tactics, however, created new problems. By breaking orthodoxy's undifferentiated totality into partially independent realms, neo-Marxists outpaced their ability to generate needed factual information. Precise data on the economic and social consequences of various public policies, perceptions of specific candidates or issues, comparative class influence, the political role of popular culture, and the world economy's influence on domestic policy, were prerequisites for leftists framing specific strategies.

These strategies, moreover, upgraded the importance of intellectuals, who contested bourgeois hegemony by enlightening and informing working class Americans. But the breeding ground of intellectuals, America's universities, were tightly controlled by mainstream behavioralists. As one struggling young graduate student put it: "To the extent that Marxist categories could be crystallized into 'testable hypotheses,' non-Marxists were willing (sometimes) to take these ideas seriously; to the extent that debate raged simply at the level of theory, non-Marxists found it relatively easy to dismiss our challenge."[1]

Finally, neo-Marxists had convincingly deconstructed materialist science without replacing it. In America's liberal culture some kind of hegemonic epistemology was needed to neutralize the impulse toward nihilism. Secular theories, then, needed a scientific imprimatur if they hoped to be taken seriously. Science was defined empirically, and was universally and unquestionably accepted by Americans as valid. Without acquiescing, neo-Marxism would somehow have to impress bourgeois empirical scientists. By doing so it would generate needed factual information and tenure its best scholars at major universities. This chapter traces how all this was accomplished.

I

Empirical science claims that all worldly things are conditioned in their existence or occurrence by causal factors within a grand system of nature. These causal factors constitute a net of determining relationships that provide a basis for accurate pre- and post-diction. Scientific method consists of rules generating systematic observation, description, and measurement based on universally acknowledged, impersonal criteria of verification. Empirical scientists generalize from collected data and postulate theories explaining the real world as a determined product of repeating patterns of events. From one general theory is deduced the behavior of a whole species of identical objects. Human perception, for example, is conditioned by received and interpreted external stimuli that are verifiable. Empirically valid generalizations regarding human attitudes and behavior are deductively applicable to all identically situated human beings. Empirical or behavioral social science, therefore, explains reflective behavior by including as research variables subjective factors—feelings, moods, desires, etc.—operationalized and verified according to accepted principles of empirical method.

The philosophical source of empirical science lies in bourgeois preconceptions regarding the natural and social worlds, particularly Descartes's dichotomy of mind and matter: his belief that human reality is qualitatively different from nonreflective matter. The logical corollary, which became the linchpin of bourgeois philosophy, is that the universe consists of "subjective" (human) and "objective" (material) components. Only the latter, factual reality, is explained by empirical scientific method. The former embodies unfettered, autonomous egos reacting unpredictably to external stimuli. Science is limited to the objective, factual world. It explains what "is," not what "ought" to be.

These seminal thoughts—man as an autonomous, nonsocial animal, the separation of fact and value, and the nonpolitical quality of science—philosophically justify empirical social science but are themselves not em-

pirically verifiable. The self-proclaimed "neutrality" and "impartiality" of empirical scientists is thus built on this naively accepted commitment to nonverifiable bourgeois values, which, moreover, embody the material interests of entrepreneurs and rationalize bourgeois institutions. Empirical science, therefore, is the methodological reflection of liberal-democratic-capitalist culture. Its unquestioned bourgeois assumptions determine what questions scientists will ask and what variables they will find relevant. Their supposedly value-free data unknowingly express foundational values that divide social reality into isolated, empirically verifiable phenomena.

Orthodox Marxian materialism, too, concerns itself with concrete empirical phenomena. But materialism is also valid prior to empirical verification. Each empirical "fact" artificially abstracts a small quantity of matter from a social and natural context that is perceived as complex and irreducible. For materialists, matter evolves dialectically. What we sensually experience as isolated elements are actually defined by the entire material totality. Hence the interpenetration of all aspects of this reality invalidates a method that seeks only cause-effect relationships among a limited number of artificially extracted variables. Materialists deny the validity of an empirical datum that is uncritically cut from its total surroundings. They seek, then, empirical illustrations of an *a priori* worldview, not empirical verification. They interpret the universal in the particular, theoretically combining facts to comprehend *a priori* social and natural laws. Although all matter must be sensually perceived, it is not accurately explained by a method that ignores underlying, pre-empirical truth.[2]

Orthodoxy, therefore, is backed into an awkward position in this age of advanced technology. The most distinctive feature of modern civilization, its extraordinary productive and technological achievements, springs from a scientific method based on the priority of specific empirical facts. The popular Marxist argument that proletarian science is superior to empirical science in terms of satisfying workers' needs comes dangerously close to rejecting the spirit of empirical inquiry and with it dreams of additional miraculous accomplishments in industrial, medical, and space technology. Since these will surely improve workers' lives, nonempirical Marxists are in effect asking workers to sacrifice practical interests to realize a workers' utopia. Consequently, motivated by a desire to improve proletarian living conditions as well as meet international political and economic commitments, orthodox Marxist states today avidly pursue a program of empirical scientific research and development. They thus subsidize two distinct kinds of science: bourgeois empiricism, which, although reified and antihuman, is invaluable for survival; and dialectical materialism, with its universal concepts that define empirical particulars. The former harnesses measurable physical laws governing organic matter. The latter protects socialism and ensures history's inherent potential for proletarian rebellion.

II

Materialists argued that empirical science, whose logic occluded the dialectical totality, is doomed like capitalism to annihilation. Just as socialism will succeed capitalism, and workers capitalists, the real science of dialectical materialism will methodologically surpass empiricism. It is this "real" (that is, *a priori*) quality of dialectical materialism that neo-Marxism denies. Marx's theories of matter, history, and revolution emerged from his extensive empirical research and are valid only when explaining a constantly increasing corpus of empirical data. The scientific laws of historical materialism, in short, are manifest in actual empirical conditions. Since empiricism focuses solely on experienced reality it is potentially exact and demystifying, exploding bourgeois myths and establishing scientifically the necessity of proletarian rebellion and socialist equality. A Marxism that is true "in itself," prior to empirical evidence, is useless to serious social scientists and dangerous to the unenlightened.

Neo-Marxism thus replaced unquestioned bourgeois presuppositions with reflective, critical generalizations regarding the social character of individuality, the indissoluble unity of fact and value, and the desirability of proletarian revolution. However, in contrast to orthodoxy, it based these solely on empirical evidence and undertook social inquiry guided by universally acknowledged principles of empirical scientific verification. Empiricism, in other words, could negate the class interests it now represents if the unquestioned myths regarding individuality, science, and politics were shattered by empirical evidence. The method of bourgeois empirical science was needed to demythologize capitalism's unspoken rules, interests, and values. Marx's critical theories and hypotheses are valid only to the extent they explain the actual empirical world and only to the degree that they are verified by modern empirical methods. Empiricism, then, is not necessarily a tool of bourgeois interests, although it is today and has been historically.

Neo-Marxists claim that Marx himself recognized this. In their view, Marx's early work tried to demystify bourgeois culture with verifiable evidence rather than empty abstractions. His later "laws" of capitalist accumulation, the falling rate of profit, and the polarization of classes were similarly founded on observed facts of capitalist development. Marx, therefore, never postulated an absolute, *a priori* principle defining capitalism as inherently unfeasible and revolution as one moment of a transcendent material totality. Furthermore, the utility of Marx's theories must now be measured against new variables that he could not have foreseen (e.g., imperialism, inflation, advertising, unionization, government economic intervention). If, as neo-Marxists anticipate, Marxism can effectively explain this behavior of real people in specified, verifiable circumstances, then its utility has not diminished and its long-run predictions are statistically valid. A neo-Marxist's "faith" in the revolutionary workers' movement and the

necessity of socialism is, consequently, purely secular and empirical, resembling a physicist's expectation as he watches the temperature of pure water approach 212 °F, rather than an ideologue's mystical confidence in the future. But by questioning the physicists' unquestioned assumptions, neo-Marxists escape bourgeois empiricism's self-imposed prison of the status quo.

In Europe, this empirical critique of orthodoxy slowly unfolded in the ideas of the Russian empiriocritics, Eduard Bernstein, Max Adler and the Austro-Marxists, the Italians Galvano Della Volpe and Lucio Colletti, Georges Gurvitch, John Desmond Bernal, and E. P. Thompson. There were, to be sure, practical and philosophical disagreements among members of this group, particularly regarding the abstract principles that will replace Cartesianism and justify empirical verification.[3] But the unifying belief in the epistemological priority of empirical data, the practical commitment to formulating revolutionary strategy in response to concrete conditions, and the professional impulse to apply Marxist theory to all empirically verifiable domains—even those heretofore ignored by orthodoxy—make it an attractive alternative for nontraditional empirical scientists.

III

Contemporary Marxists plug into empirical method by formulating a suitably radical question and then applying one of many appropriate research techniques to pertinent social behavior. Later, we will scrutinize some significant results, particularly with an eye to nontraditional neo-Marxian tactics. Typically, however, the complex project of philosophically justifying radical empirical research, without duplicating orthodoxy's opportunism, has, for the most part, been tackled by Europeans rather than Americans. In their philosophical turbulence, nonorthodox leftists have been inspired by such diverse thinkers as Kant, Mach, Hume, Lenin, Rousseau, Husserl, Bergson, Russell, and Wittgenstein; and the project has doggedly persisted since the early twentieth century. In America, on the other hand, only two full-fledged attempts at such theorizing have appeared, with the second fifty years after the first. And both, moreover, replaced Descartes with down-to-earth, practical philosophies that, once again, reflected America's frontier temperament.

Walling

During the early years of this century, William English Walling was an active member of the SP. A creative, independent thinker in a party that spurned systematic theory of any kind, Walling's reputation was built outside the SP's organization and ideology. In 1913, he became editor of *New Review*, the first radical journal in America devoted to intellectuals and artists. He later went on to become a muckraking journalist, a founder of the

Niagara movement, the institutional parent of the NAACP, and a persistent nonorthodox critic of the SP's left and right wings. In this last role Walling condemned dogmatism of any kind, and pledged to reconstruct Marxism on principles that were practical as well as empirically verifiable. Orthodox materialism, for Walling, was neither. Pragmatism, an inchoate philosophy inspired by the American philosopher John Dewey, became Walling's tool.

To the pragmatist Walling, the sole purpose of philosophy was to serve humankind, rather than to expand reputations or publications lists. It provided methods of inquiry and thought, but "in itself it is only a spirit drawn from the practical needs and activities of men."[4] As a result, an idea's meaning was determined by its real world consequences. Ideas that satisfied genuine needs or fulfilled expectations were, for those involved at that particular time and in that place, valid. As times, places, and cultures changed, so too would the definitions of truth. Ideas were therefore socially conditioned, and the mind was a social organ that reflected its evolving social environment. Marx's economic interpretation of philosophy accurately perceived the social parameters of knowledge. In this sense, that is, in its attaching ideas to their social consequences and by so doing generating useful knowledge, Marxism was part of society's natural evolution. It was, in short, scientifically accurate.

The problem, for Walling, was that most people in capitalism were not as prescient or progressive as Marx. Rather than acknowledging the unity of theory and practice, they thought like capitalists. Dogma replaced dialectics, and Marx's historical generalizations turned into abstract, objective laws that, like the market's invisible hand, were valid independent of their consequences. Marx was thus ahead of his time, but not by much. Walling believed that, in capitalism, the unsatisfied practical demands of disillusioned workers would gradually prove the epistemological superiority of Marxism, the science of worker emancipation, over capitalism. Culture was thus evolving synchronically with philosophy, "and these [two] currents are coming together in the ... pragmatism of such men as Dewey."[5] Pragmatism, which would revolutionize the way people thought, would also realize itself in revolutionary social arrangements that fulfilled humanity's historically conditioned expectations.

Walling's socialism consisted of the ideas and institutions by which workers would, intellectually and practically, satisfy their needs. It could be achieved, he argued, only by ending elite hegemony, which, in practice, meant abolishing economic classes. Liberal institutions were established purposely to secure bourgeois control over workers. Their hierarchical, antidemocratic character, and the pertinent philosophical rationalizations as well, were part and parcel of worker exploitation in America. No amount of reforming could transform such inherent elitism. Moreover, a new hegemonic class would only breed new oppressors, who would then rearrange capitalist institutions without qualitatively altering social relation-

ships. Authentic socialist theory and practice, as Walling saw it, needed always to be guided by its practical success in abolishing social classes and thereby maximizing opportunities for popular self-government. Socialists, then, should gladly sacrifice the interests of any class, including workers, if by so doing they hastened classlessness. This floating, pragmatic standard, not dogmatic allusions to "class struggle" or "materialist laws of history," was the measure of a true revolutionary. No fixed revolutionary program existed that was valid independent of its consequences; and, conversely, any tactic that expedited popular democracy—i.e., "the control of society by the human units which compose it"[6]—was authentically revolutionary.

Walling concluded that only by studying, empirically and with measurable precision, the ideas, tactics, and consequences of existing varieties of socialism could Marxists comprehend the generic meaning of this term and then frame appropriate policy proposals.[7] Marxist theory would then evolve dialectically, embodying the actual changing conditions of social life. Philosophy, science, and revolutionary politics would crystallize at the moment when, and in the place where, empirical research will have educated workers to the realities of social change.

The conundrum that all pragmatists, including Walling, must eventually confront is both obvious and devastating. All moral generalizations are relative to time, place, and culture. Thus an idea or institution can only be judged "evil" according to a society's rational perception of the extent to which its actual consequences block their own self-realization. Rationality, however, is culturally and historically defined. In Nazi Germany or racist South Africa "rational" public decisions often had grotesque, inhuman consequences. Pragmatists believe that the consequences of rational ideas and acts fulfill a people's expectations at a particular stage of their evolution in history. Even what outsiders might consider heinous policies fulfill this function. To term fascism "evil" when a society has rationally opted for it would superimpose an *a priori* truth on a culturally conditioned reality. Pragmatism can thus survive intellectually only by withholding ethical sanctions. It justifies the popular status quo, regardless of its moral quality.

Walling's dilemma steadily worsened as the post-1914 electoral popularity of socialism plummeted. Apparently, Americans were rationally satisfying their historically conditioned expectations without abandoning mainstream liberalism. A steady diet of empirical research, Walling's radical prescription for America's ills, unexpectedly didn't nourish a healthy popular criticism of capitalism. Walling's indispensable means (i.e., empirical research) had generated unanticipated ends (i.e., a rational commitment to the status quo). Radicals, for the most part, understandably disregarded the entire project of pragmatically reconstructing Marxist theory. The significant exception, Sidney Hook, confirmed their worst fears: a pragmatist-inspired commitment to empirical social science would corrode the proletariat's critical, dialectical perspective, thereby strengthening an ex-

ploitative capitalist system. Walling's legacy to leftists, consequently, was his tempered, nondogmatic, academic approach to social problems, rather than his radical theorizing. His careful case-studies confirmed empirically what orthodoxy had refused to admit: in practice, capitalism was dampening the class struggle by incorporating the petty bourgeoisie and segments of the proletariat into a hegemonic alliance. Walling also showed that successful leftist movements were equally creative, abandoning class violence for gradualist tactics that incrementally transformed laissez-faire capitalism into state capitalism, then state socialism, and, finally, real classless socialism. Walling's discredited theorizing was unremarkable. But the high quality of his empirical research and its indispensibility to realistic American radicals forged an unbreakable working alliance between modern science and the nonorthodox left.

Analytical Marxism

The only other American effort to theoretically justify this alliance began in the mid-1970s among radical young social scientists who were profoundly influenced by the predominantly British school of analytical thinkers. Analytical philosophy believed traditional discourse, including Cartesianism, haphazardly explicated grand ideas while logical and linguistic tools went unexamined. Meaning is generated by basic elements of theoretical discourse: the words, logic, and syntax that ideas hang on. Worthwhile philosophy is contextual definition, or analysis, which unpacks linguistic complexes into more comprehensible units. In Wittgenstein's *Logical Investigations*, and the work of Wisdom, Ryle, Ayers, Strawson, Austin, and others, contemporary analytical philosophy broadened meaning to include the rules, regulations, conventions, and habits governing the actual uses of linguistic expressions. It remained primarily a descriptive philosophy of language, but language as a means of social interaction, not an ideal code.

No direct connection exists between analytical philosophy and empiricism. One seeks meaning through contextual definition, the other via factual confirmation. However, both repudiate metaphysics and hence oppose idealism and materialism. The two movements congeal in the work of logical positivists like Carnap, and analytical philosophers like Ayers. Analysis cleans linguistic assertions but makes no factual claims. Science empirically verifies meaningful theory, determining its social usefulness. Despite differences, there is a natural division of labor that encourages active cooperation.

The merger of analytical philosophy and empirical method was, for some Marxists, the perfect antidote to orthodoxy's unverifiable metaphysics. Led by G. A. Cohen, John Roemer, Jon Elster, and other self-styled "analytically sophisticated" Marxists, this group used state-of-the-art methods of logic, mathematics, and model-building to clarify and elucidate the "valid core" of

Marxism that was trapped within orthodoxy's mystical shell. Paradoxically, analytical Marxists hoped to restore economics to its central position in Marxian theory.

Orthodoxy, they believed, had accurately detected the heuristic value of historical materialism. But its teleological reasoning, which overemphasized general laws at the expense of empirically verifiable specifics, was neither rigorous nor convincing. If the precepts of historical materialism could be shown "to emerge as theorems in models whose postulates are elementary and compelling," then its scientificity would be proven.[8] This process of systematically clarifying the basic concepts of Marxism and then reconstructing a more coherent, testable theoretical structure is highly abstract. Analytical Marxists thus concluded that the war against capitalism must, in part, be waged in computer laboratories and discussion groups by sophisticated intellectuals formulating theories that scientists can test and verify empirically. Marxists, in short, needed to coolly devise and test theories that could adequately explain the forms of capitalist exploitation that the rest of us are experiencing.

Rather than cleansing society of exploiters, Analytical Marxists struggled to purify minds of the false categories that, since Hegel, have polluted radical theorizing. Dialectics, "the yoga of Marxism . . . often used to justify a lazy kind of teleological reasoning,"[9] was the source of Marxism's deservedly frigid reception among respected social scientists. A method based on Hegelian logic rather than empirical verification, dialectics transformed Marx's insights into stochastic formulas that trivialized his scientific research. Analytical Marxists could discover no special "Marxist" scientific method.[10] Historical materialism, for Marx, was merely a framework for empirical research consisting of many relatively independent and verifiable observations of the capitalist economy. It was neither a general theory nor, in any significant sense, dialectical. By salvaging this research agenda, packaging it in tightly reasoned theories, and then carefully testing each one, historical materialism—like the theories of evolution, relativity, electricity, atomic particles, etc.—will become part of our accepted body of scientific knowledge. If, after completing this process, radicals wish to call some specific, verified correlation "dialectical," they can do so, provided they understand that this generalization was merely an undirected consequence of rational people functioning in a given set of external conditions.

With empirical verification their sole standard of objectivity, Analytical Marxists reduced all knowledge of society to cause-effect relationships involving individual actors and their surroundings. The foundation of social science, therefore, was verified patterns of individual behavior. These comprise what Analytical Marxists called first order or micro-foundation activities. Second order, or macro-foundation explanations are constructed from systematically related first order behaviors. Dialectics is one possible second order explanation. Scientific Marxists needed to replace orthodox

teleology, which reversed the priority of first and second order explanations, with "methodological individualism."[11] The latter included what modern scientists called "rational choice" models of behavior such as general equilibrium theory, game theory, and modeling techniques developed by neoclassical economics.

In rational choice theory actors calculate the costs and benefits of a particular action and then make the choice that maximizes their goals. Collectively, these individual choices create and maintain a social system, and generate unforeseen consequences that effect everyone. These consequences then condition each actor's goals. Thus, while rational choice models originally buttressed subjectivism and capitalism, Analytical Marxists believed they could now be used to explain how people's rational choices have been warped by a tiny hegemonic class. Capitalism, in brief, survived through favorable micro-decisions made by single actors who were rationally responding to bourgeois-created economic rules. To know how capitalism works and what precipitates social change, argued Analytical Marxists, we need specific empirical data about actors' personal motives and social opportunities. Marx's best work focused on the determining power of society's technological means and relationships of production, and proffered just such information. His so-called "laws" were merely behavioral tendencies characterizing large numbers of actors rationally pursuing their interests in societies they neither created nor controlled. The fact that capitalism, contrary to Marx's predictions, has survived, does not invalidate his research. Something (e.g., socialism) that may, in the long run, be good for the rational members of a particular group (e.g., the working class) may not be chosen because of its irrational short-term consequences (e.g., losing a job, income, citizenship, freedom, health, friends, etc.). Marxism's unfulfilled expectations actually substantiated Marx's research.

Analytical Marxism appears to be stirring America's leftist intellectuals more briskly than, in its day, did Walling's pragmatism. In major universities, on professional panels, and through academic publishers, Analytical Marxists are highly visible. This may, however, be a consequence more of the high-tech mentality pervading contemporary academic research than any innate heuristic utility of analytic theory itself. Highly trained Marxian academics dazzle audiences and peers with technical expertise heretofore found only in mainline social science. As the number of such methodologically sophisticated graduate students in America rises, so too will the percentage of radical intellectuals trained analytically. But the quantitative increase has not been matched by qualitative leaps in radical theorizing.

Cohen's *Karl Marx's Theory of History* is considered by many as the movement's clearest logical exposition of historical materialism, and Roemer's *A General Theory of Exploitation and Class* the most innovative leftist application of equilibrium and game theory. In the former, method and style outweigh substance. Cohen's academic, precise, logically struc-

tured monograph justifies old-fashioned economism, particularly the "technological" version that places final priority in the productive forces' level of technical development. It provides a grand theory of long-run trends based on the functional correspondence of productive relations to forces of production, but doesn't explain how change occurs. Moreover, the rationale for Cohen's dismissal of vulgar economic determinism is precluded by the nondialectical rules of the game. Technology apparently dominates in some undefined and unprovable "nonvulgar" sense.[12] Among Analytical Marxists Cohen's book has generated highly refined debates regarding the logical and empirical utility of functional explanations that are light years removed from real life problems of average workers.

Roemer, on the other hand, creates a general category of exploitation which embodies specific Marxian, capitalist, feudal, status, and socialist variations. Based on what he calls the "class exploitation correspondence principle" (CECP)—i.e., "every agent who is in a labour-hiring class . . . is an exploiter, and every agent who is in a labour-selling class is exploited"[13]—Roemer reconstructs some of Marx's economic theories in a manner that is logical and empirically confirmable. Economism is thus redesigned for the computer age. But, as the saying goes, looks are only skin deep. Like traditional orthodoxy, Roemer's version implicitly reduces all social injustice to class exploitation. Race, gender, religion, subjectivity, and politics remain residual categories in a unilinear, economically determined totality. Even Roemer's extravagant display of logical and empirical dexterity can't twist economism's square peg into the multidimensional, overdetermined round holes of modern social life. In the context of socially conditioned moral and political dilemmas that splinter America's working class, Roemer's presentation, like Cohen's and those of other Analytical Marxists, becomes as useful, or useless, as its vulgar counterpart. For Analytical Marxists, linguistic clarity, thus far, has had a high cost: avoiding any issue that cannot be adequately framed by nondialectical logic and confirmed empirically.

It would, in sum, be as foolish for American neo-Marxists to ignore empirical science as to naively accept either the pragmatist or analytical rationale. For practical reasons, leftists need empirical data. For moral reasons, modern social scientists need to critically reevaluate the consequences of Cartesianism. The working alliance between Marxism and empirical science is justifiable on both levels. More importantly, however, this century's Marxist-inspired empirical research agenda has borne fruit, in spite of the precious theorizing of radical pragmatists and analytical thinkers. Countless valuable empirical studies have been generated by and organized around classical Marxist concepts and explanatory assumptions. The exploding corpus of empirical knowledge, some of which we shall now examine, has propelled Marxian theorizing beyond dull economism to encompass life's inexhaustible richness. Although dialectical inquiry is contingent upon per-

tinent measurable real-life experiences, it has not been, and perhaps cannot be, philosophically reduced to bourgeois categories.

IV

Since the mid-1960s, at least three phenomena have conjoined to create a favorable environment for radical empirical studies. First, liberal America's unquestioned cultural bias toward empirical definitions of science has waxed, particularly among secular intellectuals. Second, tenure at major universities has been linked to the quantity of a candidate's published scientific studies. Finally, radical intellectuals have increasingly chosen university employment over the economic and social anxieties of life in the counterculture. Thus, in disciplines ranging from sociology to proctology, a steadily rising number of radical scientists have married traditional empirical methods to nontraditional Marxian questions. Their issue keeps many radical journals and several presses filled with words, numbers, and correlations that confirm Marxism's usefulness in explaining how we live and die in capitalist America. This expanding corpus of high quality published research has slowly congealed around three core issues related to nonorthodox theorizing: class structure, the state, and the capitalist world system. Accumulated data have, in some cases, substantiated familiar neo-Marxian theories, and in others generated new ones that could dramatically alter leftist tactics. At the very least, these areas of research highlight the vital role empirical science now plays on America's nonorthodox left.

Class

Perhaps the central concept of Marxism, class, was never adequately defined. The last section in the final chapter of the third volume of *Capital*, entitled "Classes," unexpectedly stops after only one page, following Marx's admonition "The first question to be answered is this: What constitutes a class?" Engels later commented "Here the manuscript breaks off."[14] Marx's work nonetheless repeatedly refers to class. It insinuates two potentially contradictory ways of conceptualizing this key term.

The first, which was adopted by Engels and the orthodox movement, depicts classes as groups of people characterized by similar relations to the means of production. In capitalism, people naturally split into two major groups: those who own labor power and those who own capital. The former are workers. The latter, capitalists. From this perspective, the social organization of production determines objective class relations as structures filled by people. As productive relations mature, objective class relations become increasingly antagonistic, until they explode in violent conflict. People are merely the vehicles by which objective structures such as classes logically evolve in history.

Primarily in the historical works, however, Marx occasionally acknowledged the contingency of class formation, that is, the importance of subjective factors such as shared struggle, identically perceived interests, common lifestyles, and political organization as prerequisites for objective classes to realize their potentials. Each concrete stage of history, in this view, needs to be studied empirically to see whether the conjuncture of objective and subjective factors have gelled into authentic classes mobilized to fulfill their destinies. If books like *The Class Struggles in France, 1848–50* and *The 18th Brumaire of Louis Bonaparte* are any indication, Marx had detected a gap between the objective and subjective factors of class formation that inhibited authentic class behavior. Instead of polarizing working and capitalist classes, Marx discovered that "middle and intermediate strata . . . obliterate [objective] lines of demarcation everywhere," and create an "infinite fragmentation of interest and rank" among both workers and capitalists.[15] The latter, for example, are fragmented into industrial, financial, landed, social, and political sub-groups, with each subdivided according to the quantity of members' assets. The former are split into workers (urban or rural, large or small industry, manual or intellectual, unionized or nonunionized, well or poorly paid), peasants, and lumpenproletariat. The intra- and interclass lines of demarcation fade, and at times disappear entirely. Marx assumed, perhaps naively, that as capitalism matured all but industrial workers and capitalists would eventually disappear. Disregarding, for the moment, abundant contrary evidence, there still remains a theoretical problem involving the relationship of existing concrete historical classes to abstract structural classes: at what point, if any, do "objective" workers who live, think, and behave like capitalists actually become capitalists? Do classes, in other words, automatically evolve in a structurally determined history, or are they created by people collectively struggling to be free? Marx's inchoate theory of class begs the question.

Bourgeois social scientists replace Marx's dialectical, historical perspective with unilinear statistical descriptions of the entire spectrum of social differentiation. For them, one's objective position in the relations of production is no more significant than one's ranking in society's relations of distribution (e.g., status) or relations of authority (e.g., power). Interconnections between and among all these variables are entirely arbitrary and empirical. Radical social scientists, on the other hand, employ empirical methods to clarify and verify Marx's dialectical hypotheses, including those related to class. Raw data depicting the heterogeneity of both of Marx's "objective" classes can aid in constructing clear, forceful, and verifiable Marxist theories that will also reshape proletarian tactics.

The relevant data have been interpreted by American radicals in several ways. Not surprisingly, some researchers used evidence to support Marx's structural definition of class.[16] Capitalist society, they claimed, really is polarized into workers and capitalists. Deep internal segmentations generate

intra-class frictions but don't qualitatively alter members' relations to the mode of production, and hence leave the basic class structure untouched. Workers especially have been split into several subgroups, each with distinct empirically verifiable characteristics. Some subgroups are based on ethnicity (religious, linguistic, racial, and cultural differences); others on social, economic, and educational factors (blue and white collar, intellectuals, professionals, and managers). All workers, however, regardless of living standards or self-perceptions, remain workers because of their location in the productive process, that is, because they sell their labor power. Privileged workers often become the functionaries of capital. Such inauthentic behavior occurs within the capitalist class structure, and, of course, complicates the process of mobilizing an enlightened, radicalized proletariat. Tactics must reflect real life, which is determined by examining empirically the quality of intra-class capitalist and proletarian divisions. The goal remains proletarian authenticity, that is, to convince the so-called middle classes to acknowledge long-term, objective proletarian interests. The means are set by factual evidence regarding what issues might effectively reclaim these privileged workers and further split the bourgeoisie. Workers, in other words, realize their class potential by struggling to reduce the exploitation inherent in the relations of production in which they are objectively situated. By struggling politically the objective class becomes manifest in its own self-activity.

Some scientists, echoing Marx's historical works, believe that struggle, rather than facilitating an objective identity, actually creates classes. In other words, no valid structural theory of objective class exists. In E. P. Thompson's words, "class is defined by men as they live their own history, and, in the end, this is its only definition."[17] These struggles don't just happen haphazardly. They are conditioned by the totality of economic, social, political, and cultural factors comprising the context for class formation or disintegration. Social relations, which are contingent in history, structure the struggles that create classes. Thus socialist movements are conditioned by capitalist social relations, even if they are not determined by capitalist relations of production. In America, where workers are conditioned to ignore classes, socialist tactics needed to emphasize the linkage of class and everyday experiences. Only when mobilized collective actors organized around their objective position in the relations of production could a class exist concretely. Political struggles about class formation, in other words, must precede economic struggles between classes, for the latter can't exist until the former succeeds. Politics and ideology thus autonomously condition the process of class formation because they generate struggles in the course of which classes organize, disorganize, and reorganize. The so-called middle classes, nontraditional laborers who sell intellectual rather than manual labor power, often for surprisingly high wages, are fair game for any political movement that can successfully mobilize them. Socialists who tac-

tically embrace these powerful middle groups will likely maximize their political success, but at the cost of traditional blue-collar hegemony. Those who exclude them reinforce a pristine laborism whose post-industrial political future is cloudy. In short, America's class map will be determined by leftist ideology. Only by empirically analyzing specific societies and specific conjunctures of social relations can Marxists determine what political struggles are most pertinent to creating socialism.

Gouldner

A third perspective on class, in America associated mainly with Alvin Gouldner's *The Future of Intellectuals and the Rise of the New Class*,[18] proffers empirical evidence to substantiate a revision of Marx's structural argument: classes *are* determined by objective relations of production, but, as Marx foresaw in the *Grundrisse*, modern society embodies three rather than two such classes. High-tech capitalism has begotten, in addition to its old capitalist class and the traditional proletariat, a New Class consisting of humanist intellectuals and technical intelligentsia. Members of this New Class comprise a cultural bourgeoisie whose control over cultural capital produces saleable utilities that bring to its possessors sizable incomes. Thus, like old capitalists, they derive incomes from capital. However, their capital takes the unorthodox form of knowledge and ideas on how best to manage society's conventional productive capacity. This new type of capital is significant because it engenders in those who control it attitudes that in key respects resemble those of traditional workers more than those of old capitalists. New Class ideology, in other words, rationalizes and reinforces the special material interests of its members. These include upgrading the professional quality of their work, applying their own sophisticated skills to controlling work activities and environments, raising their income, and— with all this in view—gaining the requisite political power. Moreover, New Class members, all of whom are highly educated, express themselves ideologically through what Gouldner called a "culture of critical discourse" (CCD), which verbally and intellectually justifies assertions rather than merely pulling social rank or threatening violence. Potentially, therefore, New Class rhetoric negates all forms of profit, rent, and interest that is critically unjustifiable, advocates self-government, and seeks higher salaries— goals that are thoroughly proletarian. What they lack, however, particularly the technical intellegentsia, is the broad historical perspective that might thwart their innate elitism and explain their ideological ambitions. A nonorthodox, flexible, methodologically sophisticated Marxism could do both, and thereby align workers and New Class members into a coalition based on common emancipatory interests. Surprisingly, a realistic left, using the tools of modern science, could dialectically transform capitalism's so-called middle class buffer into a socialist vanguard.

Wright

Eric Olin Wright refined this neo-structuralism in the influential book *Classes*.[19] In earlier work, Wright had concocted several classificatory schemes in which exploitative relations were distinguished from dominating relations in production, and occupations in which these two relational sets didn't correspond were called contradictory. *Classes*, discarding domination, recycled a version of John Roemer's conceptualization of exploitation as "the economically oppressive appropriation of the fruits of the labor of one class by another" based on the unequal distribution of productive assets.[20] Wright's unique contribution to class theory was his distinction between four types of productive assets: labor power, capital, organization assets, and skills. When any of these assets are unequally distributed in a society, those with less are exploited by those with more. Feudal exploitation, for example, was marked by inequalities in the ownership of labor power, permitting lords to coercively extract surplus labor from serfs. Capitalism rationalized inequalities in the ownership of capital that produced unequal market exchanges of labor power and commodities. State socialism (e.g., the Soviet Union) exploited by creating inequalities in the possession of organizational assets that permitted bureaucrats to appropriate and distribute planned production surpluses. Socialism, potentially, exploits because those with needed skills will appropriate, through negotiation, a disproportionate share of excess production. Only in pure communism, where every individual equally develops his or her human potential and skills are thereby equally distributed, will exploitation finally cease.

In addition to workers and capitalists, American capitalism also creates occupations in which actors are exploiters in terms of one kind of asset (e.g., organizational and/or skill) and exploited in terms of another (e.g., capital). These occupations, neither proletarian (exploited on all productive levels) nor capitalist (always the exploiters), comprise the middle classes and occupy what Wright called "contradictory locations within exploitation relations."[21] In relation to some productive assets these classes are exploited; in relation to others, they exploit. They have, in short, material interests, and thus political interests as well, that are fundamentally different from and opposed to those of workers and capitalists.

Wright's data indicated that proletarianization is progressing in America, despite the continued growth of relatively nonproletarian service industries.[22] Of the large wage-earning population, approximately 25 percent belong to the middle classes, with the remainder performing routinized, dull, nonresponsible, and nonautonomous activities. America's objective, worker dominated class structure, based on the unequal distribution of its productive assets, is thus empirically verifiable. However, other data showed that the effects of class structure are mediated by politics, that is, while structures set the environment, political activism actually shapes the process of class formation. Sweden and America, for example, are both economically

developed capitalist societies. But Swedish proletarian class consciousness—i.e., shared working class perceptions, which influence intentional choices, of a common relationship to productive assets—is more widespread and intense than in America. Wright attributed this, in part, to pro-labor Swedish state policies initiated by powerful proletarian interests, which have reinforced working class identity. Relatively autonomous institutions such as politics, then, "determine the ways in which class structures are translated into collective actors with specific ideologies."[23] Historical materialism correctly described the trajectory of maturing classes gradually forming as self-conscious entities with concrete political interests. Only empirical research, however, could uncover the causes and consequences of change. Wright's evidence supported the causal relevance of politics and the contingency of socialist revolution.

Wright's class theory, if correct, means that the prospects for a viable socialist movement in America depend on the capacity of working class organizations to create favorable political and ideological conditions. One indispensable tactic is to draw the middle classes into a socialist working class alliance based on shared material and nonmaterial interests. Workers needed to allay middle class fears that their financial, professional, and political interests are threatened by socialist equality. Socialism's goal of eliminating capital and organizational assets as sources of exploitation raises the specter of real democratic control over economic and bureaucratic resources used in production. Workers and most members of the middle classes would gain substantially by such decentralization. The struggle for socialism and the struggle for democracy are thus two aspects of one mutually beneficial process. In capitalism, however, this message is virtually invisible. Consequently, socialist forces needed to back potentially popular political reforms that available data indicated might promote proletarian class formation, intensify class consciousness, and create that interclass democratic socialist alliance.

In sum, America's empirical left has applied accumulated data to reconceptualizing Marx's ambiguous class theory. The theoretical results, which are tethered to Marx's structural-political dichotomy, recapitulate the explanations Marxists have always employed when discussing class, ranging from orthodox to subjectivist. Each major perspective—structural, neostructural, and political—has discovered a large and significant group of workers who identify as neither proletarians nor capitalists. Each also rejects orthodoxy's sanguine fatalism. Classes don't coalesce or disintegrate automatically. Like all of reality, classes react to external, verifiable stimuli. If change has occurred, or will occur, it was or will be caused by factors that, when discovered, can be duplicated. Empirical neo-Marxists all agree that class formation occurs, in part at least, because self-conscious class members struggle politically to achieve shared interests. They differ theoretically on whether interests are structurally or subjectively determined.

Practically, however, they advocate proletarian political activism, particularly strategies of allying with or absorbing the middle groups, to create propitious conditions for the transition to socialism. Here, too, empirical class theorists merely verify the old SP Right's primitive but profound insights. Despite the occasionally staggering displays of technical dexterity, the theoretical and practical payoff of empirical class theory has been minimal. Perhaps it's not so much *what* empirical class theorists say as *how* they say it: Marxian class theory has been legitimized by its adopting the language and methods of America's hegemonic mode of empirical scientific inquiry.

The State

Left empirical studies of the state, like those of class, translate significant competing Marxian theories into state-of-the-art conceptual and methodological terms. We have seen that Marx neglected systematic political theorizing. Orthodox Marxists are instrumentalists. They see the state as an instrument in the hands of the ruling class for enforcing and guaranteeing the stability of the class structure itself. Nonorthodox Marxists, on the other hand, emphasize the state's relatively autonomous powers to legislate significant reforms that, over time, can structurally alter capitalism's productive relationships. The former reject political activism except as a means of destroying the state. The latter electorally contest the bourgeoisie in order to control the policy-making apparatus. Both are rooted in aspects of Marx's incomplete and ambiguous theory of the state. Empirical Marxists have merely renovated the categories and supplied supportive data. Instrumentalism, for example, is transformed into a factually verifiable theory of the priority of economic structures over politics. Conventional nonorthodox state theories, such as Harrington's, are reformulated and tested as neostructuralist theories in which society's productive relationships guarantee the state a measure of autonomy in devising means of reinforcing capitalist hegemony. Finally, some empirical Marxists present data to support a subjectivist commitment to proletarian struggle as the only means of raising a mass-based, insurrectionary consciousness that can, when expressed politically, smash unjust capitalist structures. Like its nonempirical ancestor, each empirical state theory has an enthusiastic Marxian following.

Domhoff

In 1956, C. Wright Mills discovered that power in America was concentrated in and exercised by those who managed major social institutions.[24] This "power elite" encompassed what Mills felt were the most important hierarchies in America: corporations, the executive bureaucracy, and the military. Although common backgrounds bound these institutional elites, Mills emphasized their professional careers rather than their class, and con-

demned Marxists for reducing military and political power to economics. The source of social power, for Mills, was control over important institutions, rather than class.

G. William Domhoff transformed Mills's institutional elite into a class, composed primarily of corporate and banking interests that "owns a disproportionate amount of the country's wealth, receives a disporportionate amount of the country's yearly income, and contributes a disproportionate number of its members to the controlling institutions and key decision-making groups of the country."[25] This small upper class shared a privileged social background and constituted barely .5 percent of America's population. Either directly or indirectly it controlled all major institutions in America, including the state. Consequently, it was what Domhoff called a "governing class." The American state was an instrument by which this class politically reinforced its cultural hegemony.

This instrumentalist conclusion, however, emerged inductively from Domhoff's data, not deductively from an *a priori* logic. The data also showed that capitalist class power is occasionally mediated by individuals who, although wealthy, are outsiders. Through educational, social, and professional training, these individuals have been gradually coopted into becoming functionaries of the dominant class. Although capitalists directly control the executive and judicial branches of the state, there is evidence that the national legislature and most state and local governments are run by such functionaries.[26] The state, in short, is "grounded" in the capitalist class and is its "operating arm," but is not always managed directly by capitalists. Often capitalist-controlled private foundations, interest groups, universities, and mass media do the dirty work, indirectly shaping the legislative agenda by molding public opinion or influencing significant legislators. Moreover, intraclass disputes over how best to protect the capitalist system can generate conflict among national policy-makers and between state and federal governments. Capitalist power, then, is pervasive but not unlimited, and can be constrained somewhat by non-elites who organize effectively. Domhoff left unanswered the question of how much proletarian politics can alter this structure.

Przeworski

As laissez-faire capitalism evolved into the welfare state, and Keynes intellectually supplanted Adam Smith, instrumentalists encountered nonorthodox theories that reevaluated bourgeois politics. Similarly, radical empirical scientists in the 1970s and 1980s reexamined the bourgeois state in the light of its expanding functions and proffered revised, non-instrumentalist theories. Domhoff, they argued, had depicted the centrality of production relationships, but failed dismally in conceptualizing and measuring the state's new economic role. Although structurally linked to capitalism, the

welfare state could no longer be immediately bound to either the capitalist class or capitalist interests.

The Analytical Marxist Adam Przeworski found evidence that, in advanced capitalism, rational workers may under certain economic and political conditions choose capitalism as the best of all feasible social systems. These conditions appeared in America after the crash of 1929, when workers experienced first-hand the brutal consequences of economic collapse and capitalists were forewarned of the impending disaster brewing within an unregulated free market. A social-democratic compromise between these two rival classes was quickly negotiated. Workers, who bore the brunt of capitalist economic crises, agreed to moderate economic demands. It is better, they rationally opined, to be secure and exploited than to provoke a potentially disastrous, self-destructive catastrophe. In response, capitalists, for whom socialism would be costly, agreed to reinvest at artificially high rates, thereby stimulating the economy and raising salaries. This compromise turned the state from capital's instrument into "a coalition which includes important segments of organized workers."[27] Its job was to award economic concessions to capitalists, stimulate consumption, enforce the compromise, and generate support among the public at large. The state had become the instrument of a capitalist-proletarian class coalition that was rationally committed to reproducing capitalist relations. Politics still reflected the material interests of the dominant class, but was now mediated by workers' rational cooperation. The second best choice for both exploited workers and wealthy entrepreneurs was to maintain a vigorous, expanding capitalism. This rational consensus became the underlying motive of all public policy.

The compromise can erode, thereby legitimizing socialist activism, if either of two situations develops: entrepreneurs renege on delivering higher wages, or dramatic improvements in wages and material conditions are not matched by an improving nonmaterial quality of working class life. Marxists have traditionally emphasized the first scenario by organizing in factories and then exercising economic pressure when negotiating new union contracts. Using a mathematical simulation model, Przeworski discovered that in such negotiations militant workers needed to "go all the way," in effect seizing factories and public institutions, to stand any chance at all of success.[28] If they failed or hesitated, capitalists would lose confidence in the social-democratic compromise, disinvest, and precipitate a painful economic crisis. The consequences of success, however, are equally problematic because rational entrepreneurs won't invest under duress. Rebelling workers could also be crushed by an authoritarian, even fascistic, rightist coalition. In short, militant socialist activism, even if "successful," would likely hurt workers severely.

In terms of material interests, then, workers do better accepting capitalism than militantly opposing it. The rationale for democratic socialism cannot be

based on proletarian material gain. Marxists must therefore identify a non-material need that capitalism, despite its material advantages, neglects. The satisfaction of this need must be proven a necessary and sufficient condition for workers to rationally choose socialism. Przeworski suggested that Marxists initiate a cultural offensive geared toward the moral issue of freedom, that is, the maximization of quality time that is free from the constraints of scarcity or toil.[29] Capitalism generates this need and the resources required to meet it, but, in general, does not deliver. Most people with free time are unemployed, and those lucky few who aren't are funneled into prepackaged, profitable leisure activities that ignore real needs. Marxists, therefore, need to milk the multi-class state for every achievable material working class reward, and then emphasize capitalism's moral and cultural emptiness. Socialism can be sold to rational workers as the only system that democratically allocates material resources to maximize free time and self-improvement opportunities for everyone.

Block and Skocpol

Fred Block and Theda Skocpol applied rational choice Marxism to understanding the behavior of state officials or managers (i.e., "those at the peak of the executive and legislative branches of the state apparatus"[30]), not classes, and by so doing further reconceptualized the state's role in reproducing capitalist social relations. They believed workers, capitalists, and state managers occupied three different structural locations in capitalism. Every actor rationally maximized her material interests, which were conditioned by the structural location of her class. Workers, for example, sought higher wages and improved living conditions. Entrepreneurs accumulated capital and profits. And state managers hoped to remain in power.

Domhoff's instrumentalism was thus empirically and conceptually unsupportable. The dominant capitalist class is neither class conscious nor in direct charge of state activities. Even when recruited from corporations to serve the state, actors behaved as self-interested state managers rather than as capitalists. Capitalism reproduces itself as a result of the structural conflict between capitalists, state managers, and workers, not through the direct political hegemony of capitalists. State managers realize that it is in their interests to appease both capitalists and subordinate workers, and try to do so. Faced with widespread demands from below, for example, state managers have expanded public services to alleviate the consequences of proletarian exploitation, and to acquire mass support. The state's expanding social powers then threatened capitalists, whose interests were nullified by public regulations. State power could, as in Nazi Germany, reach the "tipping point" where capitalists lose their ability to resist further intervention. This danger peaks during crises, when state managers claim, and usually receive, expanded powers. However, the consequences, in normal times, of alienat-

ing capitalists in this manner—e.g., disinvestment at home, economic and political decline abroad, blocked access to privately owned media, and worsening social and economic conditions for workers—are, for state managers, rationally unjustifiable. So, in spite of occasional conflicts with capitalists, state managers reproduce capitalism because, as the German Claus Offe has also argued, their legitimacy depends on a healthy capitalist economy where capital accumulation, profits, and public revenue are all growing.

From this point of view, state power is not reducible to class power. But the exercise of state power occurs within particular class configurations that limit its form and content. These are generated by concrete relations of production. Thus, production relations in a particular society determine the class structure, which conditions how state power will be exercised. The exercise of state power, in turn, although conditioned by class power, also impacts on extant classes. The rationality of the capitalist state thus "emerges largely behind the backs of the social actors involved,"[31] in the economic structure and the actual conjuncture of class forces.

The state, therefore, has a life of its own, a life that in good measure reflects the class struggle going on around it. Social scientists needed to examine empirically the constellation of orbiting class forces as well as the pertinent political institutions and actors. In this hyperempirical vein, Skocpol asserted that no theory of the capitalist state was possible, only case studies of concrete political institutions each of which has its own key explanatory variables. Skocpol's state supports capitalism by setting flexible outer limits for public policy beyond which capitalist relations will be threatened. Within these, the political behavior of state managers is, on the surface, irreducible to any single variable or set of variables, including class.[32] Thus, on the one hand, Skocpol admitted that states are influenced by class forces. On the other, however, she claimed state activities "have an underlying integrity and a logic of their own" that is keyed to international, geopolitical, and personal factors.[33] State autonomy, neither fixed nor impossible, is linked to internal and external institutions that are always changing. Only by empirically examining the causal regularities surrounding specific states in specific circumstances—what Skocpol called "analytical induction"—can one know about the nature and role of the state, particularly the degree to which its behavior reflects the class struggle.

For Block, Skocpol, and others on the "analytical-inductive" left, the contradictions of contemporary capitalism are centered in its productive relationships, especially the antagonistic material interests of workers and capitalists. The state's policies in resolving economic antagonisms will determine the quality and pace of social change. If the state is now biased towards capitalists it is because rational state managers depend on capitalist accumulation for revenues. In effect, the capitalist economic structure now defines what "rationality" will mean to rational public decision-makers. Not, however, because of some ineluctable logic, but because, in specific

observed instances, this was shown to be the case. Also shown was the fact that legitimate state managers react to working class dissatisfaction by redistributing resources to an extent that will not undermine business confidence. Leftist strategy, therefore, must make the consequences of capitalist-state manager cooperation intolerable to rational state managers. In short, Marxists must transform the economic structure by intensifying the class struggle and persuading state officials to switch sides. The most important conflict in understanding social change is that between the dominant economic class and the state.

Tactically, this means that America's working classes must mobilize to act in national and international political arenas.[34] Proletarian electoral victories, by democratizing major social institutions, can pressure state managers into expanding progressive public policies, thereby fracturing the alliance with capital. On the other hand, a peaceful, demilitarized world order, by eliminating military rivalries, can delegitimize authoritarian political structures that have traditionally protected world capitalist interests. Leftist strategy, then, must support democratization at home and peace abroad. The success of such a policy, both in America and throughout the industrialized and developing worlds, will create a strong and independent socialist movement that can, first, coopt the capitalist state, and then restrain rational socialist state managers who, after all, will also protect their own, not workers', interests.

Many on America's empirical left were unhappy with rational choice Marxism, particularly as conceptualized in Przeworski's, Block's, and Skocpol's state theories. For as long as "rationality" is linked to productive relations, the material interests and behavior of classes and state managers is inseparably tied to the structural needs of capitalism. The state's autonomy is then relative rather than absolute. It is free to respond rationally to concrete stimuli but incapable of escaping the economic forces that condition the form and content of its freedom. Empirical case studies alone can unwrap the quality of freedom a particular state, in specified conditions, displays. However, Skocpol, especially, flirts with apostasy. If rationality, as she occasionally implied, is conditioned only or primarily by a state manager's perceived self-interest, than the state, potentially, is free to do whatever its managers wish. The class struggle, from this non-Marxian perspective, becomes vestigial for state managers, and empirical inquiry serves Descartes rather than Marx. If the state is—even potentially—absolutely free, then, as Poulantzas and others have correctly observed, we are dealing with a pluralist, not a Marxist, theory of the state.

Sweezy and Mandel

In Europe, Marxian state theorists tapped into a rich structuralist tradition that Louis Althusser had already radicalized. Radical scientists in America, on the other hand, were never comfortable with continental abstractions.

Their task was to conceptualize a nonorthodox, dialectical, structural theory of the state that was also empirically verifiable. Surprisingly, this was accomplished with the help of two old-line Marxists—Paul Sweezy and Ernest Mandel—who had tried gainfully to translate orthodoxy into the complex, quantifiable language of America's academic economists.

Following the New Deal era, instrumentalists couldn't adequately explain reformist policies that, at least in the short run, penalized substantial segments of the dominant class. Both the American Sweezy, a life-long Stalinist, and Mandel, a Belgian national widely read in America and a leader of Trotsky's Fourth International, hoped to reconceptualize orthodoxy's theory of the state with the help of neoclassical (Marshallian and Keynesian) economics. Both, apparently independently, also developed underconsumptionist theories based on critical, highly empirical reexaminations of modern capitalism.

In *The Theory of Capitalist Development* (1942) and, with Paul Baran, *Monopoly Capitalism* (1966),[35] Sweezy held that the distinctive problem in advanced capitalism was not falling rates of profit, but the absorption of surplus. Large American corporations were producing more than could be profitably consumed. This crisis of underconsumption could be temporarily blocked only through an irrational, wasteful utilization of surplus, i.e., unnecessary consumption, built-in obsolescence, burgeoning sales and advertising expenditures, and militarization. Monopoly conditions exacerbated the problem by slowing economic growth and modernization without significantly reducing output.

Mandel, in *Marxist Economic Theory* (1962) and *Late Capitalism* (1975),[36] eclectically substantiated and extended Sweezy's analysis. Modern automated capitalism, he argued, has increased capital-intensive at the expense of labor-intensive investment, thereby reducing the total hours of human productive labor and limiting the expansion of real wages. Workers, however, still demanded higher wages and more jobs, and capitalists still sought wider markets for their proliferating commodities. The ensuing contradiction between the material interests of capitalists and workers, in Mandel's view, was unsolvable. Automation symbolized this contradiction by manifesting the best and worst of capitalist production. It simultaneously portends the end of need and misery, and the advent of unanticipated proletarian insecurities, anxieties, unemployment, and demoralization.

Without entirely abandoning instrumentalism, Sweezy and Mandel nevertheless defined state activities within the context of capitalism's structural contradictions. The welfare state, from their view, eased surplus absorption by averting actual or anticipated recessions and boosting demand. It was an economic, not a political, necessity. Moreover, its structurally caused activities were likely, at times, to briefly hurt some capitalists in order to enhance capitalism's long-term prospects for survival. In this sense, the state

was relatively free from the immediate interests of particular capitalists, except insofar as the latter's acts conflicted with the need for the state to act for the class as a whole. Both Sweezy and Mandel were unrepentant materialists. The state, they implied, can be conceived both instrumentally *and* structurally, as the tool of capitalists *and* the unshackled embodiment of capitalism's internal contradictions. Empirical social inquiry needed to isolate instances of state activism and determine, in each case, the relative significance of each factor.

Sweezy's and Mandel's neo-orthodox state theory was anchored in society's economic base. State activities, whether directly or indirectly controlled by millionaires, mimicked the structural contradictions of an economic system that produced more than could be profitably sold. Both authors observed the state through an economic filter. Hence, they discovered the causes of, and remedies for, capitalist state policies in the substructure. In postwar Europe, on the other hand, neo-Marxian theorists like Poulantzas, Offe, and Habermas, were investigating the state's irreduceable role in reproducing capitalism. Their empirical studies, which were eagerly received in America, defined the state as an organizer of capitalist class interests as well as the legitimate representative of all citizens, including workers. The crisis of the state, therefore, was dialectically linked to capitalism's economic contradictions but not reduceable to them. The state's multifaceted role as defender of both capitalism and democracy generated a unique set of problems that evolved by its own logic. Moreover, state activities often displaced the class struggle from base to superstructure. The perceived fusion of economics and politics in modern capitalism had thus altered the form, content, and locations of class struggle, in effect legitimizing state theorizing as a means of understanding the structural crisis of capitalism. In brief, the work of Sweezy, Mandel, and the Europeans provided the pieces for an empirically based, nonanalytical, noneconomistic structural theory of the American state. James O'Connor, in *The Fiscal Crisis of the State* (1973), melded them into shape.

O'Connor

O'Connor found the structural contradictions of capitalism rooted in the class struggle, the consequences of which were exacerbated by the expansion of monopoly production. As modern technology improved and capitalist production became more specialized and efficient, an increasing percentage of industries were taken over by large, wealthy firms. This expanding segment of capital required continual replenishing of technically and administratively skilled workers. It also needed physical overhead capital such as transportation and communication facilities, research and development programs, worker education programs, energy supplies, etc., all of which were very expensive. Simultaneously, organized workers were negotiating to improve wages, health and old age benefits, factory and living

conditions, and recreational facilities. These clashing material interests produced an accumulation crisis among entrepreneurs, who lacked the ready cash needed for capital investment and the confidence that profits would soon improve. Workers, whose demands were perceived by management as exhorbitant, were layed off, fired, or forced into inferior jobs. Monopoly capitalism, consequently, discouraged economic growth and bred, in its place, poor, unemployed, angry workers.

For ideological reasons, the American state, except in rare cases involving unprofitable but needed services, cannot get directly involved in production. Its dilemma, therefore, was to somehow rectify the worst evils of modern capitalism without turning illegitimate to capitalists, whose economic interests it represented, or to workers, for whom it claimed to impartially mediate social conflicts. In response, the state in America has, in effect, kicked class conflict upstairs, into the state bureaucratic apparatus, by regulating not only interclass conflict but intraclass conflicts as well. All this increased state activity is, of course, enormously expensive. The costs incurred by the state's efforts to rescue capitalism from its inner contradictions engender what O'Connor called "the fiscal crisis of the state."

More specifically, the state has tried to fulfill two basic and often contradictory functions: sustaining or creating the conditions for profitable capital accumulation, and sustaining or creating the conditions for social harmony. O'Connor called the first state function "accumulation," and the second "legitimation." State expenditures have a twofold character corresponding to these two functions.

"Social capital" expenditures include social investments in "projects and services that increase the productivity of a given amount of labor power and, other things being equal, increase the rate of profit" (e.g., physical items like roads, airports, and railroads; and human services like education, administration, and job training). They also include social consumption expenses for "projects and services that lower the reproduction costs of labor and, other factors being equal, increase the rate of profit" (e.g., goods and services—such as urban renewal, hospital, child care, and development programs—consumed collectively by workers; and social insurance programs old age, unemployment, health, and medical—which expand reproductive powers of workers and simultaneously lower labor costs).[37] These social capital expenditures, by lowering costs and increasing productivity, provide incentives for higher capital investment and thereby alleviate capital's accumulation crisis.

On the other hand, "social expenses" are the "projects and services which are required to maintain social harmony—to fulfill the states 'legitimation' function. They are not even indirectly productive."[38] Social expenses include all the components of what O'Connor called the "warfare-welfare state": an elaborate system of social welfare benefits that protects surplus labor and preserves social peace; a sophisticated military machine that

employs surplus population and stabilizes domestic and world capitalist systems; and a foreign aid program that uses surplus capital to strengthen friendly nations and guarantee foreign markets. Social expenses mollify workers at home and abroad, assuring favorable environments for profitable investment and trade.

Although the federal government emphasizes social expenses, and state and local governments social capital expenditures, nevertheless nearly every public agency is to some degree involved with both accumulation and legitimation functions, and nearly every public expenditure has this twofold character.

Social capital outlays enhance both productive capacity and aggregate consumer demand. Social expense outlays expand aggregate demand, without affecting productive capacity. By adjusting capital and expense allocations the state can, and does, manipulate economic growth through its budgetary process. In short, the state sector has become indispensable to the expansion of private industry, which, in an unregulated free market, will not be able to generate needed investment resources. Moreover, as the state sector grows it stabilizes monopoly capital and makes itself indispensable.

The core of this process, however, is diseased. For as the state continually socializes the costs of production, private corporations are appropriating the profits, creating a fiscal crisis, or "structural gap," between public expenditures and revenues. "The result is a tendency for state expenditures to increase more rapidly than the means of financing them."[39] Neither of the feasible stopgap solutions—issuing debt and borrowing against future tax revenues, or raising taxes—are acceptable. The first generates inflation and deficit spending, worsening the accumulation crisis. The second penalizes successful middle class workers, the fount of increased public revenue, and irritates the legitimation crisis.

The state's financial difficulties are worsened by moral and cultural features of America's liberal totality.[40] Individualism promotes an insatiable appetite for personal aggrandizement. Special corporate interests are constantly seeking more social investment, and labor groups more social consumption. The poor, unemployed, small farmers, marginal entrepreneurs, and other special interest groups all desire increased social expense allocations. In this mad pursuit of self-interest, classes are fractured and the class struggle is obscured. State employees, for example, who seek increased social consumption allocations, battle private sector workers, who want lower taxes. Wealthy and marginal capitalists disagree on the need for more social investment funds. Decentralized, pluralist institutions tend to maximize each group's potential political influence. Public decision-making is thus characterized by waste, duplication, inefficiencies, incrementalism, even contradictory policies—all of which aggravate the state's fiscal predicaments. In the cherished name of liberal democracy, workers, capitalists, and special interests—by blindly pursuing their own interests—have unknow-

ingly blocked capitalist accumulation and intensified the state's crisis. Consequently, as state activity reproduces capitalism, it also manifests the economy's internal, class-based contradictions. Capitalism's inner economic contradiction is thus dialectically realized in the state's unsolvable political dilemma. But the state nonetheless has a life and logic of its own. It is structurally linked to the base without being reduceable to it. Its activities are both relatively autonomous and inseparable from the class struggle.

The state's relative autonomy opens new vistas for proletarian tacticians. O'Connor stressed the importance, even priority, of class struggle in production. By organizing workers in factories, and catalyzing workplace demands for higher pay and improved conditions, Marxists can strain the accumulation process and propel the state—always trying to protect the capitalist system—further into America's social and economic affairs. O'Connor also, however, sought potentially progressive alliances between, for example, state employees and state dependents to maximize public programs; and state workers and private sector workers, to oppose regressive tax structures. Militant demands on the part of these united workers and recipient groups will either undermine the state's legitimacy or hurt capitalists. If Marxists can simultaneously cultivate a widespread, anticapitalist "social individuality" ethos, then from the state's worsening fiscal crisis a compelling solution will arise: costs *and* profits must both be socialized.

Wolfe

O'Connor accented the economic aspects of state policy, implying that legitimacy among workers was contingent solely on the amount of material benefits they received. Alan Wolfe, on the other hand, applied O'Connor's basic structural critique of the state to understanding its ideological, rather than fiscal, crisis. Money alone, he forewarned, won't legitimize a state whose liberal democratic rhetoric has created irreconcilable expectations among capitalists and workers, and turned the economic class struggle into an ideological skirmish between two antagonistic worldviews, one "liberal" and the other "democratic."

Wolfe argued that the state's accumulation function, its commitment to reproducing capitalist social relations and liberal freedoms, clashes with its role as the public voice of the masses, the vehicle by which citizens can democratically control policy-making.[41] Neither role can be forsaken without trivializing the liberal-democratic values that Americans still cherish. This structural contradiction leads not only to O'Connor's fiscal crisis, but also to a profound intellectual crisis in which the state has, in effect, promised to concurrently run in opposite directions. If either capitalists or workers perceive a failing of public commitment, the state will turn illegitimate and be replaced by one more in tune with the wishes of the stronger of these two classes. The American state is thus plagued by

ideological as well as fiscal crises, both of which dialectically embody capitalism's internal class struggle.

Rather than attempting what, as capitalists and workers continually escalate their demands, is obviously impossible, today's state occludes its ideological crisis with the illusion that it is somehow above the class struggle. Loyalty, in effect, is now based not on what the state accomplishes, which is very little, but on what the state represents. Although states can, in changing conditions, adopt alternative tactics by which to reify itself,[42] and although each residually survives today, in general Wolfe describes a process in which state power—not useful policy—is consecrated, and political institutions gradually deteriorate into public relations forums for glamorous personalities. Late capitalism is eventually characterized by an absense of politics, where the state legitimizes itself simply by becoming more visible. For Wolfe, the state's reification and the alienation of politics grow together in history. A powerful bureaucratic apparatus expands ambitiously without ever resolving the problems that caused its expansion. No wonder, then, that America periodically discards Keynesianism and, until popular discontent once again swells, resigns itself to either laissez-faire or corporatist alternatives.

Like O'Connor, Wolfe suggested that the best short-term tactic for workers and poor people is to organize economically and escalate their demands on the state, in effect "exploding" its relief and public service roles and inflaming the legitimacy crisis. In the long term, however, Wolfe advised left intellectuals to repoliticize the masses by arousing self-governing, grassroots, reformist movements. A mobilized proletariat will, Wolfe hoped, sense the bankruptcy of capitalist politics. The state will be perceived in its true light, as a relatively autonomous institution that dialectically manifests the class struggle and structurally reproduces capitalism. Ultimately, voters must choose between liberalism and democracy, capitalists and workers, capitalism and socialism. If democracy wins, so will socialism.

Castells

Instrumentalism treats both workers and the state as unwitting tools of impersonal economic laws. Nonorthodox structural theories of the state, analytical and nonanalytical, are keyed to the objective processes of capitalist economic development. State actors dialectically embody society's objective, class-based contradictions. Political conflicts therefore represent disagreements between ideas, or representations of classes, rather than in-the-flesh workers and capitalists, blacks and whites, females and males. From structuralist perspectives, the state is dominated by a ruling class, but is also conditioned by ideological demands that prevent one concrete class from becoming hegemonic. A relatively autonomous bureaucracy can, within the bounds of the system's own logic, create public policy.

We have already examined the left subjectivist critique of Marxian science, and its enormous popularity among progressive Americans. It is not surprising, therefore, that some empirical social scientists, more than likely with New Left credentials, have conjured their own verifiable subjectivist theory of the state. They contend that the state's crisis is the inevitable outcome of neither impersonal economic laws nor objective structures defined by determining inner logics. Instead, the state reflects direct, human confrontations between dominant and subordinate groups that self-consciously struggle to maximize their own material and ideological interests.

The transition from structural to subjectivist state theories was effected by Manuel Castells, a French national who nevertheless for years has taught in American universities and published in American scientific journals. His rigorously empirical studies supported the structural conclusions of O'-Connor and Wolfe: an accumulation crisis has forced the state to subsidize capital by financing needed social expenses. The resulting socialization of costs and privatization of profits has engendered unsolvable fiscal and political crises. Castells found that these are experienced most intensely in urban areas, where working class requests for expanded public services go unanswered while municipal governments, to attract new capital investment, creatively funnel public resources into large corporations.[43]

Castells, however, felt that structuralism was detached from the real needs and aspirations of living workers. Although it accurately depicted the conditions within which states acted, by ignoring the human variable structuralism also denatured the political process. Bricks, by comparison, may objectively determine the kind of building that can be constructed; but architects and builders self-consciously put them in place. Similarly, the activities of public officials transpire within structural constraints, but actual political conflicts and decisions are determined by the self-conscious struggles of people seeking their own best objective interests. A united working class, in league with professional and managerial workers, through struggle can alter state policy and eventually transform the political structure itself. The structurally defined economic context is a framework for, not an inhibitor of, self-conscious class activism.[44] In the end, both the state and the objective economic structure embody the interests of the most powerful class.

Bowles and Gintis

Samuel Bowles and Herbert Gintis epitomized this perception of the state as a demarcated arena of struggling classes. Their empirical work confirmed that the liberal state is torn between upholding the material interests of hegemonic capitalists and satisfying workers' insistent demands. In Bowles's and Gintis's terms, the democratic political rights vested in citizens conflict with the economic rights vested in property owners, producing, for the state, the unenviable task of balancing incompatible material in-

terests. In America, the state has already tried and abandoned several different political strategies. The Lockian solution, for example, enfranchised only propertied and educated citizens. Jeffersonians encouraged everyone to own property. And Madisonians institutionally balanced competing interests. Currently, Keynesians employ public policy to integrate workers into the state and stimulate capitalist accumulation—the fiscal and political consequences of which have already been noted. These tactics have all failed, primarily because "as a social process, capitalist production is inherently antagonistic and always potentially explosive."[45]

Capitalism's contradictions, for Bowles and Gintis, are merely verifiable facts of social life. The spooky structures others see are neither scientific nor practical. The state, for example, has reinforced capitalist relations because it accurately perceived the social hegemony in America of a united, mobilized capitalist class. It knew, so to speak, where its bread was buttered, and public policy went straight to the corporate fridge. Because individual preferences, including those of state actors, are "both socially conditioned and susceptible to development through individual choice," the notion that some mysterious inner structural logic molds state policy is untenable.[46] Indeed, Bowles and Gintis have traced the patterns of American state expenditures and discovered, surprisingly, that they grow during periods of private corporate expansion, when economic times are favorable, but then unexpectedly create an atmosphere that dampens corporate optimism, thereby initiating recession. It seems that redistributive state policies, by severely draining the pool of reserve workers, have limited capital's ability to discipline labor and lower wages. What others have defined as capitalism's structural inner logic, in fact, is illogical, and accentuates rather than resolves the contradictions. A better, nonstructural explanation of state policy, for Bowles and Gintis, interprets the state as a field populated by competing classes. During healthy economic times, confident and assertive workers mobilize to pressure both the state and employers for improved benefits. The state, historically, has responded favorably to such tactics. As costs and wages rise, capitalists mobilize and threaten the state with disinvestment and worker layoffs, which will inflame the state's fiscal and political crises. Workers, traditionally intimidated by such economic tactics, fracture and fearfully stand by. Predictably, state policy will once again reflect the interests of the dominant capitalist class.

The implications for tacticians are clear: state hegemony can be won through building working class consciousness and struggling gainfully against capitalists. Economic mobilization is a necessary but not sufficient step. If workers are to successfully bond into unified, powerful, and radical collective actors they must identify morally and culturally as well as economically. Radicals needed to build islands of self-government and direct democracy within the capitalist system, especially in schools, unions, neighborhoods, congressional districts, etc.. Bowles and Gintis proposed a

practical program, including an "Economic Bill of Rights," they believed could spur proletarian bonding.[47] Neither orthodox nor liberal, it blended elements of both to appeal particularly to educated and professional workers.

As proletarian consciousness matures incrementally in these cultural, economic, and political adventures, the state, sensing a new conjuncture of class forces, will incrementally democratize procedures and policies. Neither quick nor easy, this tactic has nonetheless already proved itself in the transition from laissez-faire to welfare state capitalism. New proletarian pressure can force the state to abandon entirely its role as reproducer of capitalist class relations. Then, argued Bowles and Gintis, the long struggle for proletarian hegemony will have finally conquered the state.

In sum, empirical Marxian state theorists have formulated concise, logical, and verifiable theories by which to organize political research. The notable signposts of conventional Marxian political theorizing have been replicated, including orthodox economism and neo-Marxian alternatives that linked politics to the economic class struggle, and believed political activism an authentic mode of working class struggle. Empirical Marxists reconceptualized these normative assertions into analytically sophisticated, testable hypotheses, both structural and nonstructural. It appears, once again, that empirical Marxists have translated normative theorizing into the language and methods of modern social science—an essential task in this computerized world, but one that is somewhat less innovative than advocates would have us believe. Empirical state theorists, including even instrumentalists, have nonetheless reinforced the central message of neo-Marxian political theory: the economic class struggle has generated, and in part is now defined by, a capitalist state with unexpectedly expanded social and economic powers, and an unanticipated potential for significantly altering productive relationships. The state, in short, dialectically manifests the class struggle, but runs on its own track. Proletarian political activism, within the reformed capitalist state, is as legitimate a means of effecting social change as mobilizing workers in factories.

The World-System

All this empirical work has reconceptualized Marx's notions of class and the state as these relate to typical life experiences in contemporary nation-states, particularly America. Americans, of course, are also inhabitants of planet Earth, and their everyday perceptions are, often unknowingly, influenced by inter-*and* intranational factors. When goods, services, and communication flow cross-nationally, class is defined not only by a person's position in her nation's relations of production, but also by that nation's position in the world's relations of production, the so-called "World-System." Informally but effectively, this system reproduces itself by delimiting

the economic alternatives available to specific nations, thereby conditioning the quality of domestic class formation. Although it lacks legal standing or the power to legitimately sanction deviant behavior, it quietly accomplishes internationally what the state does domestically, that is, to reproduce capitalist relations of production. The ruinous economic consequences of anti-system domestic activities are usually enough to narrow any state's room to maneuver politically. Class and state theory are thus linked to the workings of the World-System.

Marxists have always been interested in these worldwide dimensions of the class struggle, but have sorely lacked reliable and comprehensive economic data bearing on the issue. This is no longer the case. Astounding advances in computer technology have recently placed mounds of heretofore hidden facts in the hands of eager, technically sophisticated Marxists. They have pioneered a new and exciting area of Marxian studies, World-System Theory, the results of which have both impressed and disturbed Marxian scholars and activists everywhere.

The seedbed of World-System Theory lies within orthodoxy, particularly its growing awareness of, and sensitivity to, empirical data. In retrospect, Marx's thoughts on this topic were ambivalent. Colonialism, he originally argued, was progressive and necessary, a means of setting Asia on the same economic track as Europe. In *Capital*, he belatedly acknowledged that British colonialism had hindered India's economic development by siphoning resources into Europe, where they served the economic needs of the Crown. Neighboring Ireland, on the other hand, was, in comparison to India, a laboratory for studying the effects of colonialism. Here, Marx and Engels clearly saw how cheap Irish labor and agricultural exports nourished British industry and drained Ireland of needed capital resources. Irish independence, they argued, was a prerequisite for Irish economic development. This kind of case by case, hit or miss strategy for understanding international capitalism fell far short of Marx's usual, refined scientific standards.

Lenin hoped to more systematically describe the underlying causes and consequences of imperialism. He foresaw in capitalism the concentration of production into large industrial monopolies, and the concentration of money into powerful banking monopolies that controlled investment capital. These industrial and bank interests combined into what Hilferding had called "finance capital," that is, capital controlled by banks and employed by industrialists. Faced with a surplus of domestic capital, banks decided to export capital abroad in search of cheap resources and ready export markets, thereby linking domestic and world markets. Finance capital, in short, split the world into international capitalist associations, each of which bore the flag of one powerful nation-state. These associations fought each other for the most profitable undeveloped territories. A financial oligarchy was forging an international capitalist order and assigning supportive roles to each participant. Imperialism had emerged as the highest stage of capitalism.

Magdoff

Harry Magdoff, since 1969 the editor of the respected orthodox journal *Monthly Review*, has measured, and bridged, the gap between Lenin's hypotheses and today's actual conditions.[48] Lenin, he contended, correctly linked monopoly capitalism and imperialism, but mistakenly assigned causal priority to finance capital. The process of capitalist expansion into virgin territory was due to many factors, ranging from the need to export excess capital and discover cheap resources and labor, to political, military, and even religious considerations. All of these "principle levers" are related features of the general logic characterizing monopoly capitalism's impulse to expand. Any single factor, or cluster of factors, could be crucial in determining, at a particular time, the behavior of particular capitalist powers. Careful empirical inquiry, not dogmatism, could ascertain the intricate linkage of monopoly capitalism and imperialism.

In this scientific light, Magdoff discovered that the power of finance capital to shape capital investment has been eclipsed by multinational corporations, which could easily marshall enormous funds, as well as the political backing of capitalist nation-states, to support their own brand of economic expansion. American expansionism, therefore, was rooted in the economic crises of monopoly capitalism, especially the needs of multinationals. However, Magdoff believed that each concrete example must also be understood within the broader constellation of relevant noneconomic factors characterizing that particular economic moment. The world order was, in short, designed by multinationals but mediated by extant cultural factors that determined precisely where, when, and how capitalist material needs would be sated.

Baran

Despite a swelling sensitivity to the need for empirical verification, orthodoxy's vision of world capitalism remained nonetheless rigidly ethnocentric, formulated from a First World perspective that accented the needs and problems of industrial capitalists and organized urban workers. Paul A. Baran, a Russian-born, naturalized American citizen who for several years after World War II was the only prominent orthodox Marxist employed by a large American University (Stanford), expunged this cultural bias.

His *The Political Economy of Growth* (1957) began conventionally enough.[49] Combining features of neo-classical price theory of "imperfect competition" with the national income analysis popularized by classical political economists, Baran highlighted the relative distribution of income between labor and capital, and thereby defined the causes and limits of capitalist economic growth. He argued that competitive capitalism expanded during the 19th century by fostering the growth of investment and, indirectly, of national income. As economic power congealed into enormous monopolies, capitalists were forced to restrict output in order to bolster prices.

This depressed investment and generated a redundant surplus that was gradually funneled into several profitable but wasteful activities, ranging from advertising to war production. Capitalist investment, in short, supported economically questionable ventures that would neither manufacture needed commodities nor stimulate industrial production. Monopoly capitalism, in Baran's view, was a system characterized by stagnation.

Baran then confronted orthodoxy's analysis of imperialism. Traditionally, we have seen, orthodox Marxists viewed capitalism as a troubled but dynamic global system encompassing, eventually, the entire underdeveloped world. Baran discovered, however, that modern capitalism had programmed Third World nations into perpetual economic backwardness. Imperialism, in effect, had transformed colonized nations into economic fodder for stagnating colonialists. In order to solve domestic economic problems, western capitalists disrupted native internal markets, uprooted potentially competitive native industries, and created a local comprador class joined to their own material interests. These activities, by inhibiting Third World economic growth, assured western imperialists cheap resources and labor, and provided them an export market that would boost domestic prices. An international capitalist structure emerged that guaranteed Third World underdevelopment.

Although Baran's dire economic predictions for western capitalism were, in retrospect, somewhat inflated, he did redirect American Marxists toward the special conditions and problems faced by Third World nations trying to modernize in a capitalist world. The world's division into developed and underdeveloped areas was not accidental. Baran taught that underdevelopment results from unfavorable universal economic constraints that evolve historically and are reinforced by western capitalists.

Dependency Theory

Baran, with André Gunder Frank—a German-born product of American colleges and universities—and the Brazilian Ruy Mauro Marini, is considered by many as a founder of the so-called Dependency School of Marxian theory. Dependency theorists saw the economic and social development of Third World nations profoundly conditioned by an international environment dominated by capitalist industry. The latter extract from underdeveloped lands—forcibly in colonial times, through market mechanisms today—raw materials and light consumer items that are no longer profitably manufactured in highly mechanized western factories. These are appropriated into domestic economies in order to fuel development. Wages in underdeveloped areas are kept low, internal markets are thereby aborted, and accumulation thus severely deformed. Dependent nations feed international capitalists cheap resources and small commodities, and consume their expensive manufactured goods, with little hope of ever producing their own. These unequal terms of exchange strengthen the system as a whole, even as

it impoverishes some of its actors. A surplus, in short, is produced in under-developed lands, which Frank labeled "satellites," and then appropriated by and at the centers of capitalist production, the so-called "metropoles." This surplus is realized in the form of profits for western capitalists and improved wages and living standards for western laborers. Third World efforts to shat-ter this cycle of poverty can barely get off the ground. By modulating import quotas and prices of exported manufactured items, and coopting feudal and comprador bourgeois allies, capitalists can economically humiliate under-developed nations, who then must meekly conform to the system's expecta-tions.

The entire process is controlled by the needs of industrialized nations, who develop the international division of labor and accumulate capital from it. As technology matures and capitalist organization alters, capitalists as-sign pertinent new tasks to underdeveloped nations, in effect transforming the international division of labor to meet their new needs. The role assigned to the state in dependent nations is to reproduce their own dependency, that is, reproduce at home the international division of labor that serves monopo-ly capitalist accumulation. Because the state is itself financially, technologi-cally, ideologically, and militarily dependent on foreign monopoly capital, it quickly becomes its tool. As the capitalist accumulation crisis worsens, and domestic pressures intensify for even more capital extraction and accumula-tion in the Third World, dependent states become more authoritarian in sub-jugating their own strained populations. The nature of the dependent state is thus conditioned by the same universal process of underdevelopment that shapes the dependent economy. Dependency is functionally necessary in a capitalist dominated world order.

World-System Theory

Orthodoxy's evolving theory of imperialism punctuated the needs and problems of western capitalism as it squeezed profits from undeveloped lands. Dependency Theory surveyed the same worldwide process, but em-phasized the needs and problems of underdeveloped nations located on the wrong end of a capitalist dominated international division of labor. The transition, in America, from Dependency to World-System Theory involved a barely noticeable shift in perspective. World-System theorists began by as-suming that the world, not developed or underdeveloped perceptions of the world, is the only meaningful framework from which to understand the his-tory of particular groups or nations.

Societies, they argued, are merely parts of an irreducible whole that is reflected in every aspect of social life. This whole, the World Capitalist Sys-tem, must be studied on its own terms in order to understand the behavior of any of its components. Consequently, a particular developed or under-developed state's mode of production, the central factor determining its in-

digenous living patterns, has worldwide boundaries. To explain that state's internal class and political struggles, one must carefully detect its place in the world economy, and then find its function. Exploitation, therefore, has two aspects: capitalists using workers, and industrialized nations using underdeveloped nations. The latter conditions the former. Urban workers, for example, are economically coopted with the extracted surplus. Rural workers are politically coopted into multi-class anti-western alliances. The system reinforces itself by muting internal national class struggles and polluting authentic working class consciousness, which should direct workers toward the World-System, not their feeble state institutions. Moreover, the variations in economic development that characterize different regions originate in the historical process of capital accumulation on a world wide scale. Each region is assigned, by the World-System, a mode of production that will correspond to its particular role in the total process. A determining World-System, in short, is mediated by, and embodied in, concrete national and regional modes of production. The notion of a "national economy" is, simply, unwarranted.

Wallerstein

The predominant figure in World-System Theory is Immanuel Wallerstein. Originally, after earning a doctorate from Columbia University in the early 1960s, a mainstream social scientist, Wallerstein was gradually pulled left by Lenin's theory of imperialism, Dependency Theory, and the Annales School of economic history—particularly Fernand Braudel's absorbing masterpiece on sixteenth century Europe—which furnished an indispensable historical dimension to radical theorizing. His post-doctoral Marxian education bore fruit in *The Modern World-System* (1974), still Wallerstein's most significant venture at model-building. Certainly not the first model of the world capitalist system, Wallerstein's is nevertheless the most empirically and analytically sophisticated, capable of explaining a far wider range of data than any other.

The Modern World-System traced today's capitalist world order back to sixteenth century Europe. By employing sophisticated military and commercial powers, the technologically advanced northwestern region of Europe managed to subdue and exploit underdeveloped regions in eastern Europe and South America. It then forcibly extracted raw materials and molded indigenous economies into suppliers of capitalism's budding industries. Northern Europe, reaping the economic benefits of its surplus, industrialized rapidly, and politically reinforced its worldwide hegemony. Eastern Europe and South America, on the other hand, were forced onto developmental paths that made economic and technological growth difficult or impossible. The essential structure of our modern capitalist World-System, then, has been in force since the sixteenth century. Moreover, the fates of millions of people were determined by the internal logic of world capitalist economic

development, which, Wallerstein later argued, would unfold in wavelike spurts of expansion and contraction.[50] Henceforth, regional or national differentiations in ethnicity, religion, language, and institutions would be articulated in response to systemically assigned economic roles in the international division of labor. Similarly, significant regional and national events that unfolded in the next four centuries, the corpus of modern world history, could be understood only in the context of this historically conceived world capitalist system. The growth in power of nation-states, especially, needed to be seen in the context of capitalists' desire to both protect their privileged access to overseas resources and to reduce free market risks. International wars were caused by capitalists either seeking economic hegemony in the world market or preventing others from doing so.

Wallerstein has broadened his empirical base enormously since 1974, and clarified several analytical concepts, but has not deviated from this basic materialist Weltanschauung. His model's most interesting conceptual twist is its trimodal, rather than the usual bimodal, worldwide system of unequal exchange. Wallerstein sorted the world capitalist system into core, periphery, and semi-periphery. The core and periphery comprise, respectively, the industrial centers and underdeveloped satellites that Leninists and Dependency theorists had already acknowledged. The semi-periphery, Wallerstein's innovative contribution, acts like a middle class in the international system, doing the core's dirty work while simultaneously competing for core status.[51] As a buffer between core and periphery, semi-peripheral states are a haven for core investments when wages rise too suddenly in the old industrial centers, and a lightning rod for angry Third Worlders, who envy their ability to attract foreign investment. They also balance the international system by providing a cushion for displaced core states, and a ladder up for ambitious states in the periphery. In brief, by supplying quick profits, security, and hope, they help the system avoid devastating economic crises. As a seedbed for future core states, the semi-periphery also performs a socializing function similar to Ivy League Universities in America: training new actors to perform necessary old tasks. Actual changes in any state's world status follow the dynamics of world capitalist expansion and stagnation, particularly the relation of that state's economy to the world economy's rising and declining technologies and economic sectors.

The tactical implications of World-System Theory are problematic. Certainly, according to Wallerstein, capitalism has been exploitive, and a socialist World-System—which would involve reunified, transnational boundaries of economic and political activity, coordinated by some kind of hegemonic world government—would be rational, humane, and liberating.[52] However, with social change conditioned by changes in the World-System as a whole, not by national events, in this nationalist age how do we get from capitalist to socialist World-Systems? Anti-system socialist states, when they appear, find the short-run costs of withdrawing from the World-System

greater than they can politically sustain. In power, they operate a state-level "catching-up" strategy by competing economically with core states on the latter's terms. Each participant in the capitalist World-System, regardless of ideology, treats other participants as a capitalist would. Playing by these rules, communist states have evolved into "collectivist capitalist firms," searching the world over to extract surpluses and accumulate capital. Socialist nation-states thus embody a conundrum: organizational survival is purchased at the cost of accepting (or modifying somewhat) the rules of the World-System, which only strengthens that system in its struggle to survive.

World-System theorists have reacted in several ways. At one extreme is André Gunder Frank's fatalism, which relegates proletarian political activism to the dustbin of history. There is no certain or probable way out of dependency and underdevelopment unless and until the capitalist World-System expires. Marxists, in Frank's view, must await patiently for the world structure itself, at its own time and through its own metropole-directed mechanisms, to self-destruct. This, of course, will succeed the severe crises attending the transformation of the metropole's productive forces.

At the other extreme are Third World scholars like Samir Amin, for whom the economic and political consequences of successful regional liberation movements can actually explode the worldwide capitalist division of labor. Amin believed that regions, that is, combinations of peripheral states with common bonds, have the resources to break, or delink, from the capitalist World-System and create viable new social and economic formations. As opportunities for additional peripheral accumulation diminish, core states, and the World-System they represent, will economically collapse. Fernando H. Cardoso and Enzo Faletto modify Amin's activism somewhat by focusing on the actual intra-and interclass struggles that determine how different periphery nations react to world structures.[53] Their research into dependent economies found that a domestic market linked to internal wages does, albeit slowly, expand. So does the hegemony of local entrepreneurs who are linked to, but not controlled by, core capitalists. These two findings, which flatly contradict Frank's conclusions, mean that unrelenting domestic class struggles in dependent nations can generate meaningful reforms that significantly improve workers' conditions, even within the capitalist World-System. As specific instances of proletarian political victories in the Third World proliferate, the political outcome of the World-System's crises will be skewed leftward.

Wallerstein's position is somewhat ambiguous. On the one hand, he, like Frank, acknowledged the World-System's causal priority in explaining social movement. Socialism is clearly impossible until the entire global system has changed. On the other, however, he foresaw progressive aftereffects from flawed or even failed socialist movements, which, at a minimum, would likely favorably impact on the worldwide class consciousness of the

proletariat.[54] While national or regional class struggles clearly are no match for capitalism's structural hegemony, they nonetheless contribute to the growing collective strength of anti-systemic movements worldwide, and thus nudge the World-System in the direction of socialism.

Marxism's dilemma of needing national power to survive but world power to succeed, in Wallerstein's view, affects leftist politics in at least two noteworthy ways. First, it purges revolutionary movements of their urgency. No single event or revolution will transform the World-System. Events must cumulatively build to the point of systemic crisis.[55] Because the system is so much larger and more powerful than any of its national or regional actors, this incremental passage to crisis is neither inevitable nor imminent. Wallerstein ruefully suggested that another 150 years of capitalist hegemony is not an unreasonable prospect.[56] Left tactics, consequently, should be geared toward long-term, system-wide payoffs rather than rousing but fruitless national campaigns.

Wallerstein's second counsel, then, was that proletarian movements needed to be internationalized. Since classes are transnational actors, the world's "upper classes" are located primarily but not exclusively in the core. Most of the world's exploited proletariat are in the periphery. The upper classes remain hegemonic by using core states to consolidate and defend their control over the periphery. Given the organization and domestic political influence of core laborers, as well as their economic cooptation, core states increase their wealth primarily by exploiting the periphery. This, the periphery, must therefore become the focus of socialist revolution, even for core Marxists. As the number of new peripheral spaces to be incorporated into the capitalist World-System diminishes, and as the proletarianization of peripheral labor progresses, the system's vitality ebbs. These crisis tendencies, argued Wallerstein, are gestating today in capitalism's accumulation crisis and the proliferation of radical Third World anti-system movements. The latter intimidate multinational corporations, who fear that indigenous political turmoil will tarnish short-term profits. As MNC's withdraw from the periphery economically, the system's crisis is exacerbated, and the economic pressures on core workers intensify. Then, in rapid order, core states will be forced to expand their economic functions, MNC's will break free of their states in search of linkages among increasingly state-controlled production systems, and anti-system states and movements will coalesce transnationally. Capitalist relations of production, which since the sixteenth century have evolved toward a fully planned, worldwide organizational network, will eventually collapse, leaving a structure that has already been rationalized. The World-System's path to socialism will have been paved by international capitalists.

Given these structural trends, Wallerstein suggested that attaining state power should be a Marxian tactic, not a goal.[57] Core Marxists, instead of plotting governmental takeovers, needed to petition those in power to equal-

ize world wage levels, thereby undermining capital's ability to play off one set of workers against another. They also needed to demonstrate clearly the racial, ethnic, and sexual bonds uniting core minorities with peripheral majorities. These noneconomic factors, by uniting emotionally much of the world's exploited population, can internationalize the proletarian cause. Finally, core Marxists, particularly in America, needed to affirm the linkage between their internal struggles and comparable struggles in the periphery. Foreign policy debates in America over policy toward socialist Third World regimes or movements, for example, are central to a realistic left politics. Not only can they, potentially, mobilize politically and morally America's fractured progressive coalition, but, contested successfully, their consequences can shorten the duration of world capitalist hegemony. Core laborers have a vested material interest in enthusiastically endorsing anti-system Third World activism.

Conclusion

Like lustful suitors from opposite sides of the social fence, empiricism and neo-Marxism need each other badly, but don't know exactly why. Philosophically, Americans are neither inclined toward nor capable of justifying the relationship. Empiricism, factual and politically neutral, arose and flourished with the bourgeoisie, and is now hegemonic among capitalist intellectuals. Nonorthodox Marxism used facts to reconstruct a dynamic, fluid universe of internally linked phenomena, the purpose of which was to vindicate democratic, socialist activism. One is individualist, the other dialectical. One carves reality into separate pieces, the other melds these into a multidimensional whole. Those, like Walling and the Analytical Marxists, who have tried to explain systematically the proposed union, have hopelessly failed. Empiricism's static, formal categories can accommodate neo-Marxism's mutability only by surgically expunging either dialectics (e.g., Analytical Marxism) or radical politics (e.g., pragmatic Marxism). Intellectually, the coupling just won't work.

In practice, however, each desperately needs the other, and the relationship blossoms. Radical social scientists have reconceptualized and verified many key Marxian hypotheses, legitimizing them for legions of empirically trained scholars. Along the way, they have reaffirmed the radical, dialectical quality of neo-Marxism. Marxian empirical analyses of class, the state, and the World-System have accented—theoretically and tactically—the linkages among blue-and white-collar workers, and between classes, the state, and the international environment. Many of these correlations merely quantified nonempirical Marxian theorizing. By so doing, however, they sanctioned a scientific critique of capitalism and materialism, both of which are unilinear and reductive. Empirical Marxists factually confirm the insidious, exploitative side of capitalism, but also its imaginative survival mechanisms, its in-

genious blending of economics, politics, international relations, and culture into a sweet but debilitating working class elixir. Materialism's crude categories can't capture this odd mixture of economic and noneconomic exploitation. Orthodoxy finally trivializes itself by confronting a sophisticated twentieth century class enemy with a 19th century economistic weapon. On the other hand, by operationalizing innovative radical theories and crunching relevant data, empirical Marxists have confirmed the internal unity of relatively autonomous spheres of activity. Their grandiloquent, highly quantitative studies have a sterling message: the working class must struggle in many locations, not just in factories, and will win everywhere, or nowhere at all.

Notes

1. Eric Olin Wright, *Class, Crisis, and the State* (London: New Left Books, 1978), p. 9.
2. See Maurice Cornforth, *The Theory of Knowledge* (New York: International, 1963), p. 146.
3. See my "Empirical Marxism," *History and Theory*, 20 (Winter 1981), pp. 403–23, and *Neo-Marxism—The Meanings of Modern Radicalism* (Westport, CT: Greenwood, 1982), pp. 163–209.
4. William English Walling, *The Larger Aspects of Socialism* (New York: Macmillan, 1913), p. 29.
5. *Ibid.*, p. 27. See also pp. 4–113.
6. *Ibid.*, p. 135. See also pp. ix-xvii.
7. Walling's *Socialism As It Is* (New York: Macmillan, 1912), describes socialist movements in the U.S., Britain, Italy, and Germany. *Progressivism—And After* (New York: Macmillan, 1914), describes the evolution of Progressivism as a relatively successful leftist response to the evils of capitalism. Other works describe empirically the historical evolution of America's labor movement and radical literary themes.
8. John Roemer (ed.), *Analytical Marxism* (Cambridge: Cambridge University Press, 1986), pp. 1, 2, 201.
9. John Roemer, "Rational Choice Marxism: Some Issues of Method and Substance," in Roemer (ed.), p. 191.
10. See Daniel Little, *The Scientific Marx* (Minneapolis: University of Minnesota Press, 1986), p. 196.
11. See the pertinent work of Roemer, Jon Elster, Robert Brenner, Alan Wood, Allen Buchanan, and Terence Ball.
12. See G.A. Cohen, *Karl Marx's Theory of History* (Princeton, NJ: Princeton University Press, 1978), pp. 166–69.
13. Roemer, "New Directions in the Marxian Theory of Exploitation and Class," in Roemer (ed.), p. 90.
14. Marx, *Capital* (3 vols.: New York: International, 1967), vol. III, p. 886.
15. *Ibid.*
16. See especially the pertinent work of Maurice Zeitlin.

17. E. P. Thompson, *The Making of the English Working Class* (New York: Vintage, 1963), p. 11.
18. Alvin W. Gouldner, *The Future of Intellectuals and the Rise of the New Class* (New York: Seabury, 1979).
19. Eric Olin Wright, *Classes* (London: Verso, 1985).
20. *Ibid.*, p. 77.
21. *Ibid.*, p. 285.
22. See *ibid.*, p. 285, and Wright and Joachin Singelmann, "Proletarianization in the Changing American Class Structure," *American Journal of Sociology*, 88 (Supplement, 1982), pp. 176–209.
23. Wright, *Classes*, p. 14.
24. C. Wright Mills, *The Power Elite* (New York: Oxford University Press, 1956), esp. p. 277.
25. G.William Domhoff, *Who Rules America* (Englewood Cliffs, NJ: Prentice-Hall, 1967), p. 5.
26. Domhoff, *Who Rules America*, p. 152, and *Who Rules America Now* (Englewood Cliffs, NJ: Prentice-Hall, 1983), p. 2. The following quoted phrases are in *Who Rules America*, p. 9.
27. Adam Przeworski, "Economic Conditions of Class Compromise" (University of Chicago, mimeo, 1979), p. 37.
28. Przeworski (ed.), *Capitalism and Social Democracy* (Cambridge: Cambridge University Press, 1985), pp. 42–43.
29. See Przeworski, "Material Interests, Class Compromise, and the Transition to Socialism," in Roemer (ed.), pp. 177–88; and *Capitalism and Social Democracy*, pp. 245–48.
30. Fred Block, "Beyond Relative Autonomy: State Managers As Historical Subjects," in Ralph Miliband and John Saville (eds.), *Socialist Register, 1980* (London: Merlin, 1980), p. 241, n.9.
31. Block, "Marxist Theories of the State in World System Analysis," in Barbara Hockey Kaplan (ed.), *Social Change in the Capitalist World Economy* (Beverly Hills, CA: Sage, 1978), p. 33.
32. Theda Skocpol, "Political Response to Capitalist Crisis: Neo-Marxist Theories of the State and the Case of the New Deal," *Politics and Society*, 10, 2 (1981), p. 200.
33. Skocpol and Trimberger, "Revolutions and the World-Historical Development of Capitalism," in Hockey (ed.), p. 128. The following phrase is in Skocpol *et al.*, *Bringing the State Back In* (Cambridge: Cambridge University Press, 1985), p. viii.
34. On tactical issues, see Block, "Beyond Relative Autonomy," in Miliband and Saville (eds.), p. 240; Skocpol, *State and Social Revolutions* (Cambridge: Cambridge University Press, 1979); Skocpol, "Bringing The State Back In," in Skocpol *et al.*, pp. 15–27; and Ellen Kay Trimberger, *Revolution From Above* (New Brunswick, NJ: Transaction, 1978).
35. Paul Sweezy, *The Theory of Capitalist Development* (New York: Oxford University Press, 1942); and Sweezy and Paul Baran, *Monopoly Capitalism* (New York: Monthly Review Press, 1966).
36. Ernest Mandel, *Marxist Economic Theory* (London: Merlin, 1962), and *Late Capitalism* (London: New Left Books, 1975).

37. O'Connor, *The Fiscal Crisis of the State*, p. 7; *ibid.* See p. 101.

38. *Ibid.*, p. 7. See also p. 150.

39. *Ibid.*, p. 9. See also pp. 40, 179, 221.

40. See O'Connor, *Accumulation Crisis* (New York: Blackwell, 1984), esp. p. 56.

41. See Alan Wolfe, *The Limits of Legitimacy* (New York: Free Press, 1977), esp. pp. 1–10, 258–59, 328–29.

42. *Ibid.*, pp. 308ff.

43. See Manuel Castells, *City, Class, and Power* (New York: St. Martin's, 1972), p. 170, and *The Economic Crisis and American Society* (Princeton, NJ: Princeton University Press, 1980), esp. pp. 130ff.

44. See *ibid.*, p. 224.

45. Samuel Bowles and Herbert Gintis, *Schooling in Capitalist America* (New York: Basic Books, 1976), p. 10. The preceding argument is in Bowles, David M. Gordon, and Thomas Weisskopf, *Beyond the Wasteland* (New York: Doubleday, 1983), pp. 62–97; Bowles and Gintis, *Democracy and Capitalism* (New York: Basic, 1986), pp. 3–8 and 27–63; and "The Crisis of Liberal Democratic Capitalism: The Case of the United States," *Politics and Society*, 11, 13 (1982), pp. 51–93, esp. p. 52.

46. Bowles and Gintis, *Democracy and Capitalism*, p. 151. The following study of American state expenses is in "The Crisis of Liberal Democratic Capitalism," *Politics and Society*, 11, 13, (1982), pp. 73–78.

47. See Bowles and Gintis, *Democracy and Capitalism*, pp. 205–208, and Bowles, Gordon, and Weisskopf, *Beyond the Wasteland*, pp. 263–70.

48. See Harry Magdoff, *The Age of Imperialism* (New York: Monthly Review Press, 1969) and *Imperialism: From the Colonial Age to the Present* (New York: Monthly Review Press, 1978). The following is on pp. 30–40 of *The Age of Imperialism*.

49. Paul A. Baran, *The Political Economy of Growth* (New York: Monthly Review Press, 1957).

50. Wallerstein, *The Politics of the World-Economy* (Cambridge: Cambridge University Press, 1984), p. 6; and Research Group on Cycles & Trends, Fernand Braudel Center, "Cyclical Rhythms and Secular Trends of the Capitalist World-Economy: Some Premises, Hypotheses, and Questions," *Review*, 2, 4 (Spring 1979), pp. 483–500. These trends resemble the so-called Kondratiev cycles.

51. See Wallerstein, *The Capitalist World-Economy*, pp. 95–118.

52. Wallerstein, *The Politics of the World-Economy*, pp. 9, 157.

53. Fernando H. Cardoso and Enzo Faletto, *Dependency and Development in Latin America* (Berkeley: University of California Press, 1979).

54. See Wallerstein, *The Politics of the World-Economy*, pp. 25–26, and *The Capitalist World-Economy*, p. 293.

55. Wallerstein, *The Politics of the World-Economy*, p. 23.

56. See *ibid.* and "The Three Stages of African Involvement in the World-Economy," in Peter Gutkind and Wallerstein (eds.), *The Political Economy of Contemporary Africa* (Beverly Hills, CA: Sage, 1976), pp. 30–57.

57. Wallerstein, *The Politics of the World-Economy*, p. 96. See also pp. 78ff.

5

Progressive Pluralism

In politics, especially among revolutionaries, utopianism is often mistaken for compassion. American neo-Marxists were so obsessed with slaying the economistic dragon they had neglected their own army, which was stuck in a harsh reality of sexism, racism, and religious bigotry. Granted, dialectics was a powerful weapon. By depicting the internal linkages of class, the state, and the world system, and acknowledging the reality of raw subjectivity, dialectics had traced the passage mobilized workers would journey on their final, revolutionary charge. It also had made Marxism intellectually respectable. But thus far the payoff, for most Americans, lay in a far-off future or in ivory towers that few lived in. Meanwhile, everyday troubles went unnoticed because they were not solely, or even primarily, experienced as political or economic phenomena.

In a liberal society that encouraged the formation of special interests, Americans found solace and strength with those bound, biologically or by choice, to a common fate. More often than not these fates were joined to a constellation of noneconomic factors, including gender, race, and religion. Those who shared socially proscribed traits formed large, bonded associations, each of which filtered social reality through its common plight. These associations became integral parts of capitalist social life. For victims of bigotry, they explained the inexplicable. They also provided the warmth and understanding that everyday reality so noticeably lacked. Of course, as safety valves for economically oppressed workers they were important to those in power as well. In any case, gender, race, and religion were central to understanding how workers thought and acted.

Aching to unmask capitalist exploitation and liberate humanity, neo-Marxism had disregarded the noneconomic substance of everyday working class life. It now had to flesh out hidden economic and political linkages, to show how bonded interests fulfilled a human need and reinforced an inhuman system. Neo-Marxism needed to follow its dialectical logic into the nasty sites of everyday life to reveal fully the contours of capitalist exploitation, and catalyze a socialist opposition.

131

I

American pluralism is marked by two related features. First, pluralism is a policy process characterized by conflict between multiple interests in society that operate within a constitutional framework of limited government, fragmented institutional power, multiple points of access to decision makers, and a decision style marked by persuasion, bargaining, and compromise among competing interests. And second, pluralism is a social process characterized by a multiplicity of independent groups formed on the basis of shared religious, moral, racial, ethnic, professional, or vocational interests, each of which has the same publicly guaranteed legal and political rights. Both meanings are rooted in liberal social theory. Locke's belief that self-interested actors possessed inalienable prerogatives to life, liberty, and property meant that government's role was limited to protecting, not creating, political rights. A pluralist policy process was seen by Locke and liberals generally as the surest means of institutionally guaranteeing laissez-faire government. With citizens fending for themselves, their relative strength was maximized by uniting with others who shared a common interest in order to compete for desired goods and services. A pluralist social process was, consequently, the best means of surviving in a fractured, competitive world lacking a centralized decision-making apparatus.

American liberalism thus encouraged the formation of diverse, self-centered, autonomous social groups. Each furnished a collective identity as well as access to the political process. Although several factors determined a group's effectiveness, invariably the wealthiest groups were also the most powerful politically. Corporate and professional interests, already economically dominant, soon controlled society and politics as well. American pluralism, in short, embodied a decentralized, competitive framework that guaranteed capitalist hegemony. Nevertheless, the ideologically sanctioned psychological benefits of joining voluntary associations, particularly among the poor and powerless, have made them indispensable. Liberal freedom, after all, is a formal-legal guarantee of individual liberty. Social and political pluralism institutionalized the only kind of freedom Americans knew.

For orthodoxy, pluralist procedures were created by and for the dominant economic class to obscure substantive inequality. The rights of individual workers, regardless of gender, race, religion, or ethnicity are realized in and through the working class, which represents both the collective interests of all humankind and history's inevitability. When workers are exploited economically they suffer culturally as well. The difficulties experienced by women, blacks, and other victims of discrimination are, in the last resort, caused by workplace exploitation. Pluralism hides this, magnifying instead physical and psychological factors the satisfaction of which will leave the economic system untouched. It splits workers into feuding, powerless tribes

whose occasional small victories are insignificant. Socialism, which frees all workers and eliminates discrimination, awaits the gelling of workers into a revolutionary force. The Party's mission, therefore, was to convince capitalism's victims that their misery is the misery of all workers, and their emancipation is a victorious working class.

American pluralism is procedurally, not substantively, democratic. By formally dividing power between autonomous social, political, and economic realms, and within each between different groups and institutions, it guaranteed elite hegemony. On the other hand, orthodoxy's tight categories promised material equality but obliterated the unique experiences of millions of Americans whose individuality was defined by race, gender, and religion at least as much as class. From within this dormant Marxism, that was unable and unwilling to change, emerged new ideas that would sculpt historical materialism to the American experience and redirect Marxian dialectics toward the real world.

II

Gender

Orthodoxy's position on the specific problems of being female in a capitalist society, which, apart from preliminary remarks in the *Manifesto*, Marx never explicitly addressed, are rooted in Engels's *The Origins of the Family, Private Property, and the State* (1884). Adopting an evolutionary paradigm popularized earlier by J. J. Bachofen and Lewis Henry Morgan, Engels traced the history of sexual relations through early forms of social organization. A sexual division of labor has always existed, he argued, with each sex dominant in its own sphere. Men have traditionally performed social functions associated with production, women with maintaining family and household. Gender status varied from society to society, but the prevalence of indiscriminate and promiscuous mating patterns, where paternity was often unknown, more often than not engendered matrilineal kinship systems and assured female supremacy. The invention of agriculture and the domestication of animals dramatically expanded society's forces of production. Private property and economic classes replaced undifferentiated communal production, and economic surpluses produced unimaginable wealth. Men, traditionally in control of production, became rich and powerful. They imposed patrilineal kinship systems by introducing monogamy, which reinforced women's household obligations while eliminating most of their social influence. Patriarchy, "the world historical defeat of the female sex,"[1] thus paralleled the rise of private property. It is the essential feature of class

society, simultaneously nurturing male workers and a female proletarian reserve. Male fears of economic competition eventually instigated a patriarchical morality that psychologically crippled females and channeled male frustrations into their own sexuality.

This, claimed Engels, is the current state of capitalist social relations, as well as the source of contemporary female exploitation. However, as capitalist production expands, so do the opportunities for female liberation. Engels, with Clara Zetkin and August Bebel, urged women to enter the labor force en masse, struggle alongside males to unionize and improve factory conditions, and, ultimately, bring the system down. By providing everyone gainful employment and decent wages, socialism would annihilate patriarchy by guaranteeing full independence for all men and women. Engels, Bebel, Zetkin, and most other interested Marxists believed monogamy would survive under socialism but the family would be transformed from a compulsory economic institution into one of voluntary emotional relations that permitted both sexes to develop full personal lives.

Feminists believe that the primary social contradiction is that between men and women, and consequently women's subordination is caused by the system of male power known as patriarchy. Orthodox Marxists, on the other hand, view what they call the "Woman Question" in the context of, and as shaped by, the struggle between capitalists and workers. Female subordination is primarily due to a particular social organization that is based on private property and characterized by elite hegemony. The former emphasize the centrality of sexuality, the latter, of class struggle. Predictably, America's orthodox SP and CP, with eyes toward Engels, rejected feminism.

After flirting with organizational autonomy in the late nineteenth and early twentieth centuries, progressive feminists decided, instead, to join and integrate into the SP. The SP Platform of 1901 promised women "equal civil and political rights," and, indeed, the early SP fought for feminist reforms, especially enfranchisement. Female membership, in 1901, reached about 20 percent of the Party's total, and included luminaries like Ella Reeve Bloor, "Mother" Mary Jones, Helen Keller, Kate Richards O'Hare, Margaret Sanger, Anna Louise Strong, and Rose Pastor Stokes. But even during these early years, the SP's dedication to women's issues seemed perfunctory, more lip service than real commitment.[2] Very little money or energy was spent on women's needs. Male SP leaders relegated specific women and internal women's organizations, especially the Woman's National Committee (WNC), to subordinate party positions. Moreover, SP feminists were often their own worst enemies. They vacillated between encouraging women to reenter the workforce and urging them to avoid exploitation by staying at home. They also split over key issues affecting women, such as birth control, marriage, and sexual equality. In brief, a factionalized group of SP females, most of whom naively accepted popular gender stereotypes, were no match for male leaders who sensed neither an immediate nor urgent need

to liberate women. A substantial bigoted minority in the SP opposed equal rights and female enfranchisement altogether.

After 1919, this sorrowful condition further deteriorated. The SP rapidly lost most of its women members to the CP or the liberal League of Women Voters. The Leninist CP dismissed as bourgeois silliness all vestiges of feminism except women's strikes. Female CP membership, by World War II, had equaled males', but female autonomy was prohibited. When, in 1940, a CP member and West Coast journalist named Mary Inman surprisingly argued that women were exploited as unpaid labor that supported male wage labor, she was quickly isolated and forced to resign.[3] Thereafter, similar protests led directly to expulsion or demotion. Even as late as 1975, when opposing the ERA, the CP contended that labor reforms, not sexual liberation, were most beneficial to female workers.

Firestone

Radical women chafed at orthodoxy's unwillingness to confront the specificity of their oppression. The Marxist Simone de Beauvoir's assertion in *The Second Sex* (1952) that the experience of feminine sexuality is not epiphenomenal motivated women somehow to transcend the feminism-socialism dichotomy. This was largely accomplished by Shulamith Firestone, whose *Dialectic of Sex* marked a definitive break with orthodoxy and a signpost Marxists henceforth couldn't ignore. By broadening the critique of political economy to encompass sex, class, and culture, Firestone was the first to bring materialist analysis to bear on patriarchy. She concluded that sex, not class, is seminal for understanding women's social exploitation because the subordination of females is rooted in reproductive biology. Marxian dialectics, in short, negates its own materialist presuppositions.

After first critiquing Engels's reductivism, Firestone dialectically examined three levels of social activity: sex, class, and culture.[4] She discovered that female exploitation and subordination is endemic to all modern societies, regardless of ideology or class structure. It is, she concluded, based on human biology, especially the female's reproductive function within the biological family, which leaves her at the mercy of her female bodily functions and responsible for the care and nurture of the dependent young. "Materialism," in Firestone's view, embodies the physical realities of male and female biology, and the political and social structures that assured biology as the determining force of the social order. The science of dialectical materialism explains how economics is determined by, and reflects, sex-class. Capitalist exploitation, which Marx and Engels fully documented, is therefore based on sexual inequality. Social change, on the other hand, requires reconstructing society's dominant sexual relationships.

The biological family is an inherently hierarchical institution because women need men's protection during reproduction and hence become dependent. To rationalize and maintain the family, male rulers created

ideological justifications of their dominance, such as the cult of romance and the ideals of feminine beauty and male strength. Given the biological facts of life, the patriarchical family, which prompted men to act creatively in society and women to passively stay home, was therefore as natural and inevitable as were the values and capitalist institutions that rationalized it. Only by abolishing the family could women be liberated "from the tyranny of their sexual-reproductive roles."[5] Firestone argued that today's new technology proffers women dramatically new options in the areas of fertility control and reproduction, freeing them from their fundamental biological condition and the sexual class system built on it. Henceforth, childbearing could be diffused to society as a whole, men as well as women. The family's collapse, now technologically feasible, would also bring down all of its exploitative institutions, such as patriarchy and capitalism, and usher in a truly egalitarian, nonsexist socialism. Then, with both production and reproduction no longer necessary, women and men, adults and children, would all be equal and fully developed. Complex forms of play would replace routinized and menial tasks. Real emotional love and liberated polymorphous sexuality would be rejoined outside the constraints of exploitative personal and social relationships.

Marxist Feminism

The Dialectic of Sex shaped feminist discourse in America and Europe. On one side, radical feminists emphasized its biological dimensions and the priority of gender in explaining exploitation.[6] Women of the world, they argued, regardless of class, must unite against male oppressors. The other side accented its dialectical materialist method, and discounted the author's reversal of economics and gender. Known as feminist Marxists, these essentially orthodox thinkers were inspired by Firestone to confront thorny, gender related problems that materialists had ignored, albeit from a conventional, materialist point of view.[7] Both groups reduced the subjugation of women to a single cause, either biology or economics. In the vast middle stood neo-Marxists whose research stressed the dialectical blending of gender and class in capitalism, rejecting the reductivism of orthodoxy and radical feminism. For these nonorthodox Marxists, also called Marxist or socialist feminists, feminism and socialism are compatible perspectives, each of which highlights one aspect of a complex capitalist totality.

Feminist neo-Marxists enriched dialectical inquiry by enlarging Marx's mode of production to include not only the means by which people have organized to produce and distribute food, shelter, and clothing, but also the means by which they have organized to produce and distribute sexuality, nurturance, and babies. Both forms of social organization, based on economic *and* sexual divisions of labor, satisfy a fundamental human need. Neither, alone, can adequately explain women's oppression in capitalism. Orthodoxy explains the origins and nature of a ruling class that is defined by

and dependent on the economic division of labor. It thus mistakenly isolates activities characteristic primarily of males in capitalism, ignoring entirely society's ruling gender, a product of its sexual division of labor. Control of society's means of production belongs to this ruling gender as well as to the ruling class.

America's culture is thus both bourgeois and masculine. Women are exploited on both levels, but especially by males, who have traditionally excluded them from the economic sphere. As homemakers, mothers, and wives they are subjugated primarily by personal relationships to men, the guidelines for which are learned early in life and continually reinforced. They are taught in a male-dominated culture to perform without pay the socially necessary work of child rearing and family care, replenishing society with new generations of law-abiding, respectful boys and girls. As consumers rather than producers, they maintain a high level of aggregate demand for commodities. And, of course, their untapped economic potential helps keep male wages lower than they would otherwise be. In sum, women's dependency in this so-called private sphere profoundly reinforces the basic features of public life, where men are subjugated by their dependency on capitalists. Politics is thus inescapable. It plays in families as well as factories, psyches as well as classes. Each mode of political subjugation, private and public, freezes the masculine, capitalist status quo. Consequently, economic production and sexual reproduction, class and gender, are neither identical nor autonomous systems. Rather, they are reciprocally defined and mutually dependent within a dynamic social totality that is both patriarchical and capitalist. The abolition of economic slavery is therefore tied to the abolition of gender slavery. Marxism and feminism are two aspects of one emancipatory process.

The recent explosion of published neo-Marxian research into gender related issues has yielded intellectual as well as practical fruits. Intellectually, what began as a highly charged but unfocused synthesis has gradually congealed into more restrictive research agendas that plug tightly into the unwieldy whole. In America, Marxist feminist scholars now enter the dialectical totality through the related but specialized categories of reproduction and the family, sexuality and gender roles, and female labor. Each perpective is represented by a constantly expanding number of articles and books that critically examine a limited scope of female experience and its links to the more general forces of patriarchy and capitalism.

These scholarly studies punctuate the intensely political quality of a woman's personal beliefs regarding gender identity, family, and work. They constitute an unconventional radical political agenda that focuses as much on transforming attitudes as institutions, and hence is, potentially, especially popular among large segments of exploited but passive liberals. For example, Marxist feminist scholars have sympathetically compared the processes of birthing, nurturing, and sustaining human life—traditional

women's work—to producing needed commodities in factories. America's system of producing and distributing the means of satisfying needs for children, sex, and emotional nurturance resembles in key ways the conventional economic system. Women, like men, are therefore workers, engaged, however, in reproducing society rather than producing valued items. They needed to acquire pride, fair compensation, and workplace autonomy—the treasures workers everywhere seek. The popular distinction, among Americans, between household and public labor serves primarily to devalue women and maximize corporate profits. It is purely ideological. In concrete terms, this means that women have been exploited by the male-controlled reproductive system, and that reproductive relationships must be made equitable. Women, in short, needed to control the means of reproduction.

On one level, then, women need open and free access to the technical knowledge, medication, and surgical procedures that would facilitate their control over the biological dimensions of reproduction. On another level, hierarchical, male-dominated families must change into egalitarian partnerships of loving adults and nurtured children. Such fulfilling relationships become self-sustaining as gender roles are redefined and children are socialized to achieve human, not gender-related, potentials. Their sexuality would then no longer be conditioned by the need to make profits and perpetuate male domination over women. On still another related level, women shouldn't be victimized by sex segregation in the labor market. Employed women in America are informally clustered into restricted occupations that pay, on average, little more than half the wage of male workers. Economics thus reinforces gender stereotyping, making it rational for women, not men, to stay home. Uninhibited access to all job categories, even those traditionally dominated by males, as well as compensation (for work in the public or private sphere) equal to comparable work performed by males, both needed to be guaranteed. When both parents choose to labor in the public sphere, or for the growing number of single parent families, affordable post-natal day care must be available. In sum, the linkages between women's biological, emotional, social, and economic experiences are unbreakable. Emancipation in one realm requires emancipation everywhere.

This entire Marxian feminist political agenda attacks exploitation at its patriarchical and capitalist sources. As gender roles, marriage and family relationships, and economic opportunities for women all change, the material foundations of both capitalism and patriarchy are cracked. The concept of work is creatively redefined by emotionally liberated men and women. Mindless consumerism becomes less appealing. A united and mobilized class of male and female workers dramatically expands. Mass-based demands for progressive public programs proliferate. Capitalism's fiscal and ideological crises are both stretched to the limits, and the old sexist cultural bromides no longer keep the lid on. The political consequences of sexual emancipation, in short, are revolutionary.

Race

For most nonwhite females in America, Marxian feminism had witnessed the conjoining of class and gender exploitation through Caucasian lenses, unmindful of racial oppression. Its political agenda ignored the traditional economic role of black women, the variety of family forms that evolved among persecuted blacks, the black family's indispensable role in outliving white bigotry, and the economic consequences of racial, rather than gender, discrimination. Its call for gender equity in the reproductive system ignored the cries of many black women who *wanted* to conceive and bear children, but without the fear of poverty and degradation. Its critique of patriarchy misrepresented the social position of black men, who often had less social power than white women. In short, the viciousness of economic and sexual exploitation, for all women, was not, in racist America, sufficient to make black women bond with white women at the expense of black men. For blacks, racial consciousness has always been a more potent force than class or gender consciousness. The inability of Marxian feminists to recruit black women, many of whom were unemployed, poor, and powerless, meant that exploitation in America was not restricted to workers and women. Marxism could no longer disregard the explosive issue of race.

Marx's legacy regarding racial issues, particularly America's so-called "Negro Question," is ambiguous. He foresaw the revolutionary economic impact of the Civil War, and realized that a Union victory over Southern landowners augured the decline of a major hindrance to free capitalist development and the rise of an independent working class movement. Moreover, he opposed slavery on moral as well as economic grounds. The now famous warning in *Capital* that "Labor with a white skin cannot emancipate itself where labor with a black skin is branded," intimated the need for interracial working class solidarity. However, Marx was always concerned primarily with capitalism as a mode of production, and with emancipating Europe's predominantly white workers. He never understood the intensity and complexity of racial bigotry in America. Aside from some passing remarks in correspondence with Engels regarding the importance of the black franchise, and several tentative comparisons of American blacks and the Irish, he largely ignored the condition of American blacks during and after the Reconstruction period. This legacy of neglect on such an important issue, viewed in the context of the *Manifesto*'s occasional characterizations of nonwhites outside of Europe as "barbarians," "semi-barbarians," and "peasants," likely means that Marx never fully transcended the hegemonic racial bigotry of his own time and place. In any case, his followers in America were left without explicit answers to the vexing "Negro Question."

Orthodox Marxists, in America and elsewhere, have, like Marx, always reduced concrete experiences of racial bigotry directly to capitalism. From

this point of view, both began at roughly the same time in the sixteenth century. As white European entrepreneurs penetrated the New World in search of cheap labor power, raw materials, and markets, ideas depicting the inferiority of nonwhites rationalized their activities. In colonial America, racist ideas similarly justified the vital economic institution of slavery. When, in the nineteenth century, slavery hindered capitalist economic expansion, racism was briefly abandoned by Union forces mobilizing for war. However the subservient roles of ex-slaves in the post-Emancipation economies of debt peonage, tenant farming, sharecropping, and eventually wage labor, reinvigorated American racism. For wealthy whites it justified the brutal conditions on their farms and in their factories, and the low wages of their workers. Poor whites salved their anxieties and powerlessness with racial bigotry, which was stiffened when accomodationist blacks scabbed during white union strikes. Racism, in short, was caused by, and reinforced, the material interests of society's dominant capitalist class. When capitalist economic exploitation died, so would bigotry. Blacks, therefore, needed to mute or disregard entirely racial issues, and emphasize instead interracial working class solidarity. They had to mobilize *for* socialism rather than *against* racism.

Economism has remained the operating formula of America's orthodox political parties. Both the SLP and SP, for example, rhetorically pronounced blacks' economic and political equality, but refused to condemn segregation, lynching, and race riots in order not to alienate white workers. The SP Constitution equated the interests of American blacks, in spite of their unique experiences as an oppressed racial minority, to those of whites. Notwithstanding the entreaties of concerned individuals like Haywood, Debs, Walling, Charles Edward Russell, and other black and white members, the SP simply ignored blacks until they moved North during the First World War.[8] Even then, although relevant intra-party dialogue expanded and SP Platforms demanded full black citizenship and an end to the most egregious and violent racist practices, SP tactics were directed primarily at organizing workers rather than eliminating the social consequences of bigotry.[9]

There were no black delegates to the CP's founding convention in 1919, nor did it actively recruit blacks until 1921, and then only at Lenin's behest. Until 1928, it dogmatically reiterated that the character of black oppression in America was essentially proletarian rather than racial. Yet the Comintern, and indirectly the American CP, knew that urban blacks could provide the Party needed energy and strength. At the Sixth World Congress of the Communist International, Stalin issued his "Theses on the Revolutionary Movement in the Colonies and Semi-Colonies," which committed America's CP to acknowledge blacks as a "nation within a nation," with unique economic and cultural characteristics, striving for "self-determination." By championing a Southern based Negro Socialist Soviet Republic of the U.S., Stalin risked splitting America's working class into separate races and nations.

This appeared to violate the teachings of Marx and Engels, but the Comintern chose Lenin's obscure *Capitalism and Agriculture in the United States of America* (1917)—which depicted black oppression only within the particular historical and social development of the semi-feudal, agrarian South—as its seminal text.[10] Stalin believed, correctly, that by accenting the specificity of the Southern black experience he could entice blacks into the CP. Given the Comintern's reliance on an unconventional but nevertheless strictly economic analysis of the South, and its otherwise unpolluted economism, this was less a theoretical change than a pragmatic decision to reassert hegemony over America's CP and coopt black discontent. With regard to the "Negro Question," it remained—except for the United Front years—official Party policy until the 1950s, and generated Party support for meliorative programs aimed at blacks, as well as for a variety of predominantly black working class front organizations.

By 1956, as black and white CP membership dropped precipitously, a desperate Party declared that blacks were, officially, no longer a nation. Henceforth, it would work to secure full equality for all workers, regardless of race or nationality. The CP, apparently, had decided that the "Negro Question" was no longer pertinent. However, the orthodox project of somehow preserving the specificity of racial oppression in the U.S. while also reducing it to economics was undertaken, usually outside the Party, by a cluster of highly sophisticated materialist scholars and social scientists.[11] Stretching and twisting economism with new conceptual tools such as internal or domestic colonialism, black power, racial stratification, marginalized workers, nation-class, segmented work, and split labor markets, in the last resort they always retracted into class as the central determining variable.

The CP's legacy, on racial issues at least, is mixed. Its race program was heavy-handed, dogmatic, and opportunistic, and the few gains made by blacks as a result of it have always been incidental to the Comintern's needs. Yet, in the words of one critical scholar, "No other organization in the United States, with the possible exception of the NAACP, has done more to publicize the Negro's plight than has the Communist Party."[12] In a hostile, racist world, one can't, apparently, be too choosy about friends. The unscrupulous CP, a party that dutifully endorsed Stalin's decision to finance Italy's slaughter of Ethiopian blacks, nonetheless had struggled courageously against bigotry at a time when white moralists were sleepwalking. Why, then, despite the hypocrisy and given its singular concern with racial issues, didn't America's most exploited citizens—black workers—join and/or remain in the CP?

For black neo-Marxists, the answer lay in orthodoxy's reduction of black consciousness to objective economic categories. America's "Negro Question," like its "Woman Question," was answered with complete disregard for specific circumstances, events, and experiences. The complex reality of black workers in America was reduced to a grossly idealized, impersonal

proletarian image. CP leaders who had studied and memorized this frigid version of black America felt justified in manipulating blacks to join the Party and become authentic. White orthodox radicals, in short, established theoretical dominance over blacks, and then sought to control their practical activities as well. Admittedly, orthodoxy's perceptive critique of the economic origins and consequences of racial bigotry meaningfully structured blacks' contradictory, often painful experiences. Similarly, orthodoxy's valiant attempts to organize workers and fight discrimination had, on occasion, improved conditions for thousands of black families. But had blacks swallowed economism and acquiesced to CP political hegemony, their collective racial, cultural, and psychological identity—the embodiment of their actual experiences as black Americans—would have perished. Orthodoxy's price for economic deliverance, which amounted to black spiritual suicide, was unacceptably high.

The initial indication of racial discontent on the Marxian left in America was the surprising popularity of black socialist preachers in the late nineteenth century. As a group, they reflected the basic economist positions of the SLP, but they also declared that blacks would gain most from socialism because they were exploited more intensely than whites. At a time, however, when American blacks were neither courted by, nor attracted to, materialist Marxism, socialist preachers dressed their revolutionary message in the liturgy of the black church, harking to early Christian values and emotionally testifying to Marx's cooperative socialist commonwealth as the realization of Christ's teachings. Since the church was a dominant influence over blacks, more black Americans learned of socialism through the spoken and written words of the Revs. George W. Slater, Reverdy C. Ransom, James T. Holly, and George Washington Woodbey than in all the publications of socialist organizations.[13] The message that Marxism needed to be realized in and through black culture, rather than in spite of it, went unheeded everywhere except in black Christian churches and periodicals. These, however, spawned a new generation of socialist black intellectuals concerned as much with racial pride as with economic dignity.

Harlom Radicals

By the 1910s, they came of age in two black controlled socialist institutions. The New Negro Harlem Radicals, established in 1917 by Chandler Owen and A. Phillip Randolph, was affiliated with the SP both ideologically and politically. Its journal, *The Messenger*, was the first national socialist magazine edited by and for blacks in America. It published and popularized the work of black socialists among Harlem's middle class cultural elite, and tirelessly fought to sensitize the SP on racial issues. As the SP veered Right, so did Chandler and Owens, and the journal was sold to non-Marxists in 1924. In its seven active years, however, both the *The Messenger* and the Harlem Radicals, using indigenous cultural images and vernacular to elo-

quently depict the linkages between racial and economic emancipation, were a potent force among black intellectuals, particularly those opposed to Marcus Garvey's black Zionism.

African Blood Brotherhood

The African Blood Brotherhood, founded in 1919 by black West Indians and Americans, was more a secret fraternal order than a political organization.[14] Its initial goal was to synthesize Garvey's brand of black nationalism and revolutionary, anti-imperialist Marxism. Eventually, it hoped to establish a black socialist state somewhere in Africa, South America, or the Caribbean. This enormous project was far beyond the abilities of its early leaders. By 1921, most of them had joined the CP and coopted historical materialism. They became the core of black CP leadership for many years thereafter, and the Party's most ardent proponents of Stalin's "nation within a nation" thesis.

Paradoxically, the Brotherhood's aspirations were far more important than their accomplishments. Particularly in *The Crusader*, its journal, the likelihood of success for black self-determination at home and anti-colonial movements abroad was rhetorically linked to the fate of American capitalism. Corporate power in America, from this view, had a direct financial stake in perpetuating both imperialism and racism. Correlatively, the survival of an independent and free black people obligated blacks, especially American blacks, to be socialist revolutionaries. The Brotherhood promised that socialism would emancipate blacks, not just workers, and, where appropriate, permit black rather than worker self-government. The black nationalist-socialist tension that was gripping Harlem, and had already fractured the black membership of both the SP and the Negro Harlem Radicals, was now crystallized in the Brotherhood. Without a synthesis, which was not forthcoming, Brotherhood members had to choose between Garvey and the CP. By the mid-1930s, with black energy spent and the apparatchiks in control, the Brotherhood quietly dissolved into the CP bureaucracy.

Dubois

W. E. B. Dubois was, unequivocally, the pivotal figure in modern black neo-Marxism. An expansive thinker, disciplined scholar, poet, novelist, editor, literary critic, and political activist, Dubois was fully prepared to bridge the chasm between black nationalism and black socialism.

Never fully comfortable with either economism or orthodoxy's answer to the Negro Question, Dubois nevertheless joined the SP in 1911, and carefully traced the supporting role slavery and later racism played in the growth of American capitalism. The turning point in Dubois's thinking came in 1935, when, in *Black Reconstruction in America*, he saw that despite optimal objective conditions, working class whites in America had subjugated their own class interests to racism and narrow-minded individualism. The network of capitalist cultural institutions rationalizing and propagating racism

was simply too powerful for white workers, even Marxists, to resist. Wages for a racially divided working class therefore remained low, and corporate profits rose dramatically. Moreover, since Reconstruction the failure of U.S. labor to support blacks had permitted a robust capitalism to expand cancerously into underdeveloped areas. Dubois concluded that, despite uncovering the link between bigotry and capitalism, historical materialism was unsuitable for explaining the survival of American racism. Objectively, America had been ripe for an interracial socialist uprising. Theoretically, blacks were part of an interracial, world wide exploited class of cheap laborers. But blacks, regrettably, had learned that working class whites in America valued racial purity more than class unity. Established by whites in nineteenth century Europe, conventional Marxist categories simply couldn't accommodate the black experience in America.[15]

To survive, blacks had to defend against an interclass racial enemy, primarily by coalescing around black, not proletarian, values. Dubois's own research, in part, aimed at bolstering black pride by depicting the centrality of blacks to both American and world history. Their sad plight, he argued eloquently, was due to an unbeatable racist alliance of capital and white labor, not some innate racial deficiency among blacks.[16] Dubois thus informed his shocked integrationist colleagues in both the NAACP (of which he was a co-founder in 1909) and the orthodox left that blacks comprised a nation of victims, a sleeping Leviathan awaiting the liberating shock of a bonded racial consciousness. American blacks needed to emphasize shared physical and social qualities, mobilize in pride and strength, support non-white emancipation in the colonized Third World, and pull themselves out of poverty. Racial solidarity would unite the black elite—Dubois's "Talented Tenth"—and the black masses, and the former would "pull all that are worth the saving up to their vantage ground."[17] As a mobilized nation, Dubois believed blacks would develop their own cooperative cultural, educational, political, and particularly economic associations. Black segregation, he argued, to the extent that it improved living conditions without itself inciting racial discrimination, was the key to black equality.[18]

Dubois never repudiated black nationalism. But unlike Garvey, Dubois was also a Marxist. He knit both into a seamless unity through which reality was exposed. Poverty and exploitation, Dubois knew, did cause bigotry. Bigotry, however, which hurt innocent black children more than white, also caused poverty. Blacks suffered as blacks *and* as workers, and their plight was not reducible to either category. Black liberation preceded and hastened worker liberation, but neither could succeed alone. Racial emancipation was thus "the warning which awakens the world to its truer self and its wider destiny."[19] Orthodoxy had ignored the race question in America, and black nationalism the economic question. Blacks, in Dubois's view, had therefore to liberate themselves through racial pride, cultural and economic autonomy, anti-colonial Pan Africanism, and an eye to the socialist future.

Planned investment, production, and distribution within black communities would provide the takeoff for black economic equality and political self-government. New black leaders would emerge from below to replace the Talented Tenth, whom Dubois belatedly acknowledged elevated profit over blacks' collective welfare.[20] Cooperative black socialism, in a sea of white capitalism, would enrich, employ, and empower blacks, provide an attractive model for white labor, and worsen capitalism's accumulation crisis. Without an imperialist safety valve, the domestic and international economic consequences of black liberation would destroy capitalism. Afterwards, racial differences would gradually dissolve into economic equality, and worldwide socialist comradeship would end the economic impulse to fight wars.[21] In Dubois's America, class struggle determined the general course of history, but was bound to the specifics of black liberation.

Dubois enriched orthodoxy with the insight that racism is an irreduceable material element in American and world history. Black autonomy is therefore a progressive resolution of one of capitalism's material contradictions, and also a prelude to resolving another.

James

This concept of independent black struggle as part of history's evolution toward socialism was delivered directly to orthodoxy's entrenched leaders by C. L. R. James, in a series of discussions with Trotsky that began in 1938.[22] In his *Black Jacobins* (1938), James had discovered that revolutionary attitudes among black slaves were established independently of bourgeois values, by Africans who had personally experienced the indignities of enslavement. He concluded that the black movement in America also needed to be liberated from the yoke of nineteenth century economism. Blacks comprised a distinct, organic radical force in America, unattached to the CP or trade unions. By digesting indigenous experiences, ideas, and struggles on their own they would approach the conclusions of Marxism. Blacks were, in short, the vanguard of white proletarian rebellion. James thus urged the CP to support movements for black cultural, political, and economic autonomy as a means of efficaciously intervening in American life, detonating the time bomb of black discontent. The Comintern, of course, had no intention of legitimizing what it perceived as black inauthenticity. By the mid-1940s, James and other black intellectuals were evicted from the Party. Fittingly, Dubois's legacy would henceforth evolve outside the CP among independent black socialists.

Wright

Richard Wright, along with the West Indian Claude McKay and Langston Hughes, were preeminent black intellectuals in the CP during the 1920s and 1930s. McKay and Hughes were sheltered from economism by their strong personal stands on the priority of art over politics. McKay finally left the

country, and Hughes eventually compromised ideologically. Wright, on the other hand, never lost the fervor that lured him into the CP in 1932.

Wright's disillusionment, somewhat like James's and Dubois's, concerned the Party's dogmatism and narrow-mindedness, as well as its unwillingness to acknowledge the uncertain future awaiting black American workers. The orthodox critique of capitalism, for Wright, was valid,[23] but its predictions regarding human behavior were not. Blacks in America, like Bigger Thomas in *Native Son*, were fragmented, exploited, and disillusioned. No longer could they be depended upon to carry out historical laws. They could, instead, turn left or right depending on the quality of their psychological awakening. No movement (including the CP) that blindly presumed all workers were progressive, could succeed. On the contrary, the left had to hatch a meaningful ideology that could inflame genuine socialist attitudes in black communities. To avoid irrational mistakes ("wild cataract[s] of emotion that will brook no control"[24])blacks had to transform Marxian dogma into their own nationalistic voice, one that would express their emergence as a negation of capitalism. Black nationalism was therefore the first stage of a more universal emancipatory consciousness.[25] It was logical, rational, and justified. Simultaneously "insiders" and "outsiders" in capitalist America, blacks had to cultivate a unique worldview, a "specially defined psychological type," that would unite them emotionally as well as generate knowledge, understanding and socialist revolution.[26]

Wright thus saw blacks as a separate and unique group in bourgeois society that required distinct ideas, not merely—as for Dubois—autonomy, created by their own intellectuals. Black writers needed to use orthodox Marxism without becoming imprisoned in it. "No theory of life can take the place of life. After Marxism has laid bare the skeleton of society, there remains the task of the writer to plant flesh upon those bones out of his will to live." Orthodoxy, in other words, only establishes the general, impersonal beginnings of socialist revolution. History's economic contradictions are embodied in, and mediated by, concrete movements for social emancipation, including that of black cultural solidarity. "The simple fact is, the social cat can be skinned in many different ways."[27] In America, Wright's disciples included Imamu Baraka, John A. Williams, Ed Bullins, Melvin Van Peebles, and Ishmael Reed.

Black Panther Party

In the 1960s and 1970s, amidst black partisan wrangling that came to resemble Harlem's turbulent 1920s, the subtle mingling of economics and nationalism that epitomized the best work of Dubois, James, and Wright slowly dissipated. The Black Panther Party (BPP) was established in 1966 as the first independent black party that was both nationalist and socialist. Its original Ten Point Program contained basic cultural and economic demands that confirmed the double-edged nature of black exploitation in America.[28]

Its implementation would have guaranteed blacks both economic security and cultural autonomy, freedom *from* capitalist exploitation and freedom *to* educate and govern themselves. Huey Newton and Bobby Seale, the BPP's original founders and leaders, also sought mutually beneficial alliances with a coalition of sympathetic radical white, Puerto Rican, and Chicano forces. In the highly charged emotionalism of the '60s, however, this openness proved fatal. First, Eldridge Cleaver joined the BPP as Minister of Information, touting a crypto-orthodox thesis of "lumpenproletarian revolution." Then, in 1968, the black nationalist Student Non-Violent Coordinating Committee (SNCC) merged with the BPP. Stokely Carmichael and H. Rap Brown, SNCC's leaders, became BPP officials, and almost immediately fought the Party's policy of coalition-building. Party members, and the black community generally, had to choose between Cleaver's crude Marxism-Leninism and Carmichael's cultural nationalism. The Party eventually split. Nationalists, in 1972, managed to join black politicians and radicals into the National Black Political Assembly, which was neutralized when black elites gradually drifted back into mainstream electoral politics. Internal personal and ideological divisions among progressive blacks had shredded what remained of black neo-Marxism. Mimicking its own past, the black left polarized into orthodox Marxist and nationalist (Pan African, Islamic, and cultural) factions. By the early 1970s, as segments of the latter drifted right, disillusioned cultural nationalists such as Baraka, Mark Smith, Gerald McWorter, and Ron Karenga retreated back into scientific socialism.

Marable

Dubois's forgotten legacy of nonorthodox black Marxism, his progressive synthesis of economism and black nationalism, was reborn in the contemporary scholar and activist Manning Marable. Capitalism, for Marable, expropriated the surplus value of black and white workers. The exclusion of blacks from management positions, however, funneled them disproportionately into unskilled, low paying jobs. In general, then, blacks' surplus value was expropriated to a greater degree than was that of whites. They comprised an underclass of American laborers. The civil rights movement improved conditions by ending legal segregation, enlarging black voting roles, and limiting discrimination in jobs, housing, unions, etc. But by the 1970s and 1980s, argued Marable, this project had run its course and blacks, in the name of fiscal responsibility, were once again regressing economically and socially. A self-sufficient black population would raise black salaries, form competitive black entrepreneurs, and increase the supply of commodities—all of which were economically unacceptable to white capitalists. Progress in black civil rights could go only so far before encountering these structural constraints. U.S. capitalism, in short, existed "not to develop, but to underdevelop Black people."[29] Dominant class interests thrived on

worker exploitation, and blacks, who worked harder for less money, were a particularly tasty economic morsel.

Marable was especially interested in the process whereby white American intellectuals nonviolently joined the oppressed to their oppressors. Indebted to the Italian Antonio Gramsci, Marable discovered that the "ideological hegemony" of whites was reinforced by an elaborate network of cultural organizations and coercive state agencies that systematically justified and enforced racist values in order to strengthen capitalism. By culturally withdrawing whites' sympathy for an "inferior race" of blacks, and then upholding, forcefully when necessary, racist rules, black economic exploitation fluorished. Corrclatively, blacks were socialized in churches, schools, and the media to passively condone the status quo and seek personal, not racial or even class, gains. Racism was thus economically and culturally exploitative.

This melding of race and capitalist economics has eluded white intellectuals, even radicals.[30] Liberals, to Marable, were naive and unrealistic. Marxists were anchored to economic determinism. On the other hand, black nationalists tackled an agenda that was out of touch with the actual material conditions of American blacks. White racism, remember, survived by organically infecting American culture. White individuals, even good individuals, were its beneficiaries. Only blacks, the victims, could initiate a new non-racist hegemonic culture, and only by cultivating shared experiences that would unite and mobilize them as an autonomous anti-capitalist social movement. Forces of black emancipation, in other words, had to arise organically from black experiences and communities. By this standard, liberals, orthodox Marxists, and black nationalists were all alien to American blacks. Their attempts to control the black power movement, like other more blatant kinds of colonialism, were unjustifiable.

By scrutinizing black American history Marable uncovered two cultural themes that were by-products of black ideology during slavery, and were organically reinforced in slave communities.[31] One, paternalistic and conservative, propagated the Sambo personality that fulfilled whites' biased expectations and justified their exploitation of black slave labor. Today's black elite—entrepreneurs, clergy, politicians, and educators manifest this conservatism in self-indulgent "white" expectations and values. The other, called by Marable "Blackwater," taught blacks to struggle collectively for a better life. Slave rebellions, the resilient black family, black radical Christianity, black idealism, and all the unnoticed everyday acts of individual courage among common slaves, testified, then, to the Blackwater tradition. Marable believed this tradition was also the fount of progressive black unity today. It proffered working class blacks an organic, grassroots framework for building popular consensus. As a reflective critique of social injustice, Blackwater intimated today's materialist critique of capitalism. As an expression of black unity and strength in a hostile world, Blackwater embodied

today's nationalists' appreciation of black autonomy and folk traditions. Blackwater, in short, is realized today in the ideological and material aspirations of black neo-Marxism. It is the nucleus of an anti-racist, anti-capitalist hegemonic culture.

In addition to updating and rephrasing Dubois's message, Marable also devised a pertinent black radical strategy, heretofore the missing link in black neo-Marxism. Adopting Gramsci's depiction of ideological and coercive state apparatuses, and the need for complementary proletarian wars of position and maneuver, Marable suggested that American blacks engage in both ideological and coercive resistance. Independent, black-controlled political parties, military and labor unions, cultural projects, producer and consumer cooperatives, neighborhood associations, day-care centers, and educational campaigns are the weapons for Marable's war of position against liberalism. By mobilizing blacks politically, militarily, economically, and culturally, as well as sensitizing them to the racial implications of pertinent domestic and world issues, Marable hoped to crack America's unquestioned racist and capitalist traditions. Revolution, ultimately, means creating an alternative set of hegemonic cultural values in America, and this had to begin with blacks struggling to control these key segments of their own consciousness and civil society. However, to renounce violence categorically, in Marable's view, is to "forfeit any realistic possibility of black empowerment and ultimately self-determination."[32] Blacks must, therefore, realistically prepare to defend themselves against racist attacks. To Marable, this meant organizing paramilitary units in black neighborhoods to fight drug traffic and to supervise police activities, and training black youth to engage in defensive combat if and when the need arose. By itself, black violence in predominantly white America could never delegitimize the system. Carefully exercised, however, it could defend the long intellectual process of cultural delegitimization.

As blacks began reaffirming their Blackwater heritage, Marable believed they could then negotiate interracial, interclass coalitions with other progressive forces, including the blossoming middle sector of professionals and managers. A new historic bloc would slowly emerge, encompassing a wide spectrum of Americans—blacks, feminists, hispanics, native Americans, trade unions, anti-nuclear groups, environmentalists, populists, socialists, communists, neighborhood associations, school boards, professionals, etc.—each critically rejecting an unjust status quo. This progressive coalition crystallizes a new hegemonic ideology as well as a Common Program of political action. Short-term goals would include building a democratic electoral consensus around a program of "non-reformist reforms" in areas that concern coalition members.[33] This decentralized political dialogue, during which capital's anti-social corporate bottom line would surface, would nurture a long term anti-capitalist consensus. As the alliance slowly matured and coalesced politically, its control of coercive

state institutions would incrementally expand. At this point state power will have been won. With the appearance of new hegemonic values and a new dominant class, the economic and cultural sources of racism would perish. What began as a black protest against racial prejudice ends with empowered common people democratically smashing the capitalist means of production.

Religion

By embracing women and blacks the nonorthodox left had, belatedly, taken two giant steps toward relevance. But the inscrutable fact of working class religiosity remained. More time, money, and effort, by far, were spent by common people on church related activities in America than on gender and race combined. And religion, with only few lapses, had consistently been a leading force of American conservatism. If, as has traditionally been the case, the line was drawn with Marxists on one side and God on the other, then leftist rhetoric would bounce endlessly between empty barricades. The atheistic, soulless left in America needed religion badly, or it risked eternal marginality.

Marx's views on religion were more problematic than we might have expected. On the one hand, he was always hostile to religious beliefs, practices, and institutions. Early in life, he emphasized religion's palliative functions, comparing its social effects to the drug-like stupor experienced by opium addicts. In later works, he depicted religion, like all ideology, as false consciousness, enslaving humankind to unjust social conditions. Religions, he argued, are tied to economic systems. They rationalize abstractly extant class relationships, in effect sanctifying the dominant class. The "superiority" of modern Protestantism was thus due to a theology that, better than any other, justified the economic superiority of capitalists. On the other hand, however, Marx also knew that religion was often the language of suffering people seeking consolation, and not simply the invention of unscrupulous leaders. Although religion was born in and sustained by forms of material exploitation, it was also "the expression of real suffering and the protest against real suffering. Religion is the sigh of the oppressed creature, the heart of a heartless world, and the soul of soulless conditions."[34] Religion may bring us "illusory happiness," but it is also a protest against human suffering that gives meaning to harsh, empty lives. It plays an important role in society and emotionally sustains most of humanity. Marx therefore never advocated or practiced tactics that would forcibly destroy religion. Nor, for Marx, was atheism the goal of socialism. If, as he anticipated, conventional religions disappeared, it would be as a consequence of proletarian emancipation from the inhuman conditions that were their final cause. But even in socialism, "Everyone should be able to attend to his religious as well as his bodily needs without the police sticking their noses in."[35]

Beginning with Engels, orthodoxy chose to emphasize the economic component of religious activity, its existence as a "reflex of the real world."[36] Lenin, and through him the Comintern and the world's orthodox CPs, twisted Marx's sensitivity to demolishing the *sources* of religion into a militant atheism that would forcibly expunge every vestige of religious activity. Leninism favored banning religions altogether and propagandizing for atheism, which, in this view, was both progressive and objectively correct. In the Leninist tradition, orthodoxy has since regarded religion as both a cause of proletarian lassitude and as a symptom of economic illness whose only cure was socialism. Confronted by a self-consciously pious American working class, orthodoxy's response has ranged from the SP Right's hands-off policy toward religion to the CP's strident atheism.

This blatant antagonism between orthodox epistemology and American political reality has always perplexed leftists. European Marxists, with their rich and diverse philosophical traditions, have searched knowingly for a synthesis.[37] American Marxists, until recently, were ill-prepared and unwilling. Here, for over a century, a small number of leftist theologians have challenged Marxists to reject economism and somehow meet them halfway, a challenge that is now grudgingly endorsed.

The Social Gospel

The Social Gospel movement (SG) arose in America after the Civil War, beginning in about 1865, among a small fraction of Protestant theologians. Influenced by Fabian and utopian socialists, as well as by reform-minded theologians and politicians, spell-binding preachers like Jesse H. Jones, F. Monroe Sprague, Vida Scudder, W. D. P. Bliss, George D. Herron, and later Walter Rauschenbusch indicted capitalism as unchristian and—at least after 1890—urged believers to be socialists in Christ's name. They were (except for Herron in his last years) not orthodox Marxists, and as Christian moralists simply disregarded class struggle altogether. Perhaps for this reason, their national appeal, always marginal, included the middle and entrepreneurial classes as much as workers.

The SG had rediscovered the social ethics of Old Testament Prophets, especially Isaiah, and the ethical teachings of Jesus and his followers—from Apostolic Christians living soon after Jesus's death to radicals in the fifteenth and sixteenth centuries—all of whom had sought social redemption in a just Christian society here on earth. The SG delivered this prophetic tradition to twentieth century Protestant America. Jesus's Sermon on the Mount, his testament that "Thy will be done *on earth* as it is in heaven," became the SG's central unifying theme. Secular life was no longer merely a way station on the believer's passage to Heaven. Capitalism, by apotheosizing self-interest, had violated Christian teachings. Socialism, which viewed society as a cooperative unity of loving individuals, represented the essence of Christ's message and was hence the institutional vehicle whereby faithful Christians

could be redeemed. A peaceful but complete redistribution of wealth was therefore required to realize an ethical kingdom on earth. This long term goal could be realized by Christians everywhere mobilizing immediately in support of progressive measures that would nationalize public utilities, enfranchise women, institute free and compulsory public education, regulate monopolies, and improve factory working conditions. For the SG, Christ's teachings were manifest in socialist activism. God, in short, was immanent in mankind *and* society. Both had therefore to be Christianized. "The Common Brotherhood of man is at once the Gospel of Christianity and the gospel of socialism."[38]

Herron

The key intellectual figures in the SG were George D. Herron and Walter Rauschenbusch, both of whom struggled to reconcile the obvious contradictions between Christianity and Marxism. Herron, a Congregationalist, appreciated the spirituality of scientific socialism. God, in Herron's view, worked through economic tendencies that assured the triumph on earth of socialism.[39] God's earthly embodiment, Jesus, mediated these spiritual and material realms. The divinity of Jesus's life was his perfect faith that God's will could be completed in this world. His supreme sacrifice was intended to save humankind. Jesus's church, consequently, embodied his sacrificial and redemptive qualities. Sacrifice meant purging men and women of the selfishness and earthly material desires that stained capitalist America. Jesus's teaching was thus the spiritual analogue of Marx's economic laws: both fought sin through divine revelation, but the former emphasized individual redemption and the latter social redemption. The logic behind Jesus's Sermon on the Mount consisted of the natural economic laws by which industrial justice and human cooperation could be attained. Socialism actualized Christianity. Moreover, proletarian rebellion would take the form of a nationwide, classless religious movement based on Christian teachings. Herron thus rejected the conventional Christian perception of an otherworldly, impractical, neutral, "philosophically absolute" God. Christianity, socialism, and science were all progressing inevitably toward the Kingdom of God on Earth.

Rauschenbusch

Herron comfortably supported materialists in the SLP and, later, the SP. To him, it was inconceivable that scientific socialism could take any but a Christian form in America. Rauschenbusch, a Baptist, had less faith in economism, even though he admired it intellectually. Like Herron, he accepted materialism's empirical critique of capitalism and its historical prognosis, but nonetheless explicitly repudiated materialist epistemology.[40] Our world may indeed be projecting us into a socialist future, in

Rauschenbusch's view, but, ultimately, a transcendent God rather than earthly matter is in the driver's seat.

When this God created humanity in his own image, that is, as separate personalities unified in one divine substance, he meant for society to be an integrated, cohesive, and interrelated body of citizens: an organic whole living in separate human parts.[41] Individuals were thus ontologically joined to their communities in a divinely inspired totality. Every changed personality impacted directly on the community, which, of course, also conditioned all personal decisions. Sin is the triumph of part over totality, personal greed over divine cooperation, man over God; and the most sinful of all social systems is capitalism. Christianity purged sin by working simultaneously to regenerate each individual and reconstruct all social institutions. Success on one level, personal redemption, inspired success on the other, cooperative socialism. "The two aims of the Christian revolution, the perfection of the individual and the perfection of society, blend and pass into each other."[42]

Rauschenbusch believed that mainstream Christianity, by abandoning this prophetic Old Testament message and plaintively imprisoning God in an anti-social, metaphysical reality, had guaranteed its own irrelevance. Now, it needed to resurrect its own stream of faith and hope, which was embodied in the prophetic teachings of Jesus.

The Church's important task was to preach for God's Kingdom, which meant, to Rauschenbusch, that it needed to play both religious and political roles. The latter involves Christianizing the social order without taking it over, employing legitimate secular means to actualize divine patterns of justice. By preserving the immanent specificity of the secular world, but, through social activism, linking it to the transcendental word of God, the Church would fulfill its divine mission. Specifically, Rauschenbusch wanted the Church to strengthen ethical, fraternal institutions such as the family, authentic democracy, and public education, while abolishing institutionalized sin, i.e., prostitution, poverty, political corruption, and, more generally, competitive capitalism. In this, the Church needed to support America's workers, who Rauschenbusch felt were then engaged in a great economic struggle to end all classes and social inequalities. Economic struggle was thus a tool for regenerating Christianity and actualizing the Kingdom of God on Earth. Since spirit and matter were joined in God's unified whole, materially exploited workers needed to struggle cooperatively with progressive middle class intellectuals as well as with enlightened Christian entrepreneurs, both of whom manifested God's spirit. Socialism would emerge as the logical, inevitable outcome of materialist class struggle *and* spiritual redemption. Neither orthodoxy nor mainstream Christianity, alone, could grasp the complex, multidimensional fabric of God's reality.

With Rauschenbusch as virtuoso, the SG rode the crest of political progressivism in America to its greatest popularity. During the period of Rauschenbusch's influence, roughly the years 1900 to about 1915, mostly

middle class Protestant intellectuals studied and often converted to socialism in numbers that, though only a small percentage of America's practicing Christians, have not yet been attained again. At the urging of SG theologians and spin-off organizations like the Christian Socialist Fellowship and the Church Socialist League, many Protestant churches financed progressive social service programs for indigent parishoners, predating similar New Deal programs. Rauschenbusch's neo-Marxism impressed dozens of theologians and Christian politicians, and, indirectly, contemporaries like Michael Harrington and the Revs. Martin Luther King, Jr. and Jesse Jackson. Had not the roaring, affluent, decadent twenties so rudely interrupted, the nonorthodox Christian left might have made further significant inroads into mainstream Protestantism.

Protestant theologians, in general, reacted to affluence, moral decay, and incipient fascism by turning inward toward what they perceived as the cause of society's sickness: sin. Among Protestant intellectuals, Rauschenbusch's innovative dialectic of spirit and matter was soon replaced by strong doses of neo-orthodox, reductivist, old-time religion. An imminent God became, once again, transcendent, and Christian faith occupied a realm beyond society and history. The redemption of sinful creatures was by God's grace, not individual effort or social reforms. Secular life was necessarily bleak, while the Kingdom of God would appear apocalyptically at the conclusion of history.

Paradoxically, neo-orthodoxy's obsession with pessimism and sin punctuated what many educated Christians believed was the perfidiousness of capitalist America. So, while damning its theology, thousands of neo-orthodox Protestant clergy lauded the SG's radical politics. This, however, was cosmetic rather than dialectical Marxism, smugly adapting popular radical principles that Rauschenbusch and other Christians had intellectually sanctified to stanch a swelling wave of bourgeois immorality. Ten years hence, after Stalinism had blotched the left's reputation among intellectuals, these same clergy would heedfully turn right. Survival in a sinful world, not justice, comprised their political agenda. The most popular ideology—left, center, or right—could therefore do the job.

Niebuhr

This ideological fickleness is highlighted by the most formidable of neoorthodox theologians, and the leader of their socialist faction in the 1920s and 1930s, Reinhold Niebuhr. Humanity's endemic sinfulness, for Niebuhr, contradicted its endless search for earthly truth and perfection. Only Christian faith, what Niebuhr called "self-transcendence"—the capacity to resolve through spirituality what history, science, and reason could not— would restore meaning to fallen man's everyday existence.[43] There was, consequently, some hope that individuals, through faith, could become at least partially moral. Communities, however, were both necessary for sur-

vival and unavoidable, and also irredeemably sinful. Collective group loyalties tended to degenerate into irrational commitments to the false absolutes of race, class, nation, or religion. Placed in society, even faithful individuals became part of a stampeding, falsely prideful mob. Christian ethics was thus limited to the intensely personal realm of self-transcendence; it characterized saved personalities. Social justice, on the other hand, comprised political rules and regulations—and a measure of coercion to back them up—that, by balancing the forces of evil, preserved a tolerable society that at least aspired to the "impossible possibility" of human perfection. "There has never been a scheme of justice in history which did not have a balance of power at its foundation."[44]

The aim of politics, for Niebuhr, was thus an equitable distribution of power that would prevent one group from gaining control of the others. Prior to 1940, primarily in his books *Moral Man and Immoral Society* (1932) and *Reflections on the End of an Era* (1934), Niebuhr depicted Marxism as the most just of political ideologies. It accurately deconstructed the dynamics of bourgeois hegemony and floated the possibility of workers, by rebelling, receiving their fair share of wealth and power. Although, contrary to Marxism, the struggle for power expressed human finitude and sin, and hence was endless, on balance Niebuhr felt, in the early 1930s, that the consequences of Marxian utopianism were preferable to those of liberal utopianism. Marxism, like liberalism, was an irrational myth, but was "a very valuable illusion for the moment."[45] By the late 1930s, that moment had passed. Niebuhr then saw that a hegemonic bureaucracy, the consequence of concentrating economic power in the state, was as unjust as capitalism's corporate elites. By the mid-1940s, even more so. During these years, Niebuhr embraced FDR's New Deal. In the rabidly anti-communist 1950s, Niebuhr became a cautious Burkean conservative who feared that even reformist activism could yield worse forms of injustice than those being changed. Niebuhr's politics, in these last years, were premised on "an empirical wisdom."[46] Capitalism was still sinful, but it preserved order and was perhaps safer, hence more just, than the alternatives. Niebuhr's early Marxism, unlike Rauschenbusch's rich dialectical blend, was only skin deep.

Neo-orthodox Protestant theology, which easily absorbed whatever social mood prevailed, set the tone for American religious social theory during the conservative 1940s and 1950s. Among Protestants, the ex-Trotskyist A. J. Muste plaintively protested Niebuhr's divorcing social ethics from the Kingdom of God, but refused to take up the neo-Marxian cudgel. He ended by equating radicalism and pacifism, sacrificing any residual leftism to a non-ideological project for world peace.[47] Paul Tillich's idiosyncratic theology left Marx in Germany, where, in 1933, he published *The Socialist Decision*. By emphasizing the Old Testament prophetic tradition, Tillich, like Rauschenbusch, sought a dialectical synthesis of matter and spirit. After

arriving in America, however, Tillich abandoned both prophecy and this un-finished project for the more obscure task of humanizing Christian theology.[48] Only intellectuals could read and understand these later works. His mystified Marxism had become just one of several anticipated spiritual awakenings. It was the type of inconsequential radicalism that even conserv-ative Christians could tolerate. The most popular Jewish thinker during this period was the Niebuhrian Will Herberg, whose "religious realism" and waxing conservative politics merely translated neo-orthodoxy into a Jewish idiom.[49] This was just fine with mainstream Catholics, who, in general, were even more critical of Christian socialism than Protestants. A series of anti-Marxian Papal pronouncements, beginning with Pope Leo's *Rerum Novarum* in 1891, had severely restricted leftist theorizing and activism among American Catholics, and thrown the Church's moral weight behind the popular, loosely defined cause of anti-communism.[50]

Widespread social and political unrest in the 1960s injected complacent theologians back into the aching ethical dilemmas of the earthly realm, if only to defend against the counterculture's anti-clerical offensive. Important encyclicals and pronouncements by Popes John XXIII and Paul VI, as well as the conciliatory Second Vatican Council meeting, acknowledged social injustice, even in capitalism, and encouraged Christian dialogue with the left. For the first time, the Church distinguished between different meanings of Marxism, some of which, Pope Paul VI admitted, were "more attractive to the modern mind" than others.[51] The Protestant World Council of Churches reinforced Vatican II by calling for a worldwide Christian initiative against social injustice and poverty, even if this meant assisting leftist social revolutionaries. Christian theologians in Europe (e.g., Karl Barth, Christoph Blumhardt, Dorothee Solle, Helmut Gollwitzer, Jurgen Moltmann, Rudolph Bultmann, Joseph Hromadka, and Jan Milic Lochman) rediscovered the left-ist implications of the Prophetic tradition and an immanent God; Christian Marxists (e,g., Roger Garaudy, Milan Machovec, Konrad Farner, and Pal-miro Togliatti), the Christ-like ethics attached to nonorthodox western Marxism. Theologians were once again awash in the kind of political tur-bulence that for almost three decades they had disregarded.

Cox

This spiritual renaissance arrived in America in the person of a Baptist iconoclast named Harvey Cox. Like Germany's Moltmann, Cox identified with the heretical and sectarian Christian tradition of Joachim Di Fiore and Thomas Muentzer. Orthodox and neo-orthodox Christianity believed that sinful individuals were redeemed after, not in, history. Cox, on the other hand, espoused a "heretical" Gnostic belief in the evilness of matter and the power of a believer's holy knowledge to transform evilness into justice. Whatever abolished evil, heretical or not, was therefore Godly. For mainstream Christians, Cox embodied the same heresy as Rauschenbusch:

he believed that sinful woman and man could perfect themselves and master the world. Since Christians, in Cox's view, could achieve the Kingdom of God on Earth, Cox's God, like Herron's, is "natural," working "in, with, and under the natural processes of history."[52]

God, in Cox's view, has historically unfolded in three epochs: that of the tribe, where people worshiped magic; in towns, where a metaphysical divinity ruled; and in the modern technopolis, where God appears in secular, technical logic. The secular city is thus divine. Cox became somewhat more mystical in later works, unveiling the political and religious functions of fantasy, myth, and utopia, but the substance of his theology always remained a secular emancipation from earthly oppression.[53] Secularization, which freed humanity from dogma and supernatural myths, was God working to free men and provide them a holy personality. Aspects of modernity that sociologists so casually condemned, such as urban anonymity and unbridled mobility, for Cox epitomized God's surprising means of preserving privacy and inhibiting idolatry. Profane man had found God here on earth. He was, in this sense, profoundly spiritual.

Here, the link with Marxism was forged. Cox believed the Church needed a "theology of politics" to tether humanity to the secular political process.[54] Its source, for Cox, was the ethical words of Jesus, particularly His Sermon on the Mount, which attached God's will to progressive, emancipatory secular movements and events of our time. The foremost of these, Marxism, represented our liberation from capitalist domination and manipulation into a nonalienated, classless, egalitarian, self-governing secular community. Since the logic of modern life generated these values anyway, democratic socialist revolution was divinely sanctioned, truly the Spirit of the Age. The dialectic of matter and spirit informed a radical theology as well as a spiritual, noneconomistic radicalism.

Liberation Theology

Cox's popularity in America, particularly in middle class, educated, predominantly white urban parishes, cultivated a relatively well-heeled Christian audience that needed ethical advice to help answer the difficult questions raised by the New Left. In the Third World, Latin America especially, a religious movement known as Liberation Theology was spreading rapidly among an urban and rural poor also thirsting for Christian answers to pressing social problems. It, however, was responding to the troubles of dependent nations, whose labor and resources were fueling foreign economic expansion. Hence, it was primarily—though by no means exclusively—a movement composed of indigenous, politically active Catholic priests, who redefined sin to embody social, economic, and political structures that violated one's Christian personhood. Marxism was their tool for explaining and destroying "structural sin," because it alone had synthesized the interrelated

processes of economic colonization, liberation, and revolutionary organization. Christian faith thus required acknowledging the possibility of social *and* spiritual emancipation, and acting *in* history, as revolutionary Christian socialists, to at least begin achieving salvation. This spiritual and political rebellion would take the form of self-governing neighborhood base communities ("Communidades ecclesiales de base," or CEBs) that organized and mobilized the poor to battle their class oppressors in God's name. In sum, predominantly Catholic, rural, and Third World-oriented, Liberation Theology was entirely unprepared to struggle in the U.S.A. Christian neo-Marxism in America desperately needed to expand beyond the small constituency served by Cox, but the potential of Liberation Theology to duplicate its Third World successes here in the U.S. was, in the late 1960s, still untapped.

But not for long. By the early 1970s, James H. Cone, joined soon thereafter by his colleague Cornell West, remodeled Liberation Theology along North American lines. Building on the traditions of Rauschenbusch and the SG, as well as on the blossoming black power project and its religious analogue, black theology, Cone translated the periphery's theology of emancipation into a familiar vernacular and style that could touch America's dispossessed masses.

At the center of America's Liberation Theology, predictably, was the by now familiar inclination of progressive Protestants toward the Old Testament's Prophetic tradition, the New Testament's ethical doctrines and especially Jesus's Sermon On the Mount, the notion of an imminent rather than transcendent God, and, finally, the commitment to bringing Christian ethics to bear on perfecting the Lebenswelt.

In Cone's hands, the incarnation symbolized God's recognition of human suffering and humiliation; and the resurrection, God's victory over such pain and bestowal of freedom upon the weak and helpless. The divine victory of Jesus thus epitomized a poor person's victory over poverty, an enslaved person's conquering of his master. The Kingdom of God, as Cone saw it, is for poor people, not the rich. Although its ultimate realization lies in the future, whenever God enters into a believer, through the message brought by Jesus, God's Kingdom emancipates her from human evil. Christians, therefore, "cannot waste time contemplating the next world" when faith in this world has such practical political consequences.[55] To be Christian means to fight for the oppressed. Christianity expedites spiritual and social freedom. It is a theology as well as a politics.

A Christian lifestyle, to Cone, was an empty vessel the divine contents of which depended on one's social and historical context. In the economically dependent Third World, Christians had to struggle to emancipate poor, landless, Catholic peasants. Their divine liquid, that is, the tenets of Third World Liberation Theology, was both pertinent and necessary, given the nature and context of their exploitation. On the other hand, exploitation in industrial-

ized, capitalist America is characterized by a unique blend of racial, sexual, and ethnic factors that profoundly condition the economic class struggle. American Liberation Theology therefore embodied a unity of diverse theologies, each drawn from the perspective of one set of victims. "There is not one Christian theology, but many Christian theologies which are valid expressions of the gospel of Jesus."[56] What united all Liberation Theologians was an unqualified solidarity with the victims of oppression, seeing in their emancipatory struggles God's eschatological plan to make us all one.

Cone and West, who are black, emphasized the racial components of American exploitation. They employed the victimization of blacks metaphorically, suggesting that Christians confess the universality of black suffering and catalyze America's struggle for social justice. From this perspective, black liberation symbolized God's Kingdom's being realized in America. At Cone's particular time and place in U.S. history, black power *was* Christianity. Theology had to be black because victims were black, and Christianity was God's defense of victims. Conversely, the white church had "maliciously contributed to the doctrine of white supremacy," and hence was "the enemy of Christ."[57] The sources of Cone's Liberation Theology thus included black American cultural traditions as well as scripture, because the former would mobilize blacks and the latter could justify the mobilization. To ignore the culture of suffering blacks, in Cone's view, was to ignore God's divine message of liberation. The political victory of blacks in their struggles for self-government and against bigotry would precipitate the victory of God's Kingdom on Earth. Of course, so would the victories of women, Asians, Chicanos, American Indians, and every other victimized group—each of which needed an emancipatory theology and praxis.

Through Christian faith people received a spiritual gift that could be realized only in the historical process of emancipation. But Christianity abjured the social analysis needed to enliven its eschatology. Without a pertinent social theory Christianity could not actualize in society what it confessed to in church. Although Cone at first flirted with black nationalism, he eventually followed West down a nonorthodox Marxian path to salvation. The dialectical tension of social context, scripture, and Church tradition was resolved, Cone finally concluded in 1977, only through revolutionary action that eliminated capitalist injustice. Marxian analysis, cleansed of economist dogmatism, explained poverty and victimization better than other theories, and also proffered a realistic emancipatory praxis through which faith could be concretized. With Marxism's help, Christianity, heretofore "the sigh of the oppressed," could become "a cry of revolution against the established order."[58] This rebellion, to Cone, was the meaning of Jesus's resurrection, not, as mainline Christianity had us believe, its negation. Moreover, rather than, as orthodoxy naively foresaw, eliminating religion, socialist revolution would sanctify God's Kingdom on Earth, liberating humanity's innate

potential to live in a Christian manner. Authentic Christianity thus inflamed both critique and rebellion, not passivity; and authentic Marxism both an internal critique of, and a call to action against, mainline Euro-American churches. The link between Christianity and Marxism was a theology of liberation that spiritually and politically empowered the victims of capitalist injustice. It taught believers to love humanity, but also to organize and protest—if possible, nonviolently—to emancipate the downtrodden. "The alliance of prophetic Christianity and progressive Marxism provides a last humane hope for humankind."[59]

Jewish Neo-Marxism

For over a century, then, progressive Christians in America have doggedly continued their intellectual flirtation with Marxism, even though it usually went unrequited. Unassimilated American Jews, on the other hand, had been chronic victims of discrimination and poverty throughout their history. Particularly the theologians among them had traditionally disavowed abstract intellectual syntheses of Judaism and Marxism in favor of radical political activism. Concentrated in New York City, the Eastern seaboard, and the industrial Mid-West, progressive Jews, beginning in the 1880s, established a variety of Yiddish language socialist journals, workers organizations, and unions, from which later emerged the leaders of the nonsectarian Amalgamated Clothing Workers and ILGWU. Many joined orthodox political parties, where they were gradually assimilated into America's radical secular culture. Others succeeded economically, and were, like Herberg, assimilated into America's mainstream liberal, Christian culture. These tendencies, on both ideological ends of the political spectrum, encouraging the collective suicide of religious American Jews gave birth to the only systematic attempts at synthesizing Marxism and Judaism. Unfortunately, they were, until recently, known only to some Yiddish language speakers and a small audience of knowledgeable radicals.

Jewish neo-Marxism in America, what little there was of it, grew from a tradition begun by Abe Cahan (later the conservative editor of the *Jewish Daily Forward*), whose column in the journal *Arbeter Tseltung* during the 1890s often explained socialism with quotations from the Talmud; and by Abraham Liessin, the editor of the orthodox *Di Tsukunft*, which during the 1910s supplemented standard Second International polemics with sensitive depictions of Jewish religion and literature. This emotional dedication to the survival of Jewish literature and, more specifically, the Yiddish vernacular—not the more abstract Christian project of synthesizing theology and materialism—always characterized the innovative theorizing of radical Jewish intellectuals such as Chaim Zhitlovsky, B. Rivkin, and Pesach Novick.

Zhitlovsky argued that orthodoxy lacked a spiritual component, which,

for Jews at least, Yiddish literary culture could supply. The socialist project, he concluded, could coexist with the Jewish search through Yiddish literary classics for its own identity.[60] Rivkin, in his seminal *Di Grunt Tendentsin fun Yiddishe Literatur* (1948),[61] argued that diaspora Jews found psychological refuge in the Yiddish language and the culture of Yiddishkayt. The literature of great Yiddish authors thus embodied and communicated a quasi-religious sense of alienation unique to Jews. Jewish radicalism, in America and elsewhere, was therefore bound to a distinctively nonrational Jewish impulse, and was not reduceable to the universal laws of histmat. Although socialism was necessary as the form of society's evolution, for Jews, Judaism—including its linguistic and cultural heritage—was revolutionary socialism's content. Among Yiddish speaking Americans, Rivkin altered the way Yiddish literature and Jewish radicalism could be understood. For others on the left, his work established Jewish religious and literary values as an irreducible element of Jewish working class culture. The socialist transformation that progressive American Jews supported would, to Rivkin, generate a pluralist proletarian folk culture where Yiddish literature and language would fluorish.

This message was adopted by the iconoclastic Novick, who, after 1939, was the most important spokesman for the orthodox position within the Jewish-American community.[62] In the CP as well as in the Yiddish language newspaper *Morgen Freiheit* and its cultural counterpart, Yiddishe Kultur Farband, Novick consistently stressed the anti-assimilationist character of Jewish radicalism, its irreducibility to universal economic forces. On issues relevant to Jews, Novick openly defied the CP and became, with his espousal of the uniqueness of Yiddishkayt, something of a heretic in orthodox circles.

The force of all these progressive Christian and Jewish ideas, combined with the radical activism of New Left theologians like Daniel Berrigan, finally persuaded well-known secular leftists into legitimizing the religious dimension of socialist revolution. Herbert Marcuse and other New Leftists, in the 1960s, belatedly entertained the possibility that religion might be both necessary and progressive, and in any case was not the unmitigated evil that orthodoxy feared. Then, in the 1970s and 1980s, popular secular leftists like Paul Breines, Russell Berman, William A. Williams, Christopher Lasch, and many others publicly professed that religious values in America were ubiquitous; that they often shaped attitudes and behavior; and, potentially, that they could salvage a revolutionary spirit that strives for socialist perfection on earth.[63] The critical value of a consensual, communitarian, selfless faith, which for over a century radical theologians in America had waved frantically at the secular left, has apparently been rediscovered by Marx's nonorthodox disciples. All of which may well constitute a prolegomenon to revised secular Marxian theorizing on religion.

Conclusion

Liberalism, with its formal-legal view of freedom, evoked a flood of so-cial groups each of which catered to one shared interest. The social and political haggling of these legally sanctioned interests over the distribution of desired resources comprised, for liberals, the essence of democratic self-government. Orthodox Marxism exposed the vulgarized content of pluralist structures. The procedural give and take of proliferating groups, it argued, occluded the substantive hegemony of wealthy capitalists. Orthodoxy's answer was to restrict social organization to the only groups that counted: classes. Once workers owned to the causal priority of class membership in determining the overall quality of social life, they would recognize pluralism for the ruse that it was, and quickly forsake noneconomic allegian-ces. In short, orthodoxy bet everything on a generic, irreducible, unmediated collectivity of workers; liberalism put its chips on a gaggle of legally protected, ego-centered, immediate crusades, and the fractious interest groups that would emerge therefrom.

In this chapter we have seen that healthy, empowered Americans have a differentiated set of social attachments that includes, but is not confined to, class. Without them, they would feel deprived of the dignity that has always attached to a prideful, nonself-conscious bond to one's own gender, race, and religion. Particularly in liberal America, with its pluralist tradition and heretofore ineradicable bigotries, these noneconomic commitments carry such heavy psychological and social baggage that sensible politicians would find them impossible to drop. On the other hand, the socially defined mean-ings of race, gender, and religion are infused with the material interests of society's opinion shapers. By naively adopting capitalism's anti-materialist agenda, working class women, blacks, and believers swallow whole a dena-tured self-image, deceitfully torn from its economic origins and consequen-ces. Authentic noneconomic attachments must be mediated through the prism of class, which deconstructs myth into its rational components. Authentic class consciousness, however, must also be mediated by sig-nificant noneconomic attachments, including those rooted in gender, race, and religion. Proletarian material interests may overlap, but workers' race, sex, and religions often do not—and these play vital roles in structuring everyday life. Orthodoxy's "either/or" framework is detached from the real world. It is as mystifying as pluralism. Workers, of course, have both material *and* nonmaterial interests. Leftists need to coordinate, not obliterate, these two aspects of working class culture. By demythologizing and then strengthening the mediations linking class and everyday behavior, an organic working class congeals from the bottom up, each member tempered by consensual loyalties that nourish a blossoming collective con-sciousness. This, not some undifferentiated medley of pliant bureaucrats, is the source of socialist democracy.

Lasch

The Freudian Christopher Lasch has written insightfully on these matters. He accepted Marx's critique of capitalism as an exploiting, alienating, and dehumanizing mode of production that would, if unchecked, spread its misery everywhere in order to maximize accumulation.[64] He also favored socialism, a system where humans can fully develop their potentials. Lasch's dilemma hinged on the depletion, in capitalism, of institutions to mediate individual action and the organic, consensual collectivism socialism depends on. Marxism's failure in America, in Lasch's view, was due this erosion of noneconomic attachments, particularly the nuclear family, which has left us emotionally naked and ill-prepared to live normal lives.

To Lasch, the family is our "last refuge of love and decency" in capitalist America, a "haven in a heartless world." As the locus of a child's emotional sustenance, it is the crucial link between social conditions and maturing individual perceptions, the means by which we develop predispositions to act in certain ways later in life. In a normal family, children internalize parental authority and guilt and thereby become well adjusted, properly sublimated personalities. Although, paradoxically, it was a product of early capitalism, today the family is being subverted by modern bourgeois values: rising divorce rates, falling birthrates, uncertain gender roles, and libertinism. Consequently, it has become depersonalized. Therapeutic experts have taken over parental functions, state agencies play growing roles in supervising and teaching children, written manuals govern sexual behavior and our children's emotional development, and busy parents sacrifice discipline for instant gratification and convenience. The human product of such a vulgarized family is "uncertain of its outlines, longing either to remake the world in its own image or to merge into its environment in blissful union."[65] The narcissistic bourgeois personality seeks its own aggrandizement, lives only in the present, and "does its own thing" in utter disregard of social rules or others' feelings.

Lasch's view of a healthy personality, what he called the "ego ideal," was based on acknowledging the tension and contradiction between us and the world, and then developing our potentials through excellence in practical activities. Social change had to be built on this firm conception of selfhood. But the only way out of the impasse of narcissism is the creation of social objects that restore our connection to others and fulfill us as individuals. Lasch thus concluded that the transition to socialism awaited the renaissance of the family, but also of religion, nonexploitative gender and racial stereotypes, decentralized decision-making, and the liberal values of "self-reliance, sexual self-discipline, ambition, acquisition, and accomplishment."[66] Feminist neo-Marxists like Jean Bethke Elshtain and Carol C. Gould have convincingly reiterated the importance of nonsexist nuclear families for propagating well adjusted children and promulgating democratic socialism.[67] They also observed what orthodoxy had known for

years, that no movement or party—feminist, Marxist, or whatever—could ever succeed politically in America on an anti-family platform. Politics aside, however, children raised in these fertile conditions will be capable and strong, a proletarian army committed to personal fulfillment in an egalitarian, decentralized, noncollectivist socialism. In brief, by demystifying and then cultivating intermediate social attachments a unique American socialism will grow. Lasch crystallized this chapter's central message: pluralism, perceived dialectically, is an invaluable tool for progressive change.

Notes

1. Friedrich Engels, *The Origin of The Family, Private Property, and the State* (New York: International, 1942 ed.), p. 120.
2. See Mari Jo Buhle, *Women and American Socialism* (Urbana, IL.: University of Illinois Press, 1981), esp. pp. 246–87; Joan Landes, "Feminism and the Internationals," *Telos*, 49 (Fall 1981), pp. 117–26; Lise Vogel, "Questions on the Women Question," *Monthly Review*, 31, 2 (June 1979), pp. 39–59; Vida D. Scudder, "Woman and Socialism," *Yale Review*, III, 3 (April 1914), p. 459; Sally M. Miller, "Women in the Party Bureaucracy," in Miller (ed.), *Flawed Liberation: Socialism and Feminism* (Westport, CT: Greenwood, 1981), pp. 13–35; and M. Jane Slaughter, "Feminism and Socialism," *Marxist Perspectives*, 2 (Fall 1979), pp. 32–36.
3. Mary Inman, *In Woman's Defense* (Los Angeles: The Committee to Organize the Advancement of Women, 1940) and *Thirteen Years of CPUSA Misleadership on the Woman Question* (Los Angeles: The Committee to Organize the Advancement of Women, 1948).
4. Shulamith Firestone, *The Dialectic of Sex* (New York: Bantam, 1970), pp. 1–12.
5. *Ibid.*, p. 34. See also pp. 206ff.
6. See the relevant work of Batya Weinbaum, Mary Daly, Susan Griffin, Andrea Dworkin, Susan Brownmiller, and Monique Wittig.
7. Mari Jo Buhle, *Women and the American Left A Guide to Sources* (Boston: Hall, 1983), pp. 205–26, includes a bibliography of orthodox studies of feminism.
8. Sally Miller, "The Socialist Party and the Negro, 1901–1920," *Journal of Negro History*, 56, 3 (July 1971), pp. 220–29; Ira Kipnis, *The American Socialist Movement, 1898–1912* (Westport, CT: Greenwood, 1968), pp. 130–33; Philip S. Foner and James S. Allen (eds.), *American Communism and Black Americans* (Philadelphia: Temple University Press, 1987), pp. 94–103; David Shannon, *The Socialist Party of America* (New York: Macmillan, 1955), pp. 51ff.
9. See James Weinstein, *The Decline of Socialism in America* (New York: Vintage, 1967), pp. 63–74; and Wilson Record, *The American Negro and the CP* (New York: Atheneum, 1951), p. 100.
10. In *Lenin on the United States: Selected Writings* (New York : International, 1970),

pp. 123–31. See also *The Communist Party and the Question of a Negro Soviet in Soviet America* (New York: Workers Library, June 1935), for the CPUSA interpretation of Comintern policy.

11. I.e., Oliver Cromwell Cox, James A. Geschwender, Michael Reich, Edna Bonacich, Robert Allen, Lloyd Hogan, Earl Ofari, James Forman, Mark Smith, Angela Davis, and James Boggs. A partial bibliography is in James Geschewender, *Racial Stratification in America* (Dubuque: Brown, 1978), pp. 80–105.

12. Record, *The American Negro and the CP*, p. 307.

13. See Philip S. Foner (ed.), *Black Socialist Preacher* (San Francisco: Synthesis, 1983), esp. pp. 1–2.

14. Founders incuded Cyril Briggs (Nevis Island), Richard D. Moore (Barbados), W. A. Domingo (Jamaica), and the Americans Otto Hall, Harry Haywood, Edward Doty, Grace Campbell, H. V. Phillips, Gordon Owens, Alonzo Isabel, and Lovett Fort Whiteman. At one time it had a membership of 2,500, including some black militant coal miners in West Virginia.

15. See especially Dubois, *Dusk of Dawn* (New York: Schocken, 1968), p. 205; and "Marxism and the Negro Problem," in Henri Moon (ed.), *The Emerging Thought of W. E. B. Dubois* (New York: Simon & Schuster, 1972), pp. 287–93.

16. Herbert Aptheker (ed.), *The Correspondence of W. E. B. Dubois, 1877–1934* (3 vols.; Amherst, MA: University of Mass. Press, 1973), I, p. 443.

17. Dubois, "The Talented Tenth," in Julius Lester (ed.), *The Seventh Son* (New York: Vintage, 1971), I, p. 385. See also "Pan-Africa and New Racial Philosophy," in Moon (ed.), pp. 240–43.

18. Dubois, "Segregation," in Virginia Hamilton (ed.) *The Writings of W. E. B. Dubois* (New York: Crowell, 1975), p. 151. See also "Immediate Program of the American Negro," *ibid.*, pp. 119–26.

19. Dubois, *Dusk of Dawn*, p. 138.

20. The reversal came after 1940. See *Correspondence*, III, pp. 131–32; *Dusk of Dawn*, p. 208; and *Autobiography of W. E. B. Dubois* (New York: International, 1968), pp. 236–37.

21. See Dubois, *The World and Africa* (New York: International, 1965, originally pub. in 1947), pp. 16–24; and "Pan-Africa and the New Racial Philosophy," in Moon (ed.), pp. 240–43.

22. See C. L. R. James, "Discussions with Trotsky," in James, *At the Rendezvous of Victory—Selected Writings* (London: Allison & Busby, 1984), pp. 33–64; and "The Revolutionary Answer to the Negro Problem in the USA," in James, *The Future in the Present* (Westport, CT: Lawrence Hall, 1977), pp. 119–27.

23. See especially Richard Wright, *Black Power* (New York: Harper, 1954), p. xiii, and *White Man Listen!* (Garden City, NY: Doubleday, 1957), pp. 44–45.

24. Wright, *Native Son* (New York: Harper & Row, 1986 ed.), p. 361.

25. Wright, "Blueprint for Negro Writing," *New Challenge* (Fall 1937), p. 54.

26. Wright, *The Outsider* (New York: Harper, 1965), pp. 118–19; *White Man Listen!*, pp. 34–35; "The Voiceless Ones," *Saturday Review*, 16 (April 1960), p. 72. The quote is in *The Outsider*, p. 129.

27. Wright, "Blueprint for Negro Writing," *New Challenge*, p. 61; *The Outsider*, p. 354.

28. The BPP's Ten Point Program is in Philip S. Foner (ed.), *The Black Panthers Speak* (New York: Lippincott, 1970), pp. 2–4.
29. Manning Marable, *How Capitalism Underdeveloped Black America* (Boston: South End Press, 1983), p. 2. See also *Blackwater* (Dayton, Ohio: Black Praxis Press, 1981), pp. 53–68.
30. See Marable, *Blackwater*, pp. 76, 173; and *From the Grassroots* (Boston: South End, 1980), p. 17.
31. Marable, *Blackwater*, pp. 31, 116–19, 162ff; *Race Reform and Rebellion* (Jackson, MS: University Press of Mississippi, 1984), pp. 169–72; *How Capitalism Underdeveloped Black America*, pp. 136–215; and *From the Grassroots*, p. 31.
32. Marable, *Blackwater*, p. 143. See also *How Capitalism Underdeveloped Black America*, pp. 257–58; and *From the Grassroots*, p. 31.
33. E.g., ERA, gay and lesbian rights, abortion reform, restrictions on plant closings, affirmative action, full employment legislation, job training, health care, peace, denuclearization, capital investment. See *How Capitalism Underdeveloped Black America*, pp. 256–59, and *Blackwater*, pp. 182–84.
34. Marx, *Contribution to the Critique of Hegel's Philosophy of Right*, in *Karl Marx—Early Writings* (New York: Vintage, 1974), p. 244. Interestingly, the next sentence reads "It is the opium of the people."
35. Marx, *Critique of the Gotha Program* (Moscow: Progress, 1971), p. 29.
36. Marx, *Capital*, I, p. 79.
37. See the relevant work of Bloch, Benjamin, Adorno, Horkheimer, Mounier, and Garaudy.
38. Rev. Franklin Mason North, in Charles H. Hopkins, *The Rise of the Social Gospel in American Protestantism, 1865–1915* (New Haven: Yale University Press, 1940), p. 172.
39. See George Davis Herron, *Social Meanings of Religious Experiences* (New York: Johnson Reprint Corp., 1968; orig. 1896), pp. 170–73 and *The Christian Society* (New York: Johnson Reprint Corp, 1969; orig. 1894), esp. pp. 104–29.
40. Walter Rauschenbusch, *Christianity and the Social Crisis* (New York: Macmillan, 1918), pp. 229–63; *The Righteousness of the Kingdom* (New York: Abingdon, 1968), p. 217; and *The Social Principles of Jesus* (New York: Association Press, 1916), pp. 125 and 162.
41. Rauschenbusch, *A Theology For the Social Gospel* (New York: Macmillan, 1917), p. 87.
42. Rauschenbusch, *Righteousness of the Kingdom*, pp. 114–150.
43. Reinhold Niebuhr, *The Nature and Destiny of Man* (New York: Scribner's, 1949), p. 262; *Faith and History* (New York: Scribner's, 1949), p. 67; *Moral Man and Immoral Society* (New York: Scribner's, 1932), pp. 257–66.
44. Niebuhr, *Christianity and Power Politics* (New York: Scribner's, 1940), p. 194.
45. Niebuhr, *Moral Man*, p. 277.
46. Niebuhr, *Christian Realism and Political Problems*, p. 50. See also *ibid.* pp. 50–72. The change, in the 1940s, can be traced in *Christianity and Power Politics* (1940) and *Children of Light* (1944). See also "The Religion of Communism," *Atlantic Monthly*, CXCVII (April 1931), pp. 462–70, and "Can We Avoid Catastrophe?" *Christian Century*, LXV, 21 (26 May, 1948), p. 504.
47. See Nat Hentoff (ed.), *The Essays of A. J. Muste* (New York: Bobbs-Merrill, 1967), esp. pp. 207–14, 283–95, 302–21, and 422–49; and Nat Hentoff, *Peace*

Agitator—The Story of A. J. Muste (New York: Macmillan, 1963). This contains many of Muste's letters that are not included in the edited volume.

48. Paul Tillich, *The Socialist Decision* (New York: Harper & Row, 1977; orig. 1933). Although, many years later, Tillich declared that, of all his works, he was proudest of *The Socialist Decision* (*ibid.*, p. xxv), he nevertheless ignored the topic in favor of more abstract theological and ontological themes.

49. See Will Herberg, *Judaism and Modern Man* (New York: Harper & Row, 1951) and *Faith Enacted as History* (Philadelphia: Westminster Press, 1976). The quote is in *Judaism and Modern Man*, p. 155.

50. See Arthur F. McGovern, *Marxism: An American Christian Perspective* (Maryknoll, NY: Orbis, 1980), pp. 93–105; and Marc Karson, "Catholic Anti-Socialism," in John H. M. Laslett and Seymour Martin Lipset (eds.), *Failure of a Dream?* (Berkeley, CA: University of California Press, rev. ed. 1984), pp. 82–102.

51. Pope Paul VI, "Octogesima Adveniens" (14 May 1971), in McGovern, p. 118. This was an apostolic letter, not an encyclical.

52. Harvey Cox, "Technology, Modern Man, and the Gospel," *Christianity Today*, XII (5 July 1968), p. 4.

53. Cox, *Secular City* (New York: Macmillan, 1965), pp. 6ff. and 98ff. The mystical later works included *Feast of Fools* (New York: Harper & Row, 1969) and *Seduction of the Spirit* (New York: Simon & Schuster, 1978).

54. Cox, *Secular City*, p. 108.

55. James Cone, *Black Theology and Black Power* (New York: Seabury, 1969), p. 125.

56. Cone, *Speaking The Truth* (Grand Rapids, MI: Eerdman, 1986), p. 8.

57. Cone, *Black Theology and Black Power*, p. 73.

58. Cone, *God of the Oppressed* (New York: Seabury, 1975), p. 160.

59. Cornel West, *Prophesy Deliverance!* (Philadelphia: Westminster, 1982), p. 95.

60. Chaim Zhitlovsky, *Fredrikh Nitshe and Zayn Filosofer Antviklung-Gang* (New York: n.a., 1920). Secondary sources include Itche Goldberg, "Di Shturmfeugel fun Yidish Kultur-Renasans (Chaim Zhitlovsky)," *Essayen* (New York: n.a., 1981), and Buhle, *Marxism in the USA* (London: Verso, 1986), p. 110.

61. B. Rivkin, *Di Grunt Tendentsin fun Yiddishe Literatur* (New York: Yiddishe Kultur Farband, 1948). A complete bibliography, and a biographical essay, is in my *Biographical Dictionary of Neo-Marxism*, pp. 358–59.

62. Pesach Novick, *The National and Jewish Question in the Light of Reality* (New York: Morgen Freiheit, 1971). A complete bibliography and a bibliographical essay is in my *Biographical Dictionary of Neo-Marxism*, p. 327.

63. See "Symposium on Religion and Politics," *Telos*, 58 (Winter 1983–84), pp. 115–57; Paul Breines, "Germans, Journals, and Jews/Madison, Men, Marxism and Mosse: A Tale of Jewish-Leftist Identity Confusion in America," *New German Critique*, 20 (Spring-Summer 1980), p. 103;

64. Christopher Lasch, *The Agony of the American Left* (New York: Knopf, 1969), pp. 8, n.5, 27–31, and 200–1; and *Haven in a Heartless World* (New York: Basic, 1977), pp. 7–8.

65. Lasch, *The Minimal Self* (New York: Norton, 1984), p. 19.

66. Lasch, *The Agony of the American Left*, p. 209.

67. See Elshtain, *Public Man, Private Woman* (Princeton: Princeton University Press,

1981), p. 332, and "Family Reconstruction," *Commonweal*, 1 (August 1980), p. 341; and Carol C. Gould, "Private Rights and Public Virtues," in Gould (ed.), *Beyond Domination* (Totowa, N.J.: Rowman & Allanheld, 1984), pp. 20–30. Lasch, in *The Minimal Self*, p. 253, finally acknowledged the need to progressively restructure gender stereotyping. Emancipated women are also better parents.

6

Conclusion: The Rude Awakening

Writing in 1965, Talcott Parsons, in a paper delivered at a plenary session of the American Sociological Association's annual meeting, dismissed Karl Marx as a social thinker "whose work fell entirely within the nineteenth century ... he belongs to a phase of development which has been superceded .... [His] predictions about the course of the socio-economic system have been deeply invalidated by the course of events in most advanced industrial societies .... [J]udging by the standards of the best contemporary social science ... Marxian theory is obsolete." Parsons went on to argue that Marxism was elitist, inflexible, and oblivious to "elements of what may be called pluralization." It had also mistakenly hypothesized the progressive homogenization of workers, ignored the state's role in improving living standards, and eliminated "ideal and normative factors" from its sterile social science.[1]

An anachronism when it was written, and even more so today, Parson's critique nevertheless accurately mirrors the kind of mob psychology that has always characterized American anti-Marxism. What it comes down to, from this distorted view, is a fundamental conflict between two bodies of principle—one good, the other evil; one individualist, the other collectivist; one American, the other un-American. Had it not appeared in America on its own, orthodoxy probably would have been invented by some enterprising politician. It is the ideal ploy for ambitious, patriotic liberals, the antithesis of everything America cherishes, a worthy recipient of Parsons's scathing attack. It is also the antiquated relic of a failed history that even leftists in America are eagerly abandoning. Like cheap gravy that conceals a food's genuine flavor, orthodox Marxism annihilates the specificity of American life, forcibly redefining its every activity as part of the proletariat's impersonal march through history. Subjectivity, politics, science, gender, race, religion, and family—the flesh of everyday life in America—are reduced to class and then pulverized beyond recognition by Party leaders hoping to purify a sottish population. It was as if, by fiat or perhaps through a few

169

decades of Marxian political education, orthodoxy believed it could eradicate an entire culture.

Both liberals and critical Marxists knew this, and joined the anti-orthodox bandwagon. On this ride, however, passengers such as Parsons didn't subtly differentiate orthodox and nonorthodox versions of Marxism. Parsons's critique of orthodoxy, a bit shopworn but certainly accurate, disregarded entirely the reality of nonorthodox left theorizing in America. The latter, we have now seen, unpacked the notion of class into its economic, social, political, and cultural components. A worker is not merely a worker, but also a member of a family, sex, race, religion, ethnic group, neighborhood, government, culture, nation, world-system, and generation. Everyday working class attitudes are part of this coherent totality, one important but not all-determining aspect of which is the work people do.

The distinct, complementary streams of neo-Marxian theorizing have infiltrated America's Lebenswelt by flowing into its major features: a rock-bottom sense of individualism, a faith in political activism, a commitment to empirical science, and a tolerance of deep, powerful noneconomic associations. Mass culture, which historical materialists could neither fathom nor tolerate, became for neo-Marxists a vehicle for progressive change, the body through which Marx's radical spirit would materialize. By acknowledging what orthodoxy wouldn't, that is, the dynamic linkages between base and superstructure, and then reformulating radical theory in response to America's hegemonic liberalism, neo-Marxism evoked what for liberals was the frightening spector of a homegrown, popular brand of socialism. Neither liberal nor orthodox, this indigenous Marxism became an outcast in America, unconditionally ignored by liberals like Parsons and censured by the mainstream left.

Of course, these anti-leftist subjective considerations were, until recently, buttressed by objective factors as well. These included the post-World War II fragmentation of workers into private houses, private automobiles, and isolated forms of suburban social life; the displacement of class antagonism into consumption and depoliticized wage demands; the relative decline of America's industrial working class compared to service and administrative sectors; the withering of industrial unions; and a steady economic growth that allowed average workers to achieve middle class affluence. Under these optimal conditions, only a few intellectuals and discontented fringe groups took Marxism very seriously. The combination of a flourishing economy and a naive but widespread commitment to bourgeois values turned America's middle class fantasies into reality, and also immobilized socialists. In general, workers were satisfied, and politicians held an undifferentiated left captive to America's raging anti-communism.

Persuasive evidence now exists that these objective conditions have changed, perhaps permanently.[2] In the past 25 years the bulk of America's wealth and income has been squeezed into ever fewer hands. The top 1/2 of

1 percent of American families, the so-called "super rich," now own 44 percent of America's wealth and business assets (up from 31 percent in 1963), and average $8.8 million of wealth per household (up 147 percent from 1963). Individuals in this elite category own almost 40 percent of America's net wealth (up from 25 percent in 1963). The top 10 percent of Americans own 72 percent of America's net wealth (up from 65 percent in 1963). The bottom 61 percent of Americans own 7 percent of net wealth; the bottom 45 percent, less than 2 percent.

The polarization is equally noticeable with regard to income. In 1968, the poorest 20 percent of American families received 7.4 percent of the total income for all families, and the richest 20 percent received 33.8 percent. In 1987, the figures were 4.6 percent and 43.7 percent. The richest 20 percent in America have more than nine times the income of the poorest 20 percent, and it is anticipated that the disparity will soon stretch further. In 1984, over 48 percent of new jobs paid less than $10,000 a year (up from 23 percent in 1963, with salaries calculated in 1984 dollars). On the other hand, jobs paying over $45,000 have grown by less than 5 percent since 1963. Compensation in the auto industry, for example, rose 32.5 pecent for workers during the 1980–85 period, while compensation for executive officers rose 246 percent. From 1979 to 1984, the family income of craft, clerical, and service workers fell relative to the median income of all families. During the same period, however, the median incomes of executives and managers rose over 12 percent. Since 1973, real wages, that is, income per employed person rather than income per capita, has declined for the first time since World War II, to the point where the bottom 5/6 of the income distribution not only fares worse in relation to the top 1/6 but has seen their net income in adjusted dollars actually fall.

As multi-national corporations search the Third World for the most profitable home, many types of manufacturing jobs that had propelled people into higher income brackets have, more often than not, been replaced by minimum-wage, low security jobs in the service sector. A high percentage of the new jobs created during the past eight years fit into this category. During the first half of this period, of the 5.1 million workers displaced from manufacturing jobs they had held for at least three years, 3.1 million—about 61 percent—had found work by 1984. 1.3 million were searching for jobs, and 700,000 had quit the labor force. About half the reemployed workers earned as much as their previous jobs. Pay cuts for the rest often were as high as 20 percent. Minorities, mostly blacks and hispanics, suffered the most. The percentage of part-time jobs, with low salaries and few benefits, steadily grows, so that, by 1988, 2 to 3 percent of the labor force wanted full-time work but settled for part-time. If one also includes people who work part-time voluntarily, the self-employed, and employees of temporary employment agencies that provide janitorial, secretarial, and other business services, the number of such underpaid and noninsured workers reaches 35

million, a 20 percent increase since 1980. By comparison, the nation's entire work force of 113 million men and women has grown only 10 percent in this decade. The costs to employers of these part-timers are only a fraction of what they would otherwise be. Moreover, if there were a labor scarcity, these people could be moved into full-time jobs as an alternative to raising wages.

The number of families living below the official poverty line has jumped by 36 percent since 1970. One million households entered the ranks of the poor during the 1970s, and another million in barely half that time in the 1980s. In 1988, almost 15 percent of Americans—32.5 million people (up from 24.7 million in 1977)—lived below the poverty line, 69 percent of whom were white (up 3 percent since 1979). The proportion of black Americans living in poverty was 33.1 percent, and 28.2 percent of Hispanic Americans were also classified as poor. Many millions more could barely make ends meet, despite incomes that exceeded the official minimum standards of impoverishment. Children under 18 constituted almost 40 percent of all those in poverty. In 1986, almost one quarter of America's children under six years old lived in poverty. In New York City, a shocking 40 percent. And the poor are getting progressively poorer. Adjusted for inflation, the amount by which the incomes of the poor fell below the poverty line rose to $49.2 billion in 1986, from $39.5 billion in 1980.

At stake here is the glue that fastens millions of working Americans to their economic system: the promise of smooth access to middle class lifestyles and incomes. "Middle class" is usually defined as households with incomes between $15,000 and $35,000. 1985 census figures indicate that their numbers shrank to 39 percent of America's families, down from 46 percent in 1970. During the same period the percentage of families earning over $50,000 rose from 13 percent to 18.3 percent. In short, as the gap separating rich and poor widens, a steadily shrinking proportion of Americans can now be classified as middle class.

To average workers, the material and psychological costs are potentially devastating. For the first time in post-World War II history, most men who became 40 in 1973 saw their earnings decline by an average of 14 percent by the time they reached 50. Middle class children, as individual wage earners, are now unlikely to reach the adjusted salary levels of their parents. A young man, for example, who left home in 1973 is now earning about 20 percent less than his father earned in the early 1970s. When the young man's father had left his home in the early 1950s, he could expect to earn 15 percent more than his father. Two income families are laborers' only sure ticket into the middle class. Yet in 1984, even with the enormous increase of such families (over 2/3 of young families now rely on two earners), median family income was below $26,400, down from $28,200 (in 1984 dollars) for mostly one income families in 1973. As "acceptable" rates of unemployment steadily rise and long-term solutions to inflation remain illusory, the trademark optimism

that has always attached to ambitious American workers has been replaced by anxiety. The vanishing middle class has cast a giant shadow on America's future.

When dreamers are rudely awakened they often are angry, disoriented, and vulnerable. America's blue and white-collar workers are now experiencing the end of an economic dream in which raised income, wealth, and status were routinely granted to those who worked hard and went along. As their painfully real economic situation worsens, workers must begin questioning the unquestioned in order to rationally reformulate new survival strategies.

The system they live in has its own survival mechanisms, which dampen dissent and disingenuously refocus attention away from economic hardships. Intensifying competition among a growing number of people for a dwindling number of good jobs, for example, breeds an impulse to eliminate marketplace rivals. Among white males, now a vulnerable majority in the work force, racist and sexist sentiments—which in better times would be considered disgraceful—provide a safety-valve for festering anxieties. Lacking more rational alternatives to what for many is a desperate situation, scapegoats emerge to explain the plague of financial disasters that infects entrepreneurs and farmers across the entire country. There is, of course, a plentiful supply of candidates: Jews, Catholics, communists, unions, foreigners, politicians, etc. Intensifying unemployment and powerlessness increase the likelihood of jingoism and Ramboesque foreign military adventures to restore lost national pride. A confidence-shaking pessimism born of personal failure serves to renew many frightened victims' faith in traditional hierarchical values and institutions. The implicit message here is that society is not deficient, we just expect too much. The personal contentment gained from upholding conventional power structures will more than outweigh our economic heartaches.

Liberal government will normally reinforce only those alienated social attitudes (e.g., tradition, hierarchy, jingoism) the support for which will not threaten its legitimacy. However, in times of severe economic crisis even the most obnoxious phenomena (e.g., racism, sexism, anti-Semitism, etc.) are indirectly aided by the government's unwillingness to deliver appropriate legislative remedies. Arguments that typically rationalize such inaction emphasize states rights, budgetary shackles, the sanctity of competition, and judicial restraint. Officials abstractly justify their position, setting the nation's intellectual agenda. Concretely, however, this discussion, vulgarized by the mass media, effectively rationalizes the irrational inclinations of an economically ravaged population. The very same ones that have already been over-inflated by a popular culture machine that pumps whatever base fantasy it can cash in on.

These subjective and objective conditions are the backdrop for the gelling Yankee radicalism we have been tracing. By demystifying both the cultural and economic aspects of America, it alone accurately reflects the dialectical

quality of everyday life. Orthodoxy fruitlessly tried to twist America into an economistic framework. Liberalism distorted the inner linkages between economics, politics, and culture. Only nonorthodox Marxism therapeutically massages capitalist America, neither pulverizing nor neglecting an increasingly distressed liberal population.

In the short term, it strenuously fights the bigotry that many Americans confuse with freedom, and supports progressive economic and political reforms sponsored by others. Equally important, however, is its long-term cultural struggle. Engaged scientists, artists, theologians, labor leaders, professors, intellectuals, philosophers, local community leaders, black and feminist activists, as well as factory workers labor to develop a full-blown socialist cultural alternative that can effectively explain reality, solve its major problems, and compete with liberalism for citizen support. Its inherent eccentricity contrasts starkly with the hierarchical, centralized old left. But this is a grassroots movement that cultivates each region and interest separately, and molds to indigenous traditions. Its incremental successes—economic, political, social, cultural—break down barriers that have hindered human cooperation. Eventually, a mobilized working class may coalesce, united under shared material interests and fractured into cohesive, self-governing associations. During this process, neo-Marxism's splintered worldview, its infancy in twentieth century America, will have matured and born a more organic dialectical vision.

Notes

1. The paper was published in Talcott Parsons, *Sociological Theory and Modern Society* (New York: Free Press, 1967). The quotes are on pp. 135, 109–10, 132, 113, 123. For a similar point of view, see Clinton Rossiter, *Marxism: The View From America* (New York: Harcourt, Brace, & World, 1960), pp. 7–8.
2. See especially "The Concentration of Wealth in the United States—Trends in the Distribution of Wealth Among American Families," published by the Joint Economic Committee, United States Congress, July 1986; and "Living in Poverty," a report published by the United States Census Bureau, 31 August 1988. Of related interest, see also Ravi Batra, *The Great Depression of 1990* (New York: Simon and Schuster, 1987); Frank Levy, *Dollars and Dreams: The Changing American Income Distribution* (New York: Basic Books, 1988) and "The Vanishing Middle Class and Related Issues: A Review of Living Standards in the 1970s and 1980s," *PS*, XX, 3 (Summer 1987), pp. 650–55; and Barbara Ehrenreich, "Is the Middle Class Doomed?" *New York Times Magazine* (7 September 1986), pp. 44–64.

Bibliography

Abbott, S.J., Walter M. (ed.). *The Documents of Vatican II*. New York: America Press, 1966.

Amin, Samir. *Unequal Development*. New York: Monthly Review, 1976.

Aptheker, Herbert (ed.). *Marxism and Christianity*. New York: Humanities, 1968.

___(ed.). *The Correspondence of W. E. B. Dubois, 1877–1934*. Amherst, MA: University of Massachusettts, 1973.

Baran, Paul A. *The Political Economy of Growth*. New York: Monthly Review, 1957.

___ and Sweezy, Paul. *Monopoly Capitalism*. New York: Monthly Review, 1966.

Batra, Ravi. *The Great Depression of 1990*. New York: Simon & Schuster, 1987.

Berger, Victor. *Berger's Broadsides*. Milwaukee: Social Democratic Pubs., 1912.

Block, Fred. "The Ruling Class Does Not Rule," *Socialist Revolution*, 7, 3 (1977), pp. 6–28.

___. "Marxist Theories of the State in World System Analysis," *Social Change in the Capitalist World Economy*. Barbara Hockey Kaplan (ed.). Beverly Hills: Sage, 1978, pp. 27–37.

___. "Beyond Relative Autonomy," *Socialist Register, 1980*. R. Miliband and J.Saville (eds.). London: Merlin, 1980, p. 24

Bohn, William E. "Reformer and Revolutionist," *International Socialist Review*, X (September, 1909), pp. 204–9.

Boudin, Louis B. *The Theoretical System of Karl Marx in the Light of Recent Criticism*. Chicago: Kerr, 1912.

___. *Socialism and War*. New York: New Review, 1916.

Bowles, Samuel and Gintis, Herbert. *Schooling in Capitalist America*. New York: Basic, 1976.

___. "The Crisis of Liberal Democratic Capitalism," *Politics and Society*, 11, 13 (1982), pp. 51–93.

___. *Democracy and Capitalism*. New York: Basic, 1986.

___, Gordon, David and Weisskopf, T. *Beyond the Wasteland*. New York: Doubleday, 1983.

Buhle, Paul. *Marxism in the U.S.A.*. London: Verso, 1987.

Castells, Manual. *City, Class, and Power*. New York: St. Martin's, 1972.

___. *The Economic Crisis and American Society*. Princeton, NJ: Princeton University Press, 1980.

Chodorow, Nancy. *Reproduction of Mothering*. Berkeley: University of California, 1978.

Cohen, G.A. *Karl Marx's Theory of History*. Princeton, NJ: Princeton University Press, 1978.

CPUSA. *The Communist Party and the Question of a Negro Soviet in Soviet America*. New York: Workers Library, 1935.

Cone, James. *Black Theology and Black Power*. New York: Seabury, 1969.

___. *A Black Theology of Liberation*. New York: Lippincott, 1970.

___. *God of the Oppressed*. New York: Seabury, 1975.

___. *For My People*. Maryknoll, New York: Orbis, 1984.

___. *Speaking the Truth*. Grand Rapids, MI: Eerdman's, 1986.

___ and Wilmore, Gayraud S. (eds.). *Black Theology*. Maryknoll, New York: Orbis, 1979.

Cornforth, Maurice. *The Theory of Knowledge*. New York: International, 1963.

Cox, Harvey. *Secular City*. New York: Macmillan, 1965.

___. *On Not Leaving It to the Snakes*. New York: Macmillan, 1967.

___. "Technology, Modern Man, and the Gospel," *Christianity Today*, XII (5 July 1968), p. 4.

. *Feast of Fools*. New York: Harper & Row, 1969.

___. *The Seduction of the Spirit*. New York: Simon & Schuster, 1973.

Davis, Angela. *Women, Race, and Class*. New York: Random House, 1981.

Debs, E. V. *Debs: His Life, Writings, and Speeches*. Chicago: Kerr, 1908.

DeLeon, Daniel. *What Means This Strike?* New York: SLP, 1916.

___. *Reform or Revolution*. New York: SLP, 1918.

___. *As To Politics*. Brooklyn, NY: New York Labor News, 1966.

Diggins, John P. *The Left in the Twentieth Century*. New York: Harcourt Brace Jovanovich, 1973.

Domhoff, G. William. *Who Rules America?* Englewood Cliffs, NJ: Prentice-Hall, 1967.

___. *Who Really Rules America?* New Brunswick, NJ: Transaction, 1978.

___. *Who Rules America Now?* Englewood Cliffs, NJ: Prentice-Hall, 1983.

Dubois, Ellen Carol, et al. *Feminist Scholarship.* Urbana: University of Illinois, 1985.

Dubois, W. E. B. *Black Reconstruction in America.* New York: Harcourt Brace, 1935.

___. *The World and Africa.* New York: International, 1947.

___. *Dusk of Dawn.* New York: Schocken, 1968.

___. *The Autobiography of W.E.B.Dubois.* New York: International, 1968.

Dunayevskaya, Raya. *Marxism and Freedom.* New York: Bookman, 1958.

___. *Woman as Reason and as Force of Revolution.* Detroit: Women's Liberation—News and Letters Committees, 1981.

Eisenstein, Zillah (ed.). *Capitalist Patriarchy and the Case For Socialist Feminism.* New York: Monthly Review, 1979.

Elshtain, Jean Bethke. *Public Man and Private Woman.* Princeton, NJ: Princeton University Press, 1981.

Elster, Jon. *Logic and Society.* Chichester: Wiley, 1978.

___. *Ulysses and the Sirens.* Cambridge: Cambridge University Press, 1979.

___. *Making Sense of Marx.* Cambridge: Cambridge University Press, 1985.

Engels, Friedrich. *Anti-Duhring.* Peking: Foreign Language Press, 1976.

___. *Dialectic of Nature.* New York: International, 1940.

___. *The Origins of the Family, Private Property and the State.* New York: International, 1972.

Feuer, Lewis (ed.). *Marx & Engels: Basic Writings on Politics and Philosophy.* New York: Anchor, 1959.

Firestone, Shulamith. *The Dialectic of Sex.* New York: Bantam, 1970.

Flynn, Elizabeth Gurley. *Sabotage.* Cleveland: IWW, 1916.

Foner, Philip (ed.). *The Black Panthers Speak.* Philadelphia: Lippincott, 1970.

___. *American Socialism and Black Americans.* Westport, CT: Greenwood, 1977.

___. *Women and the American Labor Movement.* New York: Free Press, 1979.

___ (ed.). *Black Socialist Preacher.* San Francisco: Synthesis, 1983.

___ and Allen, James S. (eds.). *American Communism and Black Americans*. Philadelphia: Temple University Press, 1987.

Fraina, Louis. *Revolutionary Socialism*. New York: Communist Press, 1918.

___ (aka Lewis Corey). *The Crisis of the Middle Class*. New York: Civici, Friede, 1935.

___ (aka Lewis Corey). *The Unfinished Task*. New York: Viking, 1942.

Frank, Andre Gunder. *Dependent Accumulation and Underdevelopment*. New York: Monthly Review, 1978.

Goldberg, Itche. *Essayen*. New York: n.a., 1981.

Gorman, Robert A. *Neo-Marxism—The Meanings of Modern Radicalism*. Westport, CT: Greenwood, 1982.

___. *Biographical Dictionary of Marxism*. Westport, CT: Greenwood, 1987.

___. *Biographical Dictionary of Neo-Marxism*. Westport, CT: Greenwood, 1987.

Gould, Carol C. (ed.). *Beyond Domination*. Totowa, NJ: Rowman & Allanheld, 1984.

Gouldner, Alvin W. *The Future of Intellectuals and the Rise of the New Class*. New York: Seabury, 1979.

Gronlund, Laurence. *The Cooperative Commonwealth*. Cambridge, MA: Harvard University Press, 1965.

Hamilton, Virginia (ed.). *The Writings of W.E.B. Dubois*. New York: Crowell, 1975.

Harrington, Michael. *The Accidental Century*. New York: Macmillan, 1965.

___. *Toward a Democratic Left*. Baltimore: Pelican, 1969.

___. "Why We Need Socialism in America," *Dissent*, 17, 3 (May-June 1970), p. 265.

___. "Soaking the Poor," *Commonwealth*, 97, 3 (20 October 1972), p. 57.

___. *Socialism*. New York: Saturday Review Press, 1972.

___. *Fragments of the Century*. New York: Simon & Schuster, 1972,

___. *Twilight of Capitalism*. New York: Simon & Schuster, 1976.

___. "The New Class and the Left," *The New Class*. B. Bruce-Briggs (ed.). New Brunswick, NJ: Transaction, 1979.

___. *Decade of Decision*. New York: Simon & Schuster, 1980.

___. *The Next America*. New York: Holt, Rinehart & Winston, 1981.

___. *The Politics at God's Funeral*. New York: Holt, Rinehart, & Winston, 1983.

___ and Meir, Deborah. *Theory, Life and Politics*. New York: Institute For Democratic Socialism, 1977.

Harris, David. *Socialist Origins in the United States*. The Netherlands: Van Gorcum, 1966.

Hartz, Louis. *The Liberal Tradition in America*. New York: Harcourt, Brace & World, 1955.

Haywood, William D. "Socialism—The Hope of the Workers," *International Socialist Review*, XII (February 1912), p. 462.

___. "What Haywood Says on Political Action," *International Socialist Review*, XIII (February 1913), p.622.

___ and Bohn, Frank. *Industrial Socialism*. Chicago: Kerr, 1910.

Hentoff, Nat (ed.). *The Essays of A. J. Muste*. New York: Bobbs-Merrill, 1967.

Herberg, Will. *Judaism and Modern Man*. New York: Harper & Row, 1951.

___. *Faith Enacted as History*. Philadelphia: Westminster, 1976.

Herron, George Davis. *Social Meanings of Religious Experiences*. New York: Johnson Reprint Corp., 1968.

___. *The Christian Society*. New York: Johnson Reprint Corp. 1969.

Hillquit, Morris. *History of Socialism in the United States*. New York: Funk & Wagnells, 1910.

___. *Socialism Summed Up*. New York: Fly, 1912.

___. *Socialism in Theory and Practice*. New York: Macmillan, 1919.

___ and Ryan, John. *Socialism—Promise or Menace?* New York: Macmillan, 1917.

Hook, Sidney. *Toward the Understanding of Karl Marx*. New York: Day, 1933.

___. *From Hegel to Marx*. New York: Reynal & Hitchcock, 1936.

Hopkins, Charles H. *The Rise of the Social Gospel in American Protestantism, 1865–1915*. New Haven: Yale University Press, 1940.

Horton, Miles and Adams, Frank. *Unearthing Seeds of Fire*. North Carolina: Blair, 1975.

Inman, Mary. *In Women's Defense*. Los Angeles: Committee to Organize the Advancement of Women, 1940.

___. *Thirteen Years of CPUSA Misleadership on the Woman Question*. Los Angeles: Committee to Organize the Advancement of Women, 1948.

Jaggar, Allison and Rothenberg, Paula (eds.). *Feminist Frameworks*. New York: McGraw-Hill, 1978.

James, C. L. R. *Black Jacobins*. New York: Dial Press, 1938.

___. *State Capitalism and World Revolution*. Detroit: Facing Reality, 1950.

___. *The Future in the Present*. Westport, CT: Lawrence Hall, 1977.

___. *Notes on Dialectics*. London: Allison & Busby, 1980.

___. *Spheres of Existence*. Westport, CT: Lawrence Hall, 1980.

___. *At The Rendezvous of Victory*. London: Allison & Busby, 1984.

Joint Economic Committee, United States Congress. "The Concentration of Wealth in the United States—Trends in the Distribution of Wealth Among American Families," Washington, D.C., July 1986.

Kipnis, Ira. *The American Socialist Movement, 1897–1912*. Westport, CT: Greenwood, 1968.

Klehr, Harvey. *The Heyday of American Communism*. New York: Basic Books, 1984.

Konrad, George and Szelenyi, Ivan. *Intellectuals on the Road to Class Power*. New York: Harcourt Brace Jovanovich, 1979.

Kuhn, M. and Wolpe, M. (eds.). *Feminism and Materialism*. Boston: Routledge & Kegan Paul, 1978.

LaMonte, Robert Rives. "The New Intellectuals," *New Review*, II (January 1914), pp. 35–53.

Lasch, Christopher. *The Agony of the American Left*. New York: Knopf, 1969.

___. *Haven in a Heartless World*. New York: Basic, 1977.

___. *The Culture of Narcissism*. New York: Norton, 1979.

___. *The Minimal Self*. New York: Norton, 1984.

Lenin, V.I. *Collected Works*. 45 vols. London: Lawrence & Wishart, 1960–1970.

___. *Lenin on the Woman Question*. New York: International, 1934.

___. *Lenin on the United States*. New York: International, 1970.

Lester, Julius (ed.). *The Seventh Son*. New York: Vintage, 1971.

Levy, Frank. *Dollars and Dreams*. New York: Basic, 1988.

Little, Daniel. *The Scientific Marx*. Minneapolis: University of Minnesota, 1986.

Long, Priscilla (ed.). *The New Left*. Boston: Porter Sargent, 1969.

Magdoff, Harry. *The Age of Imperialism*. New York: Monthly Review, 1969.

___. *Imperialism*. New York: Monthly Review, 1978.

Mandel. Ernest. *Marxist Economic Theory*. London: Merlin, 1962.

___. *Late Capitalism*. London: New Left Books, 1975.

Marable, Manning. *From The Grassroots*. Boston: South End, 1980.

___. *Blackwater*. Dayton, Ohio: Black Praxis Press, 1981.

___. *How Capitalism Underdeveloped Black America*. Boston: South End, 1983.

___. *Race, Reform, and Rebellion*. Jackson, MS: University of Mississippi, 1984.

Marx, Karl. *Early Writings*. New York: Vintage, 1985.

___. *Karl Marx: Selected Writings*, edited by D. McLellan. London: Oxford, 1977.

___. *On America and the Civil War*, Saul K. Padover (ed.). New York: McGraw-Hill, 1972.

___. *Grundrisse*. New York: Vintage, 1973.

___. *Capital*. 3 vols. Moscow: International, 1975.

___. *Werke*. 39 vols. Berlin: Dietz Verlag, 1974.

___, and Engels, Friedrich. *The German Ideology*. Moscow: Progress, 1976.

___, and Engels, Friedrich. *Letters to Americans, 1848–1895*. New York: International, 1953.

Mattick, Paul. *Anti-Bolshevik Communism*. New York: Sharpe, 1978.

___. "Workers' Control," in Priscilla Long (ed.). *The New Left*. Boston: Porter Sargent, 1969.

Miller, Sally. "The Socialist Party and the Negro, 1901–1920," *Journal of Negro History*, 56, 3 (July 1971), pp. 220–229.

Mills, C. Wright. *The Power Elite*. New York: Oxford University Press, 1956.

Moon, Henri (ed.). *The Emerging Thought of W. E. B. Dubois*. New York: Simon & Schuster, 1972.

Niebuhr, Reinhold. *Moral Man and Immoral Society*. New York: Scribners, 1932.

___. *Christianity and Power Politics*. New York: Scribner's, 1940.

___. *Children of Light and Children of Darkness*. New York: Scribner's, 1944.

___. *Faith and History*. New York: Scribner's, 1949.

___. *The Nature and Destiny of Man*. New York: Scribner's, 1949.

___. *Christian Realism and Political Problems*. New York: Scribner's, 1953.

Novick, Pesach. *The National and Jewish Question in the Light of Reality*. New York: Morgen Freiheit, 1971.

O'Connor, James. *The Fiscal Crisis of the State*. New York: St. Martin's, 1973.

___. *The Corporations and the State*. New York: Harper & Row, 1974.

___. *Accumulation Crisis*. New York: Blackwell, 1984.

Oglesby, Carl (ed.). *The New Left Reader*. New York: Grove, 1969.

Perlman, Selig. *Theories of the Labor Movement*. New York: Macmillan, 1928.

Przeworski, Adam. *Capitalism and Social Democracy*. Cambridge: Cambridge University Press, 1985.

___ and Wallerstein, Michael. "The Structure of Class Conflict in Democratic Capitalist Societies," *American Political Science Review*, 76, 2 (1982), pp. 215–38.

Quint, Howard H. *The Forging of American Socialism*. Columbia, SC: University of South Carolina Press, 1953.

Rauschenbusch, Walter. *The Social Principles of Jesus*. New York: Association Press, 1916.

___. *A Theology For the Social Gospel*. New York: Macmillan, 1917.

___. *Christianity and the Social Crisis*. New York: Macmillan, 1918.

___. *The Righteousness of the Kingdom*. New York: Abingdon, 1968 ed.

Record, Wilson. *The American Negro and the CP*. New York: Atheneum, 1951.

___. *Race and Radicalism*. Ithaca, NY: Cornell University Press, 1964.

Rivkin, B. *Di Grunt Tendentsin fun Yiddishe Literatur*. New York: Yiddishe Kultur Farband, 1948.

Roemer, John. *A General Theory of Exploitation and Class*. Cambridge: Harvard University Press, 1982.

___ (ed.). *Analytical Marxism*. Cambridge: Cambridge University Press, 1986.

St. John, Vincent. *The IWW*. Chicago: IWW, 1919.

Schlesinger, Arthur (ed.). *Writings and Speeches of Eugene V. Debs*. New York: Heritage, 1948.

Shannon, David A. *The Socialist Party of America*. New York: Macmillan, 1955.

Skocpol, Theda. *States and Social Revolutions*. Cambridge: Cambridge University Press, 1979.

___. "Political Response to Capitalist Crisis," *Politics and Society*, 10, 2 (1981), p. 200.

___ and Buroway, Michael. *Marxist Inquiries*. Chicago: University of Chicago, 1982.

___, et al. *Bringing the State Back In*. Cambridge: Cambridge University Press, 1985.

Sombart, Werner. *Why Is There No Socialism in the United States?* London: Macmillan, 1976.

Spargo, John. *Substance of Socialism.* New York: Huebsch, 1909.

___. *Karl Marx.* New York: Huebsch, 1910.

___. *Sidelights on Contemporary Socialism.* New York: Huebsch, 1911.

___. *Applied Socialism.* New York: Huebsch, 1912.

___. *Bolshevism.* New York: Harper & Bros., 1919.

Swerdlow, Amy and Lessinger, Hanna (eds.). *Class, Race, and Sex.* Boston: Hall, 1983.

Sweezy, Paul. *The Theory of Capitalist Development.* New York: Oxford University Press, 1942.

Thomas, Norman. *America's Way Out.* New York: Macmillan, 1931.

___. *A Socialist's Faith.* New York: Norton, 1951.

___. *Democratic Socialism.* New York: League for Industrial Democracy, 1953.

Thompson, E. P. *The Making of the English Working Class.* New York: Vintage, 1963.

Tillich, Paul. *The Socialist Decision.* New York: Harper & Row, 1933.

Walker, P. *Between Labor and Capital.* Boston: South End, 1975.

Wallerstein, Immanual. *The Modern World-System.* New York: Academic, 1974.

___. *The Capitalist World Economy.* London: Cambridge University, 1979.

___. *The Modern World-System II.* New York: Academic, 1980.

___. *The Politics of the World-Economy.* Cambridge: Cambridge University, 1984.

Walling, William English. *Socialism As It Is.* New York: Macmillan, 1912.

___. *The Larger Aspects of Socialism.* New York: Macmillan, 1913.

___. *Progressivism—And After.* New York: Macmillan, 1914.

Weinstein, James. *The Decline of Socialism in America.* New York: Vintage, 1967.

West, Cornell. *Prophesy Deliverance!* Philadelphia: Westminster, 1982.

___, et al. (eds.). *Theology in the Americas.* Maryknoll, New York: Orbis, 1982.

Williams, Ben H. "Trends Toward Industrial Freedom," *American Journal of Sociology*, XX (March 1915), p. 627.

Wolfe, Alan. *The Limits of Legitimacy.* New York: Free Press, 1977.

Wright, Eric Olin. *Class, Crisis, and the State*. London: New Left Books, 1978.

___. *Classes*. London: Verso, 1985.

___ and Singelmann, Joachin. "Proletarianization in the Changing American Class Structure," *American Journal of Sociology*, 88 (Supplement, 1982), pp. 176–209.

Wright, Richard. "Blueprint For Negro Writing," *New Challenge* (Fall 1937), p. 54.

___. *Native Son*. New York: Harper, 1940.

___. *Black Power*. New York: Harper, 1954.

___. *White Man Listen!* New York: Doubleday, 1957.

___. "The Voiceless Ones," *Saturday Review*, 16 (April 1960), p. 72.

___. *The Outsider*. New York: Harper, 1965.

Zaretsky, Eli. *Capitalism, The Family and Personal Life*. New York: Harper & Row, 1976.

Zeitlin, Maurice (ed.). *Classes, Class Conflict, and the State*. Cambridge: Winthrop, 1980.

Zhitlovsky, Chaim. *Fredrikh Nitshe und Zayn Filosofer Antviklung-Gang*. New York: n.a., 1981

Index

ABOUT THE AUTHOR

ROBERT A. GORMAN is Professor of Political Science at the University of Tennessee, Knoxville. His other books include *The Dual Vision—Alfred Schutz and the Myth of Phenomenological Social Science, Neo-Marxism, Biographical Dictionary of Marxism,* and *Biographical Dictionary of Neo-Marxism.* His writings on contemporary social theory have also appeared in journals of Political Science, Sociology, Philosophy, and History.